PRAISE FOR *THE OUTSOURCING H.*

CW01064298

'Logistics outsourcing is a complicated process that can deliver significant benefits for all parties if it is managed well, but if managed poorly can create critical business issues. Understanding the process from the initial decision to outsource or not through to the management of relationships to deliver against a business strategy is fundamental for those in procurement, in-house logistics teams and logistics service providers. *The Logistics Outsourcing Handbook* is an invaluable publication, written by experienced practitioners, that brings all the elements of the outsourcing cycle into one comprehensive guide. AS CEO of CILT UK and as a former executive within a logistics service provider I recommend this book.' **Kevin Richardson, Chief Executive, The Chartered Institute of Logistics and Transport (UK)**

'We are witnessing a period of extraordinary change within the logistics industry. The exponential growth of e-commerce is driving the need to hold inventories as close as possible to major urban conurbations to meet delivery expectations of technology-enabled consumers, propelling unprecedented demand for multiple stocking locations. This pursuit of greater agility and flexibility in logistics networks is serviced increasingly by third-party logistics providers (many being members of UKWA). Often in a shared user environment and requiring integration of IT systems and sophisticated sharing of data, the concept of outsourcing is growing. The insights shared by the authors and contributors to *The Logistics Outsourcing Handbook* are therefore very timely and relevant, and will be of interest to both seasoned practitioners and the next generation of logisticians in equipping themselves for this fast-moving, vitally important sector.' **Peter Ward, Chief Executive, United Kingdom Warehousing Association**

'Logistics outsourcing is a strategically important part of an organization's supply chain strategy. Making the wrong decision can result in product shortages that make news headlines and cause significant reputational damage. Getting it right can be a significant competitive advantage. This book provides a comprehensive overview of the different aspects to consider when making a logistics outsourcing decision. It is a must-read for all those involved in logistics outsourcing.' **Jan Godsell, Professor of Operations and Supply Chain Strategy, University of Warwick**

'If outsourcing is undertaken appropriately, an organization can "in-source" key capabilities to secure competitive advantage; if outsourcing is badly managed millions can be lost! This book, based on extensive author experience from across the UK logistics profession, provides a much-needed introduction to the opportunities and traps of outsourcing – with insights into a variety of critical areas including the logistics service marketplace, the key decisions to be made, measuring performance, and contracts and risks. It's an important reference for those already engaged in outsourced relationships or about to embark on an outsourcing journey.' **Richard Wilding OBE, Full Professor and Chair of Supply Chain Strategy, Cranfield School of Management**

'The process of outsourcing any logistics operation is always complicated and can be brimming with pitfalls along the way. For those companies embarking on their first journey through the minefield of outsourcing, the fear of change and business risk can often be their first major obstacle to overcome. Fortunately, The Logistics Outsourcing Handbook offers novice and experienced logisticians alike a practical and structured approach to the process, based upon the authors' own plentiful experience, plus valuable input and feedback from companies who have already progressed through an outsourcing programme. The book is a template for all companies to use, and the first task for any outsourcing project team should be to read it from cover to cover.' **Paul Sloan, Logistics Manager, FUJIFILM UK Ltd**

'Another useful book from Kogan Page on third-party logistics operations; in fact, probably a must-read unless you are bang up to date on outsourcing matters. Godsmark and Richards pool knowledge and give valuable insight into whether or not to outsource, size of the market, IT considerations, risks involved, and the future, and explain with recent examples of disasters that may help others to avoid similar pitfalls. Those public disasters can be remembered for many years and can add to reasons why most tendered contracts will stay with the current third-party logistics provider.' **Nick Deal, Manager, Logistics Development**

'This book is invaluable reading for providers and customers of outsourced logistics services. With hugely useful case studies and insightful new research into relationships between logistics partners, it will form a key part of the debate about the future direction of this important business sector.' **Alan Devine, formerly Managing Director, Gist Limited**

'The Logistics Outsourcing Handbook makes for valuable reading for operations managers and procurement professionals managing logistics spend for their organization. This book offers clear guidance, shares extensive years of experience by the authors, with added case studies, statistics, interviews and real-life applications.' **CIPS Knowledge**

'The Logistics Outsourcing Handbook is an invaluable guide for understanding logistics environments, different entities involved in logistics services, and the decisions to make when outsourcing logistics services. The book provides good practical learning, informative case examples and supporting academic theories. It is an important book that combines aspects of purchasing and logistics. The book will provide value for UG, PG and MBA courses with a focus on logistics and supply chain management.' **Professor Samir Dani, Professor of Logistics and Supply Chain Management, Huddersfield Business School, University of Huddersfield**

The Logistics Outsourcing Handbook

A step-by-step guide from strategy through to implementation

Jo Godsmark
Gwynne Richards

KoganPage

Publisher's note

Every possible effort has been made to ensure that the information contained in this book is accurate at the time of going to press, and the publisher and authors cannot accept responsibility for any errors or omissions, however caused. No responsibility for loss or damage occasioned to any person acting, or refraining from action, as a result of the material in this publication can be accepted by the editor, the publisher or the authors.

First published in Great Britain and the United States in 2020 by Kogan Page Limited

2nd Floor, 45 Gee Street
London
EC1V 3RS
United Kingdom

122 W 27th St, 10th Floor
New York, NY 10001
USA

4737/23 Ansari Road
Daryaganj
New Delhi 110002
India

www.koganpage.com

© Jo Godsmark and Gwynne Richards, 2020

The right of Jo Godsmark and Gwynne Richards to be identified as the authors of this work has been asserted by them in accordance with the Copyright, Designs and Patents Act 1988.

ISBNs

Hardback   978 1 78966 057 9
Paperback   978 0 7494 8462 0
eBook   978 0 7494 8463 7

British Library Cataloguing-in-Publication Data

A CIP record for this book is available from the British Library.

Library of Congress Cataloging-in-Publication Data

CIP data is available. Library of Congress Cataloging-in-Publication Control Number: 2019044220

Typeset by Integra Software Services, Pondicherry
Print production managed by Jellyfish
Printed and bound by CPI Group (UK) Ltd, Croydon CR0 4YY

CONTENTS

Additional resources to accompany this book are available at:
www.koganpage.com/TLOH

ACKNOWLEDGEMENTS

Firstly, as co-authors we need to acknowledge the help and support of our family and partners – Teresa, David and Jo's daughter Kate, who have provided cups of tea, biscuits and hours of encouragement during the long evenings of typing. Thanks also to Jo's long-term business partner, Ruth Waring, for her enthusiasm and understanding, and to Martin Port at BigChange for supporting this endeavour.

Second, we must acknowledge the help of our contributors:

- Lynn Parnell of Logistics Partners Consultancy Limited;
- Nigel Kotani of Excello Law;
- Dr Richard Gibson;
- Victoria Gibson.

Our thanks also to Kate Vitasek for her contribution to Vested®, Mark Rowlatt and Phil Wood for their case studies, John Munnelly from John Lewis, David James from Knapp, Jonathan Nutchley, David Lowther and John Gurr for allowing us to interview them and for their wonderful insights.

Thanks also to the Chartered Institute of Logistics and Transport (CILT) Knowledge Centre for their contribution, and to CILT's Outsourcing and Procurement Committee, whose work and events over many years have laid the foundation for this book. A particular thanks to Rob Krikhaar, Ana Walker and the CILT team for their work on the Outsourcing Attitudes surveys that have informed our thinking.

Our thanks also to the Chartered Institute of Procurement & Supply Knowledge Management, the Warehousing Education and Research Council, Penn State University, Transport Intelligence, eft, JDA Software, Armstrong & Associates, A T Kearney, DHL, Kirsten Tisdale of Aricia and Gavin Williams of XPO for allowing us to use some of their material and survey results in the book.

This book is the result of many years of working with, and learning from, our past and current colleagues, customers and suppliers. We appreciate all the wisdom and help that we have received, as well as the challenges that have taught us about risk and risk mitigation!

Finally, thanks to Róisin Singh and Julia Swales of Kogan Page for their patience and resilience throughout this whole process.

Introduction

In this fast-moving, global marketplace, the supply chain and the logistics services within it are taking centre stage for many companies.

Logistics outsourcing came to the fore in the 1980s in Europe, with many retailers and manufacturers outsourcing much of their transport and, to some degree, their warehousing, to third-party logistics companies (3PLs). The industry has evolved over time, and since the 1980s there have been several changes, not least to the logistics service providers themselves. According to Gadde and Hulthén (2011), the whole industry 'has undergone significant changes... as a result of mergers, acquisitions, company failures and the entry of many new competitors into niche markets'.

Many logistics outsourcing relationships are becoming increasingly complex, and management of those relationships is quite challenging to both parties.

This book has been written for both shippers and logistics service providers to give an insight into the complex nature of logistics outsourcing and to lead both existing and potential users and providers through the process. The authors are able to draw on years of experience in buying, managing and providing outsourcing services.

The writing of this book coincides with the UK's decision to leave the European Union – a decision which has already had and will have a number of effects on supply chains and logistics outsourcing – as well as five high profile logistics outsourcing events in the UK:

1 the problems incurred at KFC when DHL took over the warehousing and delivery contract from Bidvest Logistics, now known as Best Food Logistics;

2 the court challenge by DHL regarding the loss of one of their NHS contracts to Unipart Logistics;

3 the purchase of House of Fraser by JD Sports, which resulted in XPO Logistics refusing to expedite e-commerce orders until their outstanding debt was covered;

4 Aggregate Industries terminating their contract with Eddie Stobart, two years into a five-year contract, and awarding it to Wincanton;

5 retail store Debenhams taking their warehousing operation in-house due to a company re-structure.

These are only a few examples highlighting issues in logistics outsourcing and the need to ensure that the logistics outsourcing process is carried out thoroughly, risk assessments are undertaken and contingency plans are drawn up and tested regularly.

The retail world is also changing and both retailers and logistics service providers (LSPs) are having to face up to the challenge of significant growth in e-commerce. This includes becoming more innovative and proactive – a criticism frequently levelled at LSPs in the past.

E-commerce is proving to be a major force in both retail and logistics. Adidas recently commented that in 2010 their online sales were at zero, but they are projecting a turnover of €4 billion by 2020. Department store John Lewis believe that within a few years their e-commerce and store sales will be equal.

Peter Ward, CEO of the United Kingdom Warehousing Association, said recently: 'The continued demise of the high street means that retailers are having to face up to the challenge of re-shaping their routes to market to meet the ever-increasing demands of technology-enabled consumers. As a result, logistics has become the new retail' (*Forwarder* Magazine, 2018).

He goes on to say: '...a short supply of new warehousing stock in the required locations, increasing rents, a shrinking labour pool and a transport infrastructure that, in many places, is creaking, means that logistics professionals are under greater pressure than ever to deliver new and innovative solutions that meet the demand for shorter lead times and faster delivery'.

In a recent report by eft (2018), Danny Halim said: 'Among all the interesting insights captured in the report, it's refreshing to see LSPs are finally escaping the commoditization trap in 2018, as a higher number of LSPs have been able to sign longer-term, strategic contracts and less are relying on price outbidding as a strategy to create business growth'.

The 2019 Third-Party Logistics Study (Langley *et al*, 2019) found that among respondents to the study, 73 per cent of shippers and 92 per cent of LSPs consider that LSPs provide new and innovative ways to improve logistics effectiveness, and 81 per cent of shippers and 98 per cent of LSPs felt that the use of LSPs had contributed to improving services to end customers.

Company boards are continually debating whether to retain their supply chain operations in-house or outsource to a third party. Peter Drucker once said: 'Do what you do best and outsource the rest'. This statement suggests that companies should examine the logistics capabilities and competences within the business, and, if they are found to be inefficient, companies need to think about outsourcing.

If there is significant supply chain and logistics expertise within the company, then companies can continue to manage these operations in-house. However, there are also financial aspects to take into account, especially with the introduction of new technologies such as artificial intelligence (AI), augmented reality (AR), self-driving vehicles and robotics.

According to Mello, Stank and Esper (2008), there are a number of reasons for and potential outcomes which steer companies towards outsourcing. These include:

- the potential for cost reduction;
- service improvement expectations;
- opportunities to focus on core competencies;
- the possibility of improving productivity;
- upgrades to IT capabilities;
- the ability to leverage supply chain management;
- the ability to react to changes in the regulatory environment;
- access to logistics expertise;
- globalization of the business;
- the complexities of operating in a just-in-time (JIT) environment;
- rapid growth;
- limited resources to spend on logistics activities.

These reasons are mirrored in the surveys carried out by the Chartered Institute of Logistics and Transport (CILT) in the UK, and many others which are discussed in Chapter 2.

Mello, Stank and Esper also suggest that there are certain events which can trigger companies to consider outsourcing. These include:

- corporate restructuring;
- changes in logistics management;
- changes in executive management;

- corporate cost/headcount reduction programmes;
- market and product line expansions;
- increasing customer demands;
- mergers and acquisitions;
- entering new markets;
- customer use of JIT or Quick Response;
- labour costs/problems;
- instituting a quality improvement programme;
- CEO directives to investigate the feasibility of outsourcing.

This book will discuss the advantages and disadvantages of logistics outsourcing and provide models to allow companies to decide whether outsourcing is viable. The book goes on to discuss how to go about the processes of determination, choice and implementation.

This book, written by experienced operators, provides an insight into outsourcing within the supply chain. The contents of the book are as follows.

Chapter 1 examines the logistics services likely to be outsourced, including freight transport, warehousing, forwarding, reverse logistics, value-adding services and back office operations.

Chapter 2 takes the reader through the advantages and disadvantages of outsourcing, and provides models and a questionnaire to help companies decide whether logistics outsourcing is right for them.

Chapter 3 takes a look at the logistics marketplace – its size, the major players and current trends including profitability, mergers and acquisitions.

Chapter 4 looks at the different levels of supplier relationships using the Kraljic (1983) model as a guide. It discusses relationships from the purely transactional through to strategic partnerships.

Chapter 5 provides a nine-step guide to outsourcing, from strategic review through to managing an exit. This step by step guide follows a tried and tested outsourcing process which has been used successfully by the authors to outsource various logistics operations to LSPs.

Chapter 6, co-written with Nigel Kotani, a solicitor with Excello Law, examines the legal aspects of outsourcing, and goes on to discuss the various charging mechanisms in use today by LSPs, including open-book, closed-book and hybrid systems.

Chapter 7 provides the reader, both LSPs and shippers, with examples of performances measures that can be introduced into logistics contracts. It also draws on the annual survey carried out by the Warehousing Education Resource Council to provide guidelines for benchmarking.

Chapter 8, co-written with Richard and Victoria Gibson, is on managing risk throughout the outsourcing process. It includes a case study on KFC's experiences awarding a contract to DHL and QSL to manage supply chain operations in the UK.

Chapter 9 provides an insight into supplier relationship management and its importance to major logistics outsourcing contracts. It includes an interview with David Lowther, former Supply Chain, Customer Services and IT Director within the Kingfisher Group of companies.

Chapter 10 is written by Lynn Parnell of Logistics Partners Consultancy Limited, an experienced logistics IT consultant with significant implementation experience. Many logistics contracts have failed as a result of poor IT specification, integration and implementation. This chapter discusses the choices shippers need to consider in terms of IT and how to ensure a successful IT implementation.

Chapter 11 looks at the future of logistics and the future of logistics outsourcing. These are exciting times for the logistics industry with significant innovations and market disruptors such as the Internet of Things, AI, autonomous vehicles, blockchain, drones and 3D printing. The chapter looks at each of these technologies, and how logistics service providers can introduce advanced technology into their logistics outsourcing relationships.

The book includes models, case studies, interviews, tools, videos and advice on what to consider when contemplating logistics outsourcing and how to go about the process. It also gives the LSP an insight into the minds of shippers and what their expectations may be.

Some of the resources within the book can be accessed from the 'Howto Logistics' website.

Both authors are also involved with the CILT's Outsourcing and Procurement Forum, details of which can be found on the CILT website.

Providers of logistics services have been described as LSPs, 3PLs, lead logistics providers, hauliers, truckers and so on, whilst the purchasers of logistics services are classed as customers, clients, buyers, shippers and many more. In this book we generally, but not exclusively, use the term 'LSP' for the former, and 'shipper' for the latter.

Logistics outsourcing

01

Introduction

This chapter will examine each of the logistics services that are regularly outsourced by companies. The first section will define the terms 'logistics' and 'outsourcing' from the authors' point of view. The second part will outline and discuss each logistics service as mentioned in the 2019 Third-Party Logistics Study (Langley *et al*, 2019).

Throughout the book we will refer to those companies who outsource their logistics as 'shippers', and on occasion as 'customers'. The companies who provide the logistics service(s) are referred to as 'logistics service providers' (LSPs). LSPs encompasses couriers, hauliers, truckers, third-party logistics companies (3PLs), fourth-party logistics companies (4PLs), fifth-party logistics companies (5PLs), '7PLs' and lead logistics providers (LLPs).

Most of these LSPs physically handle the goods whilst under their care; however, companies such as 4PLs and many freight forwarders manage the logistics process with no physical contact with the goods.

Companies that run most of their own logistics services in-house will be described as 'own-account operators'.

Definitions

Logistics

There are many definitions of logistics available. The term can be all-encompassing, as per this description by the Council of Supply Chain Management Professionals (CSCMP):

> '...the process of planning, implementing, and controlling the efficient, effective flow and storage of goods, services, and related information from point of origin to point of consumption for the purpose of conforming to customer requirements.' (CSCMP, 2013)

Note that this definition includes inbound, outbound, internal and external movements, and the management of information. In today's e-commerce world, we also need to include the return of materials for operational and environmental purposes – nowadays described as reverse logistics.

Logistics is a fundamental part of a supply chain, comprising physical transport, storage, handling and value-adding services. The supply chain as a whole also encompasses manufacturing and customer operations.

Logistics can simply be described as getting the right product, in the right quantity, to the right place, to the right customer, at the right time, in the right condition and at the right price. These are the seven 'rights' of customer service. In an increasingly environmentally-aware world, we can also add 'at least cost to the environment' to this list.

According to Uri Dadush of the World Bank, 'As a main driver of competitiveness, logistics can make you or break you as a country in today's globalized world' (Jackson, 2011). Logistics can give companies a sustained competitive advantage, provided it is well-managed. However, in today's fast-paced economy, with ever-increasing technological advancements, companies cannot stand still, and must continually update and upgrade their logistics services offerings in order to keep pace with the competition.

Appreciation of the importance of logistics in modern companies has only recently come to the fore – and the fact that many logistics and supply chain professionals now sit on the board of directors of their respective companies is surely testament to the increasing recognition of its value. However, this does not necessarily mean that companies should retain their logistics operations in-house.

Outsourcing

Outsourcing essentially means identifying a task or function that isn't a core competency for your organization, and employing a specialist to run it more efficiently (and hopefully more cost-effectively). According to management gurus Peters and Waterman (1982), companies should 'stick to the knitting' – meaning that they should concentrate on what they're good at, and leave the rest to the experts.

The 2019 Third-Party Logistics Study (Langley *et al*, 2019) provides details as to which logistics services are commonly outsourced, and the percentage of respondents who outsource these services. Figure 1.1 outlines this.

Figure 1.1 Commonly outsourced logistics services

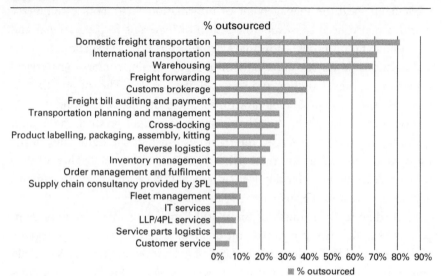

SOURCE Langley *et al*, 2019

As shown, domestic and international transportation are by far the most frequently outsourced services, followed by warehousing and freight forwarding.

In the following section, we examine each of these services in turn.

Outsourced logistics services

Freight transport – domestic and international

As evidenced by Figure 1.1, and backed up by most logistics surveys, freight transport is the service most frequently outsourced.

Freight transport modes include road, rail, inland waterways, short sea and deep sea movements, pipelines and air freight. Freight transportation can include both domestic and international movements.

As shown in Figure 1.2, freight can be moved by various modes of transportation.

Road transport

Road transport includes letter, parcel, pallet, less than truck load (LTL) quantities (sometimes referred to as 'groupage'), and full truck load (FTL) movements.

Figure 1.2 Freight transport modes

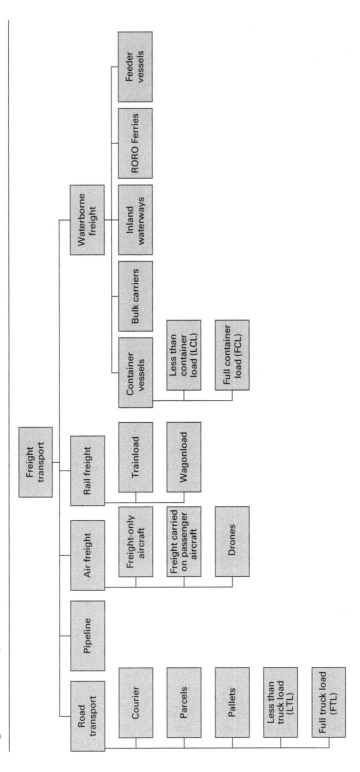

These freight movements can be:

- undertaken by the own-account company (shipper), utilizing their own fleet of vehicles;

- a contractual arrangement, where own-account companies have employed an LSP to provide vehicles and drivers to undertake deliveries on their behalf – those vehicles being supplied in the own-account company's own livery;

- an ad-hoc arrangement with vehicles supplied in the LSP's livery.

A significant barrier for shippers to operate road freight vehicles is the amount of regulation related to running a heavy goods vehicle (HGV) fleet. In Europe, with operator licence legislation, this includes loading limits, working and driving time legislation, digital tachographs, parking and vehicle limits, maintenance and service obligations, and driver and manager training and qualifications. These regulations apply to companies running vehicles over 3.5 tonnes gvw and include legal obligations for senior management.

Many companies choose to transfer this legislative burden by outsourcing. Manufacturers can opt for a restricted licence, which restricts them from carrying goods other than their own, but the compliance burden is not significantly less and it can reduce flexibility in terms of back-loading.

Another barrier is the high level of investment required in road freight vehicles, particularly HGVs, and in qualified drivers. High vehicle and driver utilization are necessary to justify this investment, and many operators struggle to achieve this. Seasonality and demand variability are easier to deal with if goods from a variety of manufacturers are being carried, and larger LSPs have set up national and/or international networks to achieve high utilization levels.

Investment levels and the scope of regulation is much lower for van fleets, although both are rising and many companies operate this type of logistics operation in-house. The exception to this is parcel distribution, which is discussed below.

Parcel distribution   The majority of parcel delivery operations are carried out by 3PLs. These include household names such as DHL, Federal Express, United Parcel Services (UPS), Yodel, DPD, Blue Dart and domestic postal services such as USPS, Royal Mail, Japan Post and Post NL. This is a sector that has seen growth over the last 15 years with the introduction of e-commerce, and will continue to grow over the next few years. According to a report by IBISWorld, the global courier and delivery services industry grew by 2.0 per cent over the five years to 2018, achieving a total revenue of $272bn in that year. In the same time frame, the number of businesses grew by 4.4 per cent, and the number of employees by 1.5 per cent (IBISWorld, 2019).

As shown in Figure 1.3, further growth is predicted in e-commerce, which will naturally lead to continued growth in the courier sector.

There has been an interesting move recently towards companies such as Amazon, Flipkart in India (recently purchased by Walmart), JD.com and Alibaba in China setting up their own parcel distribution services. The growth in e-commerce and discount days such as Black Friday, Cyber Monday and Singles Day in China has put enormous pressure on both retailers and courier companies. It is therefore unsurprising that these companies are looking to protect their home delivery operations by increasing capacity.

We have also recently seen Asda Walmart in the UK taking control of some of their last-mile delivery and returns operation through the use of click-and-collect. They also act as a third-party operator, offering this service to other retailers. In the US, they plan to use their own staff to make deliveries to their customers whilst on their route home.

Figure 1.3   Global e-commerce revenue forecast

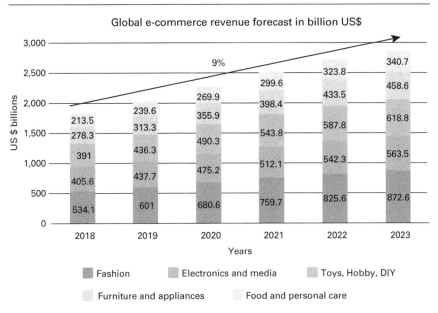

SOURCE Statista, n. d.a

Companies such as Collect Plus, Doddle and Parcelly in the UK have also built up a network of collection points on behalf of their clients.

More recent entrants into this marketplace are autonomous vehicles for last-mile delivery. These include driverless vehicles, drones and robots. These may or may not utilize the courier networks and can be despatched directly from fulfilment centres.

To supply a next-day service nationally and across borders requires a comprehensive infrastructure of local delivery depots, regional and na-tional hubs, together with large fleets of delivery vehicles (bicycles, mopeds, motorbikes, vans and light trucks) and articulated vehicles for movements between the hubs and the depots. The premise is that these parcel distribu-tion companies will have depots strategically placed within geographic areas to both collect items for delivery and make deliveries to the final customer.

These companies provide business-to-business (B2B), business-to-consumer (B2C) and to a certain extent consumer-to-consumer (C2C) services with the growth of online companies such as eBay.

Prior to the growth in parcel and pallet distribution networks, shippers would transport goods directly to the end customer, as can be seen in Figure 1.4.

Figure 1.4   Historical delivery operations without the use of a hub and spoke system

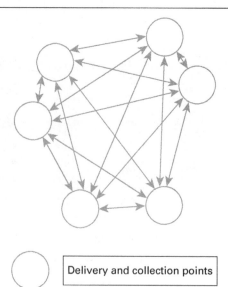

Delivery and collection points

Pallet distribution via networks   Companies who are operating their own freight transport vehicles can find it expensive to move small quantities of product around the country – hence the use and growth of pallet networks and groupage services. These networks tend to specialize in individual shipments of between one and four pallets.

In Europe there are a number of pallet distribution companies. In the main, these are either joint ventures between haulage companies, or franchise operations which utilize regional haulage companies to carry out deliveries and the collection of pallets. However, some networks will also deliver out-of-gauge freight, hazardous items and temperature-sensitive items. These networks include Pall-Ex, Palletways, Palletforce, the Pallet Network, Fortec, the HazChem Network, and many others.

The advantage of using networks and companies such as these is that deliveries can be consolidated, thus reducing the overall cost per delivery for those companies who do not have FTL deliveries. Rather than going directly from supplier to end user, as shown in Figure 1.4, deliveries can be consolidated first at local delivery and collection depots, and further consolidated at regional and national hubs to produce FTL deliveries.

Haulage or trucking companies operating in one geographic region can collect consignments from their local customers and deliver them to the hubs for onward delivery to other geographic areas. In turn, they will collect deliveries from the hub(s) which are destined for delivery into their own geographic region, as in Figure 1.5. This reduces overall mileage, and can also reduce delivery times.

The hub acts as both a consolidation and a transshipment facility. Figure 1.6 shows a typical example of a hub, where pallets are unloaded from one vehicle and re-loaded onto another. This can be done either inside the facility, loading and unloading from the side, or alternatively operating with loading docks and therefore loading and unloading at the rear of the vehicle.

Part load/Groupage/Less than truck load (LTL) deliveries   The movement of product on pallets can be relatively straightforward, as is the planning of those journeys in terms of vehicle capacity. Where shipments exceed four pallets but are not classed as FTLs, these tend to be classified as part-load or LTL deliveries.

LSPs delivering these products need to build up a network of compatible clients to ensure cost-effective delivery. This can also include the formation of local hubs to consolidate these deliveries. In the USA, companies such as

Figure 1.5   Use of parcel and pallet hubs to consolidate deliveries

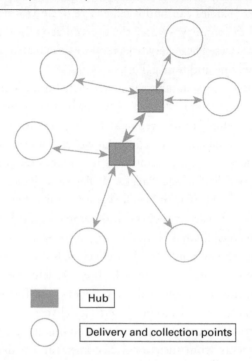

Hub

Delivery and collection points

Figure 1.6   A typical pallet distribution operation

SOURCE Palletforce

Old Dominion Freight provide nationwide LTL services for companies utilizing their own country-wide depot network.

For own-account operators, consolidating deliveries can be prohibitively expensive. Own-account operators are more likely to operate vehicles to undertake FTL deliveries only, or for specialist or niche transportation.

Abnormal or 'ugly' freight   Product which doesn't fit neatly onto a pallet is more difficult to plan and move. Where companies have not formed an alliance or network, they will utilize their own vehicles to deliver these out-of-gauge products.

Products which are classed as 'ugly' freight have been seen as a barrier to outsourcing in the past, and are more likely to be moved by own-account operators. However, we are seeing courier companies adapting their hubs in order to better deal with these.

FTL deliveries   FTL deliveries take place between shippers and end users, whether they are manufacturers receiving raw materials or components, wholesalers, distributors or retailers receiving finished goods, or retailers delivering from their distribution centres to stores.

Deliveries may be made using standard vehicles or specialized vehicles such as car transporters, tankers, temperature-controlled vehicles, tippers and crane-equipped vehicles. The decision for the own-account operator is whether to operate with their own fleet, or to outsource to a third party.

The decision will revolve around factors including control, capital expenditure, staffing and load efficiency. For example, a vehicle belonging to a manufacturer or retailer which is delivering from A to B will need to return to base. The issue is whether that vehicle returns empty or fully laden. If the manufacturer can collect components or packaging from its own suppliers on a regular basis, then vehicle utilization increases significantly. However, if this isn't the case, then outsourcing the delivery to a third-party can make economic sense.

Research from Eurostat shows that at EU-28 level, one-fifth of road freight journeys were performed by empty vehicles. The share of empty journeys increased to 23.1 per cent for national transport, but was only 12.2 per cent for international transport in 2017. At total transport level, most member states fell in the range between 15 per cent and 30 per cent empty journeys. With regard to outbound journeys, EU-28 average vehicle loads were 13.7 tonnes in 2017, with national loads of 12.7 tonnes and international loads of 15.9 tonnes. Maximum load capacity in most countries averages around 24 tonnes (Eurostat, 2018).

The onus is on the operator to find a return load, and therefore utilize the vehicle to the full, unless they have negotiated a round-trip price with the customer.

An interesting development in this market sector is the introduction of return load websites, where companies can post details of their loads, with collection and delivery addresses. At the same time, hauliers and truckers are able to post details of their empty vehicles showing location and destination requirements. The sites work in a similar fashion to dating agencies, where the empty vehicle is matched with a load, and the client and supplier are put in contact. This is discussed further in Chapter 11.

A further development is the growth of 4PL companies who do not own any truck assets, but buy in services from hauliers to provide customers with a cost-effective service. By utilizing their own transport software, they are able to optimize the movement of goods across their client network.

Rail

The movement of freight by rail is having somewhat of a revival, with companies looking to be more environmentally-friendly. There is increasing customer pressure on companies to review their freight transport operations as road congestion gets worse, and this is having a significant effect on delivery times. The shortage of HGV drivers is also an issue, together with concerns about CO_2 emissions.

The UK is committed to making an 80 per cent reduction in its carbon emissions by 2050. Transport represents around 23 per cent of UK domestic CO_2 emissions, and within that, freight transport – mostly road – contributes just over 30 per cent. On average, rail freight produces 3.4 times less CO_2 per tonne-km than road transport.

Switching goods from road to rail could mean a 70 per cent reduction in CO_2 emissions. Rail freight could save 4.6 million tonnes of CO_2 per year by 2030 for the UK alone.

There are a number of issues with this, however:

- There will often be a requirement for road transport at the start and end of the rail journey.
- The rail infrastructure in many countries is either non-existent, or has had little or no investment over recent years.
- Passenger transport takes priority over freight transport.
- There is very little competition, with too few rail freight operating companies in the market.

- There are too few rail terminals in many countries for transferring cargo between rail and road.
- Timely deliveries of goods by rail will often depend on the quality of the rail network and the service provider.
- Freight timetables may not be suitable for time-sensitive deliveries.
- There may not be a suitable rail terminal within close proximity of the origin of the goods or that of the end customers.

For large freight volumes, a train load operation is likely to be involved. For such higher volume traffic, full-length trains can be moved directly between origin and destination terminals, without intermediate marshalling with other wagons. Examples of such flows include trains that carry coal from collieries and ports to power stations, often with loading and discharge at each end undertaken automatically while the trains are still moving.

Conventional wagon services are well-suited for terminal-to-terminal movements, ie where there is little or no road transport required at each end. It is possible to load and unload freight between conventional wagons and road vehicles if required, but if road haulage is required at each end of a rail transit, intermodal services may be more suitable.

Where the volume of freight moved per shipment is less than 500 tonnes, this may be insufficient to justify operating a dedicated train service between two points. This will vary between countries. As an alternative, the wagon-load option assembles a number of less-than-trainload shipments from separate sources or customers into a whole trainload.

Figure 1.7   Full train load movements

Figure 1.8   Wagonload movements

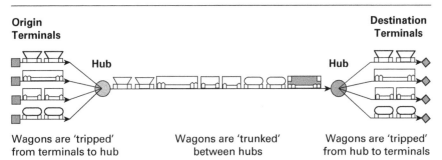

| Wagons are 'tripped' from terminals to hub | Wagons are 'trunked' between hubs | Wagons are 'tripped' from hub to terminals |

With this type of service, groups of wagons can be collected (tripped) from an originating terminal to a hub terminal, then marshalled with other wagons into full-length trains which are hauled over longer distances (trunked) to another hub, then delivered individually to destination terminals. In logistical terms, this type of operation is known as a hub and spoke network, similar to the parcel and pallet distribution operations mentioned above.

It is very unlikely that companies will operate their own rail freight stock, and therefore in most circumstances the use of a third party is a necessity. This is certainly the case when requiring a wagonload service, as opposed to a full train load service.

According to the Freight Transport Association (FTA) in the UK:

'The sector you operate in will largely dictate whether moving goods by rail is viable. For example, retailers may use rail to deliver goods to a regional distribution centre, but the final leg to store almost always has to be by road. Perishable goods and those that are time-critical may not be suited to rail.'
(FTA, n. d.)

We are now seeing the first rail freight trains operating between China and Europe. These services are cheaper than air and, although more expensive, take half the time of deep-sea shipments.

In terms of feasibility, companies need to examine their entire supply chain and calculate current costs per tonne moved. They also need to ensure that their depot location and delivery points, are within a reasonable distance of a rail hub. Finally, costs, load capacity, time slots and hub despatch options are areas that need to be examined carefully.

Inland waterways

Rivers and canal networks have transported freight for hundreds of years, and with the current level of concern over the environment are becoming more fashionable.

The use of inland waterways very much depends on the infrastructure within a country. Again, it is very unlikely that own-account operators will use their own fleet of boats and barges, and will rely on third parties to undertake deliveries.

One recent occurrence is a joint venture between Rhenus Group and LBH, bringing together freight transportation and port operations, providing clients with a single point of contact for onward shipping of goods brought to the ports via inland waterways.

Short sea movements

For deliveries made by coastal waterway, sometimes termed short sea shipments, the following vehicles operate:

- feeder vessels – short haul between local ports;
- roll-on-roll-off ferries.

In both examples, ships and ferries are most likely operated by third parties.

Short sea shipping is often an alternative to cross-border or even within-country road haulage. Sometimes this will be seasonal, and deliveries can be accompanied or unaccompanied. If unaccompanied, the transporter will need to arrange collection of the trailer at the port of destination for onward delivery.

Deep sea movements

With regard to deep sea freight movements, there are a number of transportation options. These include the following:

- Liners: cargo carried in vessels according to a fixed scheduled of routes and port calls. Most containerized transportation, as well as some break-bulk cargo, falls into this category.
- Tramp: dry cargo carried on chartered vessels. This includes mainly dry bulk cargo such as coal, grain, minerals, china clay and fertilizers, as well as steel and, in some cases, finished cars and heavy equipment.
- Tankers: liquids, such as crude oil.

As with rail and short sea, the vast majority of movements will be carried out by third-party companies, with own-account operators having very few if any ships of their own.

As Table 1.1 shows, the top 10 shipping lines hold 82.8 per cent of container capacity globally.

Air

According to the International Air Transport Association (IATA), air cargo accounts for less than 1 per cent of world trade tonnage, yet 35 per cent of world trade value is carried by air – the equivalent of $6 trillion (IATA, n. d.). A high-value industry, air cargo is critical for serving markets that demand speed and reliability for the transport of goods.

Similar to rail and waterborne transport, very few companies will own or operate their own air cargo transport and the majority of freight will be moved by third-party carriers. An exception to this is Amazon, who are

Table 1.1   The top 10 container shipping lines as at June 2019

Position	Operator	TEU	Share
1	APM – Maersk	4,157,575	18.0%
2	Mediterranean Shipping Co	3,378,356	14.7%
3	COSCO Group	2,884,153	12.5%
4	CMA CGM Group	2,687,579	11.7%
5	Hapag–Lloyd	1,700,677	7.4%
6	ONE Ocean Network Express	1,538,274	6.7%
7	Evergreen Line	1,272,845	5.5%
8	Yang Ming Marine Tpt Corp	643,180	2.8%
9	Hyundai M M	424,566	1.8%
10	PIL Pacific Intl Line	391,831	1.7%

SOURCE AXSMarine, 2019

planning to operate up to 40 Prime Air aircraft out of their own air cargo hub in Northern Kentucky. Other own-account companies running their own cargo aircraft are aircraft manufacturers such as Boeing.

According to a report by Boeing (n. d.a), world air cargo is composed of three main service sectors: scheduled freight, charter freight, and mail. Scheduled freight is the largest component, accounting for 90 per cent of all world air cargo traffic. Scheduled freight includes general and express (sometimes referred to as 'integrator') freight.

Charter air freight (sometimes referred to as non-scheduled freight) accounts for 6 per cent of world air cargo traffic. The charter sector captures traffic with urgent or special handling requirements. Nearly all urgent or special handling cargo is carried on freighter airplanes, rather than in the lower hold of passenger aircraft. Just under 50 per cent of all air freight is carried on passenger aircraft.

According to Boeing (n. d.b), world air cargo traffic is forecast to grow 4.2 per cent per year in the next 20 years. In terms of revenue per tonne kilometre growth, air freight, including express traffic, is projected to grow at a rate of 4.3 per cent per year, while airmail will grow at a slower pace, averaging 2 per cent annual growth through 2037. Overall, world air cargo traffic will more than double in the next 20 years, expanding from 256 billion RTKs in 2017 to 584 billion RTKs in 2037. Much of this as a result of the growth in cross-border air cargo.

The top 12 air cargo companies as at July 2018, according to IATA are shown in Table 1.2.

According to IATA (2019), the top 25 cargo airlines saw cargo traffic increase by 7.2 per cent year on year, to 166.5bn freight tonne kilometres.

The growth in e-commerce, most significantly in China, has seen a huge growth in Chinese airlines. The emergence of Qatar as a hub for both passengers and freight is also very noticeable.

The top 10 air freight forwarders in 2017, according to Air Cargo News (2018), were as follows:

1 DHL Supply Chain and Forwarding;

2 Kuehne + Nagel;

3 D B Schenker;

4 Panalpina;

Table 1.2 The top 12 air cargo carriers as at July 2018

Company	Position	Freight tonne kilometres (millions)
1	Federal Express	16,851
2	Emirates	12,715
3	United Parcel Service	11,940
4	Qatar Airways	10,999
5	Cathay Pacific	10,722
6	Korean Air	8,015
7	Cargolux	7,322
8	Lufthansa	7,317
9	Air China	6,701
10	Singapore Airlines	6,592
11	China Southern Airlines	6,174
12	China Airlines	5,741

SOURCE IATA, 2019

5 Expeditors;

6 UPS SCS;

7 Nippon Express;

8 Hellman;

9 Bolloré Logistics;

10 DSV.

(Note: at the time of writing, DSV have agreed to acquire Swiss rival Panalpina.)

Pipeline

Pipelines are the most efficient mode of transport for suitable commodities such as oil, gas and liquids.

Like railroads, however, pipelines are constrained by their physical network, and are generally custom-built for a particular application.

Intermodal transport

According to the European Conference of Ministers of Transport (ECMT), intermodal transport is:

> '...the movement of goods in one and the same loading unit or vehicle, which uses successively, several modes of transport without handling of the goods themselves in changing modes.' (ECMT, 2001)

As discussed, other than some road freight transportation, the majority of modes of transportation are operated by third parties. In order to move freight intermodally, therefore, there is a requirement to utilize a third-party company to co-ordinate the various modal freight movements.

It is possible for a company to manage this aspect themselves; however, it can be very complicated and requires extensive knowledge of the marketplace.

Warehousing

According to the 2019 Third-Party Logistics Study (Langley *et al*, 2019), 69 per cent of respondents outsource their warehousing operation to one or more LSPs.

Warehouses can be outsourced as a whole, meaning that companies will contract with a supplier to provide the building, the equipment and the staff. These contracts can be for three, five or even 10 years in duration, depending on the ownership of the building.

Warehouses can be purchased by the LSP and all the costs are charged to the customer. An alternative is where the shipper will own the warehouse, and the LSP will, in effect, provide the equipment and the staff to manage the outsourced operation. This gives the customer the flexibility to change supplier without having to move operations if the LSP is not adhering to the contract.

One example of this is a warehouse in the UK which is owned by Nestlé, but operated by Wincanton. Fuji Film UK has a similar arrangement with Yusen Logistics, as do B&Q and Screwfix with their LSPs in the UK.

A warehouse is a significant fixed cost, and if underutilized can increase the cost per unit appreciably. In the above example, Nestlé initially designed their warehouse for future growth, and therefore had significant additional space in which to expand. As a result of a change in strategy, this additional space was not required and therefore could have remained empty. However, Wincanton, their LSP, was tasked with finding additional clients for this space, which they have done.

Some companies such as Sainsburys, Asda Walmart, Mondelēz, John Lewis (see case study in Chapter 2) and many others will operate some warehouses themselves, and outsource others. This may be in order to benchmark internal versus external operations, to outsource warehouse operations where the operation is not a core competency, such as hanging garment storage, or to operate in a different country where the company has no expertise.

Shared-user warehousing is where an LSP will own or lease a warehouse, and will offer its services to multiple customers who share the costs of the operation. This is becoming very prevalent today with regard to e-commerce, with online retailers sharing space, staff and equipment under one roof.

In one recent example, a skincare company needed to find a shared-user warehouse in the UK as a result of the uncertainty surrounding Brexit. The LSP warehouse chosen had five other similar companies already operating from the warehouse. This not only gave the skincare company confidence in the ability of the LSP, but it also gained from the synergies present. The full case study (Apprise Consulting) can be found in Chapter 2.

Companies choosing shared-user warehousing are able to share the costs of the warehouse, including equipment and staff. They are not burdened with all the fixed costs of a warehouse unnecessarily. Shared-user warehousing enables start-up and overseas companies to set up in a country without bearing all the costs of a dedicated warehouse operation. They are also able to share costs such as outbound transportation, and take advantage of the warehouse operator's buying power.

When making the decision to outsource warehousing, there are a number of criteria which need to be taken into account when choosing a LSP. These include the following:

- the warehouse location;
- the LSP's existing clients (if shared-user);
- the LSP's experience in the market;
- the availability of value-adding services such as packing, labelling, tagging, quality control, sub-assembly, reverse logistics and repairs and refurbishment;
- outbound transportation;
- IT capability and compatibility;
- the opportunity to expand;
- the culture of the LSP;
- the LSP's financial standing.

Customs brokerage and freight forwarding

Where businesses do not have sufficient imports/exports to warrant employing personnel experienced in the complex regulatory requirements governing the transport of goods across borders, they can outsource to a customs brokerage company or freight forwarder.

Customs brokers can do their job as employees or associates of freight forwarders, independent businesses, shipping lines, importers, exporters or customs brokerage firms.

A customs broker will ensure that all the proper procedures are followed when importing or exporting goods and services. Each country operates under a different set of rules and regulations regarding the transfer of goods entering or leaving their borders. Customs regulations and laws concerning import and export of goods are subject to constant change, sometimes on a daily basis. Customs brokers will ensure that they are up to date with all of these rules and regulations.

Freight forwarding is normally associated with the movement of freight internationally. A freight forwarder is a service provider, moving goods from A to B, but usually not a carrier. It is predominantly a B2B relationship; however, with the growth of e-commerce this now encompasses an element of B2C.

A freight forwarder has specialist knowledge of the import and export market and the paperwork involved, and buys in services from carriers to effect deliveries.

A day in the life of a freight forwarder will include:

- providing quotations;
- offering advice on the most efficient and cost-effective mode of transport and usage of the correct Incoterm;
- negotiating contract rates with transportation companies;
- taking orders from clients and making bookings with transport operators;
- arranging for the collection and delivery of goods from A to B using multiple modes of transport including air, sea, road and rail;
- preparing and processing all the documents which may be required;
- completing customs formalities on client's behalf;
- tracking customer shipments.

Companies utilize freight forwarders because:

- the company doesn't possess the internal expertise;
- freight forwarders have greater buying power, knowledge and time;
- freight forwarders have the up-to-date knowledge of customs and shipping regulations;
- freight forwarders can act as an extension to a business, to help them grow through international trade.

As shown in Figure 1.9, shippers can bypass the freight forwarder if they have sufficient expertise in-house and significant volumes of freight to be able to deal directly with either the non-vessel operating common carrier (NVOCC), or even with the shipping line itself.

An NVOCC is an entity that provides ocean freight services as a 'carrier'. The NVOCC buys space from a shipping line such as Maersk or NYK, and resells the same to their customers, who can be exporters or forwarders. NVOCCs issue their own house bill of lading as a carrier, and in doing so undertake the responsibilities of a carrier subject to the terms, conditions and liabilities of their bill of lading.

The freight forwarder may or may not operate its own collection and delivery vehicles or its own warehouse or consolidation centre, instead relying on a third-party logistics company to undertake this work. Freight forwarders will have contacts globally who can arrange collection and delivery

Figure 1.9   The import/export shipping process

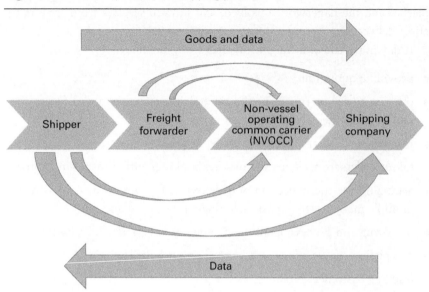

of shipments and customs clearance in those countries where they do not have a physical presence.

The larger freight forwarders such as Damco, Yusen, Expeditors and so on have become LSPs as well, providing both dedicated and shared-user logistics services.

Freight bill auditing and payment

Freight invoices can be both complicated and confusing, and frequently change as a result of additional costs such as fuel surcharges, currency fluctuation, demurrage, volume discounts and so on.

According to Inbound Logistics (2017), in addition to checking that bills are accurate, a growing number of shippers rely on freight pay firms to help analyse freight spend and produce reports with an eye toward reducing costs and optimizing the supply chain. These shippers are also 'turning to their freight payment process to unlock working capital either through improved operational efficiencies or improved cash flow'.

These companies can also provide other services including insurance claims processing, vendor management and compliance, contract negotiations, management and renewal. Payment for these services can be based on the overall savings made.

One other point to be aware of is that these companies may hold a fund provided by the customer from which to pay the transport suppliers. Any interest on this money will normally lie with the auditor.

Cross-docking

Cross-docking can be part of a warehouse operation, a regional transport service, or a standalone service where deliveries are consolidated and shipped onwards almost immediately to the end destination.

Cross-docking allows companies to reduce inventory carrying costs, since they are fulfilling exact orders immediately on arrival and don't require safety stock. This does require careful planning, supplier conformance, co-operation and order management for optimal effectiveness.

Cross-docking is increasingly used for products with a short shelf life, such as perishable or temperature-controlled items. Integrating the cross-dock operation with other logistics services can also help to streamline operations. It is also used in the automotive industry where parts are delivered on a just-in-time basis to a sequencing centre close to the manufacturing facility.

Sequencing centres can also be termed 'consolidation centres', where parts or products are delivered into a location from multiple suppliers for onward delivery to a retail store or a manufacturing facility.

Transportation planning and management

The extent to which transport planning and management is outsourced very much depends on who is operating the actual physical vehicles.

Companies who operate their own freight vehicles will plan their routes either manually or by using a transport planning tool. LSPs will also utilize this method. They will use their own sophisticated transport planning software to manage the deliveries and ensure fleet efficiency.

When outsourcing transport planning and management, the shipper can either hand over the responsibility of planning to the LSP, or plan the routes themselves and contract the LSP to execute the deliveries. With the advent of 4PLs, we are seeing the increasing use of transport management software systems to plan and manage deliveries. This will be further enhanced with the introduction of artificial intelligence.

Value-adding services

Outsourcing value-adding services as described below to an LSP can be very cost-effective. Some companies will separate these services from the warehouse operation, necessitating the company to source these services from another third party. This can be expensive in terms of logistics costs, what with transferring products between sites.

The cost of transporting items to and from a third party can be removed by having the LSP carry out these tasks in their warehouse. This has been a significant growth area for these companies.

CASE STUDY   DHL and value-adding services

In a shared-user warehouse, DHL carried out testing and repair on electronic products for Saitek, an electronics manufacturer for the computer games market, produced hampers for Crabtree and Evelyn at Christmas from their stock items, ensured products were retailer compliant and store ready for numerous suppliers, and re-packaged and re-labelled products for export.

For William Levene, a household goods manufacturer, they set up a production line to produce different configurations of products rather than store pallets of multiple product lines. The specific lines were assembled as and when ordered by their customers.

Examples of value-adding services include the following:

- labelling;
- kitting;
- sub-assembly;
- testing;
- packing;
- shrink-wrapping;
- tagging;
- kimballing – adding security tags;
- promotional work (eg buy one get one free offers);
- gift wrapping.

Some companies will also look to outsource back-of-house functions such as purchasing, invoicing, supplier and customer payment management, inbound and outbound planning, inventory management, systems and technology management and call centre support.

A further example from the DHL warehouse mentioned in the case study is Western Publishing, an American publisher and supplier of books and accessories. DHL managed all their inbound transportation, import clearances, storage, order receipt and processing, outbound transportation, invoicing and accounts payable. Western Publishing only had to provide a procurement and sales team in the UK, whilst DHL managed the whole of their logistics operation.

Reverse logistics

E-commerce returns can represent between 15 per cent and 20 per cent of all items sold, and much more in fashion retailing. Boden, a UK-based fashion company with operations in Germany and the US, has an average return rate across Europe of approximately 36 per cent, with Germany having a return rate of 54 per cent.

The growth of e-commerce has seen a significant increase in reverse logistics operations. In the above case, Boden utilize the services of DHL in Germany to receive and process the returns and authorize a credit before shipping the items back to the UK to be quality checked, cleaned (if necessary), repacked and returned to stock if the quality of the goods is acceptable.

This quality control and repacking operation can be carried out in-house or outsourced to a third party. The service can be operated within the stock-holding warehouse, or at a separate location, either dedicated or shared-user. For example, food companies will often process returns in a separate facility so that they can check for infestation before accepting the goods back. This protects their core facility.

A typical example of a shared-user reverse logistics operation is that operated by Clipper Logistics in the UK on behalf of Marks and Spencer, ASOS and John Lewis amongst others.

Reverse logistics can be complex, and as a result can incur increased costs if not managed efficiently. Gone are the days when returned items are stacked up in the corner of a warehouse. Today they need to be processed quickly to ensure consumers receive their refunds and that the goods are available for resale immediately.

This increase in returns has seen the growth of non-asset owning companies such as CollectPlus, who utilize sister company Yodel to effect the collections. Many retailers will offer customers the opportunity to return items to their stores, as opposed to using couriers or the postal service. This reduces the overall cost of reverse logistics.

Companies such as XPO Logistics also provide added value in this sector by operating an eBay account for their clients to dispose of out-of-season products, 'seconds' and end-of-line items.

A recent challenge for companies is the introduction of online 'try before you buy' facilities, introduced by companies such as ASOS, Topman and Schuh. This system could potentially result in a significant increase in returns. According to a report by Brightpearl (2018), 17 per cent of global retailers are adopting this model. With returns already costing UK retailers £60 billion per annum, this is another challenge to their bottom line.

Inventory management

Managing stock levels and (re-)ordering product is an area where many companies are reluctant to outsource. Putting the ordering of stock in the hands of an LSP is difficult, as they are unlikely to have the experience or knowledge required when it comes to replenishing product.

The use of a distributor is an alternative option. According to the Integrated Marketing Communication Council (IMCC) Europe, a distributor is:

> '...an entity that buys non-competing products or product lines, stores them and resells them to retailers or direct to the end users or customers.' (IMCC Europe, 2019)

They usually also provide a range of services such as product information, estimates, technical support, after-sales services and credit to their customers.

A further exception is Vendor Managed Inventory, in which the supplier manages the re-order levels on behalf of the customer. This can also be seen in service parts logistics operations, maintenance stores and production facilities, where the vendor will top up the parts and tools utilized.

Order management and fulfilment

We have seen a significant increase in this area of logistics services over recent years as a result of the growth in e-commerce. Start-up companies are able to utilize the services of a third-party fulfilment centre to provide an all-encompassing service.

Information technology services

The outsourcing of IT services has risen over the past few years. According to the 2019 Third-Party Logistics Study (Langley *et al*, 2019), 11 per cent of IT services were outsourced in 2018. Potential areas include cloud-based software, whereby companies rely on third parties to store data on remote servers.

An interesting development is the supply of warehousing, distribution, IT services and automation systems by Ocado to Kroger in the US, Groupe Casino in France and Morrisons in the UK. Kroger plans to roll out 20 customer fulfilment centres in the US equipped with Ocado's end-to-end technology and automation solutions (Melton, 2019).

In the UK, Ocado provides Morrisons with automation technology, logistics, distribution services and an end-to-end online platform. This includes the online shop and mobile apps, the routing and planning software, and the warehouse and head office systems needed to support and operate their online retail business. Since 2017, Ocado Solutions has also been providing Morrisons with the software required to fulfil customer orders from its store network via a store pick solution. They have recently entered into a partnership with another UK retailer – Marks and Spencer.

Supply chain consultancy

One could argue that companies who enter into an outsourcing arrangement with a 3PL will expect some form of 'free' consultancy from its suppliers. After all, they should be the experts in this area.

However, some 3PLs such as Unipart have their own supply chain consultancy division, which can work on behalf of existing logistics clients and external companies. A leading utilities company has recently contracted a consultant from a 3PL to assist them in improving their in-house warehouse operation. GSK has also gone through a similar exercise.

Fleet management

As with transport planning, this very much depends on who is operating the physical fleet. However, an own-account operator can outsource the repair and maintenance of its fleet to a third party. This may be the supplier of the vehicles, such as Volvo or Mercedes, or a commercial vehicle repair and maintenance company. Charges can be based on a cost per mile or per kilometre.

Service parts logistics

One of the factors driving the move to outsourcing service parts logistics is a company's desire to move parts inventory – and physical assets such as parts warehouses and depots – off their balance sheet and onto a third-party provider's.

Aftermarket supply involves a wider variety of different part numbers, sourced from a greater number of suppliers and distributed to a larger number of end customers. Each of these dimensions brings its own characteristics that help to make service parts logistics much more complex than manufacturing logistics.

Sourcing and supply of non-current service parts, minimum batch sizes, obsolete materials and components bring logistical challenges. Time-critical warehousing and distribution, often on a multi-echelon, worldwide basis within 24 hours utilizing multiple modes of transport over air, land and sea brings challenges too. Outsourcing to a specialist service parts logistics company can overcome many of these challenges.

LLP/4PL services – supply chain management

Outsourcing the whole of a company's supply chain is a recent phenomenon, and has resulted in the rise of the 4PL company. Operating in a global marketplace, a number of companies have recognized the value in outsourcing the management of their supply chain, either in totality, within a region or for a specific product. The cost of one-way movements of stock can be significant, and therefore the use of a company to manage this whole process and draw on under-utilized resources from other supply chains can improve efficiency and reduce overall costs.

An example of this is DHL's contract with Morrisons, in which they are managing their wholesale logistics operations. The service includes warehousing, order fulfilment, store delivery and IT services.

Not only have we seen the rise in 4PLs, but we have also seen 3PLs such as DHL, Kuehne + Nagel and XPO Logistics enter this market sector – not as 4PLs in the true sense of the word, but as LLPs, utilizing their own assets and those of their competitors to provide a 'one-stop shop' service to their customers by managing the whole of their supply chain.

The management of a company's supply chain can be very complicated, and requires sophisticated software systems, sometimes called Control Towers, and experienced staff to provide an efficient and cost-effective service.

Customers of these services also need to be aware that they are entering a new type of relationship that requires considerable investment in the relationship and cannot be regularly tendered. This is discussed in Chapter 4.

Customer service

This element of supply chain and logistics is rarely outsourced, as companies are reluctant to lose control over this part of the business. However, it can be included with other aspects of logistics and supply chain services.

A typical example is a mobile phone company which outsources its warehousing and distribution business, combined with a customer service call centre and repair service.

Conclusion

A wide variety of logistics services and added value services can be carried out by LSPs.

As discussed in this chapter, modes such as rail, air and sea freight tend to be outsourced because of the high capital outlay involved. Road transportation and warehousing also have a significant capital outlay – however, some companies will still prefer to manage these operations in-house as they do not want to lose control of their overall operation.

Whether the other logistics services mentioned such as freight forwarding, value-adding services and freight bill auditing are outsourced will very much depend on the competencies within the company to carry them out.

To outsource or not to outsource?

02

Introduction

This chapter will discuss whether logistics services are core activities for most companies, and, if so, whether they should be outsourced. For many businesses, logistics can be considered core, but the company may not have the required competencies internally to efficiently and effectively manage these services.

The chapter will go on to discuss the advantages of and barriers to outsourcing, which can be many, and will vary by company. It will also explore the risks attached to outsourcing what some companies deem to be a core part of their business.

At the end of the chapter there are specific models to assist companies in making informed decisions as to whether to outsource their logistics services.

Is logistics core or non-core?

Before deciding whether to outsource logistics services, companies need to decide whether logistics is core to their operations or not. The answer may well influence their final decision.

The 2018 Chartered Institute of Logistics and Transport outsourcing survey (and all those which have preceded it) report that one of the main reasons why companies outsource their logistics is because they don't perceive it to be core to their business.

More than 32 per cent of respondents stated that one of their main reasons for outsourcing logistics, and the main advantage they gained from doing so, was to enable them to concentrate on their own core competencies, turning to logistics service providers (LSPs) to provide the expertise and knowledge required. Quotes from respondents included:

'We can concentrate on our area of expertise.'

'We can focus on what we do best.'

'It's [logistics], not a core area to invest capital.'

'It allows the business to focus on its core competencies.'

The core functions that these businesses prefer to focus on tend to be the efficient sourcing of raw materials, research and development, product design, production, and sales and marketing of finished items.

The authors suggest that if logistics is a core part of the business, but not a core competency, outsourcing is certainly worth seriously considering. In certain circumstances there might not be sufficient critical mass in terms of logistics services for a company to deem them to be core, and therefore they can easily be outsourced.

Ensuring that getting the right product to the right place, at the right time in the right quantity, in the right condition at an economic cost is critical to most businesses, whether managed in-house or subcontracted to an LSP.

According to Power, Desouza and Bonifazi (2006), a company's logistics operation is more likely to be core than non-core. Today's logistics services are integrated into an organization's products and services and can differentiate the organization from its competitors.

Before the advent of e-commerce, many retailers would have argued that logistics was a non-core activity. However, in today's market, logistics has become one of the main battlegrounds for businesses, with companies competing for online sales by extending order cut-off times – the ability to receive orders late in the day and deliver next day – and providing clients with a myriad of ways to receive their goods, including same-day delivery, collection in-store or from other convenient locations, together with real-time information as to where their order is at any time.

Table 2.1 shows retailers competing in two areas – cost and latest order cut-off time.

Amazon Prime is offering same-day delivery to customers in the London area, and companies such as Shutl are able to deliver within 60 minutes of an order being placed.

Table 2.1   UK retail order cut-off times as at February 2019

Retailer	Last order cut-off time for next-day delivery	Cost*
Next	11pm (12pm if collected from store after 12 midday)	£3.99
Harvey Nichols	3pm	£8.00
Jigsaw	2pm	£8.00
Argos	8pm	£3.95
Boohoo	11pm	£5.99
John Lewis	8pm	£6.95
ASOS	midnight	£5.95
Very.co.uk	7pm	£3.99
New Look	7pm	£5.99
Warehouse	8pm	£4.99

* The above costs vary depending on the size of the order. Some retailers will offer free next-day delivery if the order is above a certain value.

Amazon is currently proposing to offer all their Amazon Prime customers a free next-day delivery service. This will put further pressure on its competitors to replicate this service, and will require a further enhancement of logistics capability.

According to Porter (1985), a competitive advantage exists when a firm is able to deliver the same benefits as competitors, but at a lower cost (a cost advantage), or deliver benefits that exceed those of competing products (a differentiation advantage). A competitive advantage therefore enables a firm to create superior value for its customers, and increased profits for itself.

Logistics can therefore be truly described as strategic, and worthy of the time and effort required to operate successfully. The question remains as to whether companies should operate the services internally, or work to ensure that they can buy in their logistics services cost-effectively. This will also very much depend on the size of the operation, the strategy and the competencies within the company.

By outsourcing logistics to an LSP, the shipper becomes reliant on the provider to bring their core competencies to bear, and as a result enhance the organization's service to its customers, create value and increase profits.

Power and colleagues had the following to say:

'When engaging in outsourcing, it is absolutely essential that a client organization is able to tap into the core competency of the supplier, not just for the simple task of sourcing the work but also for knowledge…. Clients are no longer only looking for cost savings but also for a business partner who can contribute to the strategic efforts of the company by providing it with expertise and competencies that are not found in-house.' (Power, Desouza and Bonifazi, 2006)

Other companies may just be looking for a transactional relationship, and don't require a partnership-type relationship.

Core competencies

Core competencies can be described as a combination of resources and skills that distinguish a firm in the marketplace. They are the foundation of a company's competitiveness.

Prahalad and Hamel (1990) suggest three tests which are useful for identifying a core competency:

- Does it provide access to a wide variety of markets?
- Does it contribute significantly to the end-product/service benefits?
- Is it difficult for competitors to imitate?

Let us take each one of these points in turn, and examine their relevance to logistics services.

Access to a wide variety of markets

Access to markets is at the very heart of logistics. However, this does not necessarily mean that logistics services are a source of competitive advantage. The ability to access different markets will often depend on the size of the business in that market, and few businesses are large enough to have a critical mass in all aspects of logistics.

Using local distributors, freight forwarders and groupage services may be the only cost-effective way to reach some markets. Outsourcing to a global, regional or even national LSP will give businesses access to markets, and they will have a ready-made network of warehouses and transport hubs. In fact, in China large e-commerce companies are purchasing logistics companies in order to access new markets.

UK food retailers Morrisons and Marks and Spencer have partnered with Ocado to strengthen their online presence, whereas Waitrose has decided to set up its own online grocery operation, identifying it as core to its future strategy.

Contribution to end-product/service benefits

With the advent of e-commerce, warehousing and last-mile delivery is certainly a great deal more important in today's fast paced retail world. Delivery on time, in full, meeting all the customer's requirements including a trouble-free returns process, can prove to be a differentiator between suppliers, and will significantly contribute to the end product.

This is highlighted by the number of consumers who abandon a purchase online when they see the cost of delivery or the fact that they would have to pay for returns.

CASE STUDY   Shipper collaboration

During a recent project undertaken on behalf of two major tyre manufacturers, it was agreed that logistics was not a core competency that led to competitive advantage and differentiation for either company, as both were able to receive orders and deliver to customers on a next-day basis. They saw differentiation in the product itself, and in overall stock availability.

As a result, the companies looked to combine deliveries, in order to save costs. They had no issue with both brands delivering orders using the same LSP vehicles and network.

Ease of imitation

How easy a logistics service is for competitors to imitate will very much depend on how innovative and sophisticated the services are, and how complicated their customers' requirements.

Companies such as Amazon, JD.com, Alibaba and Ocado are introducing innovative logistics solutions and becoming early adopters in order to remain ahead of the competition. Zara, a fashion retailer is also seen as a trendsetter in terms of its supply chain operations.

There is also an argument, discussed in greater detail in Chapter 11, that the LSPs are not innovative enough, and this is why many shippers retain critical elements of their logistics operations in-house.

A hybrid version

Outsourcing can provide access to new markets. However, many companies do not want to lose control over the operation, and want the ability to manage customer expectations and provide an enhanced delivery service.

Amazon's recent decision to operate its own warehouses, freight aircraft and road transport in many markets backs up this idea of keeping logistics services in-house. However, even they cannot handle the volume of deliveries at peak times, which is why we are tending to see a hybrid version with some logistics services retained in-house whilst others are outsourced.

John Lewis, a UK retailer, operates its own distribution centre for outbound e-commerce and store replenishment, but outsources its returns operation and last-mile parcel delivery.

CASE STUDY John Lewis – interview with John Munnelly, Head of Operations

John Lewis opened a small drapers' shop in Oxford Street in 1864. It is now one of the UK's top 10 retailers, with 50 outlets (36 department stores, 12 John Lewis at Home stores and shops at St Pancras International and Heathrow Terminal 2).

The business has an annual turnover of more than £10.2bn, and is the UK's largest example of worker co-ownership, where all 85,500 staff are partners in the business.

Johnlewis.com stocks more than 280,000 products, and is consistently ranked one of the top online shopping destinations in the UK. The company's online sales grew by 9.9 per cent year-on-year in 2018.

This case study concentrates on the store replenishment and online operation of John Lewis.

John Lewis operates its own warehouses and fulfilment centres for store deliveries and its online shopping experience. It undertakes its own store replenishment deliveries, together with its two-person home delivery operation.

The outsourced elements of its logistics include their total reverse logistics operation, pre-retailing operations, peak period relief, courier delivery to homes across the nation and abroad, and its joint venture with Clipper Group, 'Clicklink'. This is a sortation and delivery service which guarantees next-day delivery of online orders to Waitrose stores, for customer collection before noon the next day. These outsourced elements make up to 15 per cent to 20 per cent of the John Lewis logistics operation.

The current situation is likely to remain unchanged over the next few years. However, the uncertainty around the continuing growth of e-commerce and its seasonality (for example, an event such as Black Friday can generate 10 times more sales than on an average day) is likely to see growth in terms of utilizing 3PLs for dealing with peak demands, click-and-collect and returns management.

The length of outsourcing contract varies with the amount of investment made by the LSP. Clipper Group has invested heavily in its reverse logistics operation which is operated on a shared-user basis. This has resulted in a 10-year-plus contract being awarded. Other contracts are based on a rolling-year basis which, in this case, emphasizes the trust between the two companies. This is as opposed to short-termism, which can be seen in other similar rolling contracts.

The main contracts tend to be a hybrid of open-book, gain-share and closed-book. The shared-user facility enables John Lewis to pay as they use; however, there are also incentives for the LSPs to reduce costs on an ongoing basis. There is an open-book arrangement for parts of the logistics outsourcing contracts, with a percentage profit margin for the 3PL, but with a cap in place to ensure that unit costs are reduced year-on-year.

Courier charges are inevitably based on a transactional agreement.

John Lewis sees many benefits in outsourcing parts of its logistics operations, but also realizes the wisdom of currently keeping the majority of its logistics operation in-house.

The move to greater reliance on an in-house operation partly arose as a result of a bad experience with an outsourcing arrangement, but also as a result of recognizing the need to build internal capability within John Lewis. According to John Munnelly, if John Lewis staff can do it better, they should retain the operation in-house.

The company's main reasons for outsourcing include the following:

- greater flexibility at peak times;
- less capital investment;
- increased systems capability;
- increased capability in certain areas such as reverse logistics;
- the ability to share costs within a multi-user environment.

As an example of increased capability, Clipper Group manages the whole reverse logistics operation for John Lewis, including fundamentals such as receiving, checking, quality control and reporting, but also services such as cleaning, ironing, repairing, liaison with approximately 4,500 suppliers, supplier debit recovery, credits, disposal through jobbers, and so on.

The downside to this, of course, is the requirement to transfer the good stock to the John Lewis facility, which costs both in terms of transportation and time to market.

John Munnelly sees his relationship with his LSPs as a partnership – although fostering this relationship tends to be more difficult with the courier companies, as the work has to be spread across numerous companies to ensure that the volume of deliveries is covered.

As for barriers to outsourcing, the current situation still leads to multi-site orders which require either consolidation or separate deliveries to the consumer, as well as the stock transfer costs already discussed.

With regard to the dos and don'ts of logistics outsourcing, John Munnelly's main pieces of advice are to fully understand what it is you want to do when you outsource; to fully assess your in-house capabilities; and to think carefully about what may happen in the future.

John does see a role for the procurement department in final negotiations, but prefers to have the logistics team involved at the outset. He is now seeing a greater tendency towards innovation and investment by the major LSPs, but this does come at a cost, and inevitably means longer contract periods – which isn't always a bad thing. LSPs are becoming less risk-averse as a result.

Asda Walmart outsourced 72 per cent of its store replenishment operation in the 1980s. However, by 2009, 100 per cent of warehousing and 97 per cent of transport was back in-house. Having realized significant cost savings through the expertise of the LSPs, and assuming service levels will be acceptable, a shipper can confidently take an operation back in-house and save on the management fee. The ability to transfer key staff across is also advantageous.

The picture changes, however, as the complexity of the operation increases. Asda Walmart's fuel delivery to store is still completely outsourced.

Many retailers did not relinquish the buildings and transport fleets to LSPs when they outsourced their store delivery operations in the 1980s, and continued to control the assets, with contractors supplying the management expertise and the staff. The Kingfisher Group of companies in the UK is a current example of this. The reasoning behind this decision is that the company can control the quality of the assets. Owning or leasing the assets also allows shippers to transfer the operation between LSPs if they aren't satisfied with the service.

As seen in the Asda Walmart example above, a company may have competency in some but not all aspects of logistics services. Asda has outsourced specialist operations such as fuel delivery, but retained control over food distribution.

This hybrid combination can be seen in outsourcing relationships between shippers and freight forwarders where the shipper doesn't have the expertise in-house, and between shippers and couriers where the shipper doesn't have critical mass in terms of depot coverage for last-mile delivery.

People skills

Rouse (n. d.) states that 'a core competency is fundamental knowledge, ability, or expertise in a specific subject area or skill set'. This suggests more of a concentration on people skills, and therefore whether a company sees logistics as a core competency may be dependent on the calibre of staff employed. During the 1980s and 1990s, when companies outsourced significant parts of their logistics operations, they also lost a number of experienced staff in these areas to the LSPs.

There are signs that, in order to strengthen their supply chain teams, companies are again employing logistics experts. This is also resulting in companies reviewing their outsourced policy and contemplating bringing previously outsourced logistics operations back in-house.

Should companies therefore invest in people to ensure that supply chain management capability remains or becomes a core competency? Or should they outsource to an LSP to tap into their knowledge and expertise, and look at things holistically?

Outsourcing will require the LSPs to have the expertise to help clients enhance their supply chain operations. Peter Surtees, formerly European supply chain director for Kimberly-Clark, suggested when speaking at a Chartered Institute of Logistics and Transport (CILT) event that he had yet to see LSPs facilitate potential collaboration between companies within the supply chain, and it was companies such as Kimberly-Clark which were driving supply chain improvements.

Interestingly, in the tyre manufacturer case study in this chapter, both companies were utilizing the same LSP, but it was the shippers who were driving the collaboration. In fact, the LSP was reluctant to contribute to the project, and as a result it failed to materialize.

Is remaining in-house (insourcing) the answer?

Before giving up on in-house operations, a company must objectively assess its core competencies and measure them against world-class standards.

The main rationale for outsourcing decisions tends to revolve around cost, performance and productivity. PWC (Schwarting and Weissbath, 2011) add risk to this list of factors.

PWC argues that the 'make or buy' decision is built on three key pillars – business strategy, risks and economic factors, as seen in Table 2.2.

This model follows a number of others in terms of identifying whether the service differentiates the company from its suppliers, whether the capability within the company has synergy with other areas of the business, and whether the company is able to leverage its own capabilities, as Ocado has done recently.

The main criteria regarding logistics outsourcing tend to revolve around the three Cs – cost, control and competencies.

It can be argued that one of the most important elements in outsourcing is not who carries out the actual service, but who carries it out best. The company that does this is the one most likely to gain financially from the improvement in service.

Table 2.2 'Make or buy' – the three pillars of sound decision making

	Remain in-house	Pillars	Outsource
Business strategy	• In-house process differentiates the service. • Capability has synergy across the business. • Supply market is hostile or controlled by competitors. • Need to push the technology or capability envelope.	• Attractiveness of the process/business. • Criticality for overall business success. • Proprietary processes. • Service differentiation. • Industry dynamics and competitive positioning. • Dynamics of the technology or capability: 　o rate of change; 　o risk to core capabilities.	• Process/business is unattractive (hard to find labour, strict regulatory environment). • Processes are not critical to end products or marketing efforts. • Supply market is suitable for building close partnerships. • Suppliers are willing and able to meet innovation needs.
Risks	• Few or no alternative sources of supply. • High supply market risks. • Imperative to couple supply and usage (real-time/short lead time) for quick response or quality. • Sensitive IP involved in process.	• Hold-up risks. • Availability of alternative sources and switching costs. • Supply market risks if sourced overseas. • Political stability. • Exchange rate volatility. • Transportation risks. • Lead times. • Supply disruptions. • IP protection.	• Hold-up risk is low or sufficiently managed through contract of broader business relationship. • Low switching costs and easily accessible alternative sources of supply. • Uncoupling the supply chain has little impact. • No sensitive IP involved.

(continued)

Table 2.2 (Continued)

	Remain in-house	Pillars	Outsource
Economic factors	• Internal cost advantage or cost parity, high quality. • Significant recent investment in process technology that cannot be recovered. • Investments meet required ROI. • Company has strong defensible skills base.	• Relative economic and operating performance advantage. • Scale and utilization. • Efficiency. • Reliability. • Factor costs. • Quality. • Capital requirements and financial returns. • Level of skills and expertise.	• Suppliers have lower costs or better quality. • Major new investments are required. • Suppliers have lower ROI targets, insufficient or weak in-house skills/capabilities; skills are difficult to acquire.

SOURCE Schwarting and Weissbarth, 2011

CASE STUDY   Outsourcing isn't always the answer!

Gwynne Richards was engaged by the Royal Institution for Chartered Surveyors (RICS) to evaluate their warehouse operation and offer advice as to whether they should outsource it or retain it as an in-house operation. The lease on the building was due for renewal, and this provided an excellent opportunity to evaluate the situation.

The warehouse was relatively small but had a throughput of more than 27,000 books, and also undertook a number of mailing services on behalf of its marketing department.

On visiting the warehouse and meeting the staff, there was, understandably, a guardedness about his involvement. However, all the staff were very helpful and he soon had a comprehensive understanding of the operation and its cost base.

Having gathered the information, he contacted two service providers who were experts in the storage and distribution of books and reports, and explained the situation to them. Both parties were fully aware that it was a comparison exercise, and not a formal tender procedure. Honesty at this stage ensures that there is no ill-feeling at the end of the process if a contract is not awarded. From a service provider perspective, there is the possibility of involvement in a tender process in the future should the decision to outsource be taken.

Having ensured that all parties were quoting on a like-for-like basis, it became clear that the in-house operation was competitive and that with a couple of improvements and an extension of the business offering to include more mailing services, it could hold its own against any third party. Thus, in this case, RICS were the company which had the incentive to improve in order to retain the capability of the staff, but also extend their services to increase income.

The board's decision was to remain in-house. However, the company has subsequently outsourced as a result of a change in management and strategy.

Insourcing

If a contract fails or is due for renewal, the customer has to decide whether to remain with the incumbent, to award the logistics contract to another LSP, or to insource the logistics operation.

The answer can be complicated. It will depend on a number of internal factors as follows:

- the cost and level of service currently provided;
- the type of operation;
- the capital investment required;
- the existing level of expertise within the company;
- how important logistics is to the company.

If we take each factor in turn, we can determine the viability of insourcing in each situation.

a) The cost and level of service currently provided

If the current operation is working well and the supplier is proactive and continuously working towards cost reduction and service improvement, the decision to insource is likely to depend on the type of operation, the future strategy of the company and the strength and capabilities of its management team.

If the shipper is to replicate the service currently provided by the LSP, they will need to invest in resources to operate the contract. This will also include increasing the headcount within the company. It is true that LSPs make a profit on the contracts they operate (well – mostly), and that this is a possible saving for the shipper if they bring the business in-house. However, this supposes that the shipper has the expertise to operate the contract as efficiently as the LSP, and is able to draw on the synergies available to the LSPs.

Recent experience suggests that a number of shippers are not satisfied with their current arrangements, and if the option to insource was available would seriously consider it. However, companies are sometimes restricted by parent company strategy, capital investment and the will to go through another transformation.

b) The type of operation

A dedicated logistics operation is far easier to replicate, and also offers the opportunity to transfer both management and employees to the shipper through TUPE (Transfer of Undertakings, Protection of Employment). On the other hand, if the operation relies on some method of shared resource, it makes it very difficult for companies to not only replicate but improve the operation.

There is a trend emerging for companies that operate their own warehouses to rent space to other companies, in order to minimize the cost impact. There is also the appearance of collaboration between own-account operators, including Kimberly-Clark and Heinz and Nestlé and United Biscuits. Many retailers are also collaborating with their suppliers in terms of backhaul, minimizing the amount of empty running and thus reducing costs.

One of the main issues around collaboration is who drives and facilitates it. As discussed, Peter Surtees, formerly European supply chain director for Kimberly-Clark, expressed disappointment that LSPs were not driving direct collaboration amongst their customers. LSPs who run pallet networks, groupage services and shared-user warehouses are providing an opportunity for collaboration, but mainly through the service itself, as opposed to bringing parties together such as in the tyre shippers case study.

At the same event, Alan Devine of Gist stated his opinion that LSPs are proactive when it came to optimizing shared use; however, there is a risk involved if one of the partners decides it's not part of their future strategy for one reason or another.

Therefore, the expectation that LSPs are able to broker shared use amongst manufacturers isn't as straightforward as imagined. There are issues about confidentiality and a fear of losing competitive advantage, and contract length may not be conducive to these types of relationships. LSPs also tend to be more risk-averse in the current climate, and may be reluctant to share data surrounding rates.

c) Capital expenditure

The need to invest capital in logistics operations has also been a major factor in determining whether companies insource their logistics operations. However, in today's marketplace shippers are just as likely to get the same deals as their LSP counterparts, both in terms of the contract length and the overall lease and contract hire costs for warehouses and equipment.

Investment tends to be in staff as opposed to infrastructure. However, the cost of IT systems also needs to be taken into account – these include warehouse management systems (WMSs), route planning systems and workforce management systems, which may all belong to the LSP. This area is discussed fully in Chapter 10.

d) Staff expertise

Another reason why companies outsource is a lack of expertise within the company. Again, this can be rectified by employing experienced supply chain and logistics managers from either the incumbent LSP or the logistics sector. In fact, recent surveys have suggested that manufacturers and retailers are currently strengthening their supply chain teams, not only to enhance their own internal operations, but also to put pressure on their suppliers to improve performance and reduce costs. Taking on staff does increase headcount significantly, and this may not be an acceptable strategy as far as the board is concerned.

Another complicating factor here is that when companies outsourced in the past, they reduced their supply chain and logistics teams, believing that the LSPs would manage the whole process and there would be little need to oversee the logistics operation. Therefore, the decision to insource is likely to be a strategy decision for the board in terms of employing staff, assuming there are sufficient capable staff available in the market to make it work.

e) Importance of logistics to the company

Kate Vitasek's outsourcing decision matrix (Figure 2.1) looks at the relationship between the potential value of the service to the organization, and the available expertise within the company.

As shown, if the service is of high importance and there is significant expertise within the company, then remaining in-house should be strongly considered. If the value of the service is low and there is very little expertise in the company, then outsourcing is suggested.

Figure 2.1 Vitasek's outsourcing decision matrix

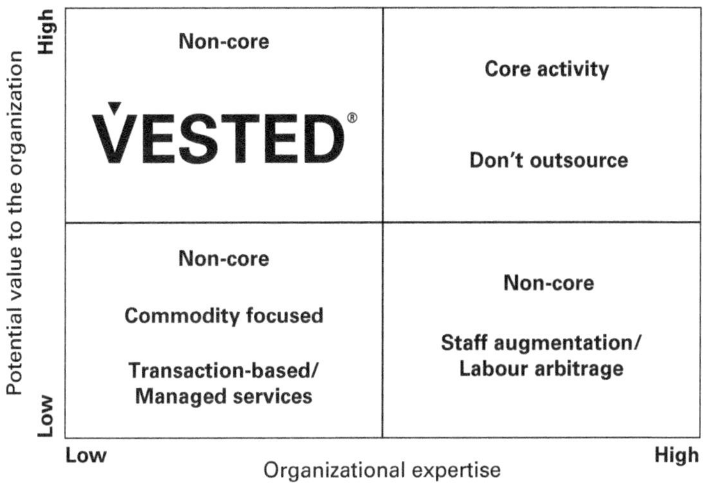

SOURCE Vitasek, 2013

Where the value of the service to the organization is high, but expertise is low then a partnership approach such as Vested® should be considered. If the value of the service is low but expertise is high, then it comes down to a financial decision – which is the most cost-effective, in-house or outsourced?

Vested® is discussed at length in Chapter 9.

Why do companies outsource?

There are a number of reasons why companies outsource.

There is an argument that if an LSP can perform activities more productively than the shipper, then the shipper should appoint that provider to do the work. Outsourcing allows companies to access competencies, knowledge and experience which they currently don't have. They can also take advantage of economies of scale – as suppliers are dealing with multiple clients, the scale of operations can reduce overall costs significantly.

Some of the main reasons companies outsource include the following.

Their own performance is poor and requires improvement

Where a company is performing badly in terms of logistics, there is always the temptation to outsource in order to improve service levels. This can be self-defeating, however, as the problems causing the poor performance may not lie with logistics, but in other parts of the business.

They need to reduce asset capital

The potential to remove assets such as warehouses and trucks from the balance sheet can be attractive. In a number of outsourcing relationships, we see service providers buying the assets and renting them back to the customer. Customers can then transfer their logistics costs from their balance sheet to their profit and loss account.

They need greater flexibility and scalability

Logistics service providers are usually able to react to changes quicker than a company operating its own assets. They tend to have a larger pool of vehicles and warehouses, allowing them to redeploy resources within the company. If outsourcing contracts are on a 'pay as you use' basis, shippers are able to reduce costs as volumes decline. With a static in-house fleet and warehouse estate, this isn't possible in the short term.

They want to transfer risk

A number of companies see outsourcing as an opportunity to transfer risk to the service provider. This is not a good idea, however – risk should be shared, as both parties have a vested interest in the outcome.

They want to concentrate on their core competencies

If logistics is not a core competency and the company is reluctant to invest in hiring those competencies, then outsourcing is certainly an option. This allows the company to concentrate on its own core competencies, as previously discussed.

They need to reduce cost

Cost reduction has always been cited as a reason to outsource. However, this is not always achieved. Service providers need to make a profit, and this can be anywhere between 5 per cent and 15 per cent – which could negate any potential savings through economies of scale, improved asset utilization and improved performance.

As Mal Walker from Logistics Bureau says (O'Byrne, 2017), cost can be a differentiator between service providers, but not the main reason to outsource.

They want to access new technology

The expectation is that LSPs invest in the latest technology, and continually assess its efficiency and cost-effectiveness.

Access to new markets

When a company is looking to expand into new markets, the ability to work with service providers who are already operating in those geographic regions is certainly advantageous. Outsourcing can be politically, strategically or financially motivated, or potentially all three.

The decision of the British public to leave the European Union has also had an effect on logistics outsourcing. In one example that we know of, one workwear company with a warehouse in the UK which serviced the whole of Europe decided to build a warehouse in Poland to service mainland Europe, due to the political uncertainty.

In a second example, as described in the following case study, a cosmetics and skincare company with a warehouse in The Netherlands decided to operate from a second warehouse in the UK to ensure supply to its UK customers.

CASE STUDY   Apprise Consulting Ltd

Apprise Consulting Ltd were approached by a cosmetics company which was worried about the potential effects of a no-deal Brexit on their business.

The company delivered throughout Europe from an outsourced warehouse in the Netherlands. In order to safeguard their UK online business, they decided to operate with a two-centre system by utilizing a third-party warehouse in the UK.

The client provided a comprehensive data pack which included sales data for the previous 12 months, storage requirement, product dimensions and delivery addresses together with specific logistics requirements, including a video of the value-adding services undertaken at the existing fulfilment centre. Apprise was asked to find a suitable 3PL in the UK who could partner with the cosmetics company.

Apprise researched the market, and found 17 3PLs who had experience within the e-fulfilment and cosmetics sector. Interestingly, of those 17, three only had a 'sales@' e-mail address and an enquiry form rather than a direct line to a salesperson. All three failed to register interest.

Each of the remaining companies was sent a Request for Information (RFI). The companies were provided with the company's background, headline data and timescale. They were also asked for the following information:

- their experience in e-fulfilment of cosmetics and skincare products or similar;
- their current relevant customer base;
- services carried out within the warehouse, including value-adding services;
- the WMS system used, and whether it would interface with the company's enterprise resource planning system;
- the ability of the WMS to allow clients full visibility of stock and real-time stock updates;
- whether their warehouse had bonded status (and if not, whether they were likely to apply for it in the near future – an important consideration if duty were to become payable on items at a later date);
- the latest order cut-off time for next-day delivery to mainland UK;
- proposed location, based on the above data and size of the warehouse;
- whether there would be space for expansion;
- which courier companies they had agreements with;
- which click-and-collect companies they had agreements with;

- the KPI currently being achieved with clients;
- warehouse operating times;
- the number of years in business and ultimate owner.

These were all areas which were very important to the client.

Based on the responses, eight companies were shortlisted and sent a non-disclosure agreement (NDA) to sign. On receipt of the NDA, the full Request for Proposal (RFP) was sent. The RFP included all the relevant data, together with the timetable and video of the current pick and pack process.

The 3PLs were encouraged to send in questions, and all responses were copied to each participant, ensuring that everyone was working with the same data and information.

The 3PLs were not given a rate schedule template. They were allowed to produce their own schedule of rates and were encouraged to be innovative.

A decision table was produced in anticipation of the replies.

Table 2.3 Criteria and weighting table

Criteria	Weight	Supplier 1	Supplier 2
Existing cosmetics customers	25		
IT capability – WMS and online portal	25		
Enterprise resource planning integration experience	25		
Cost and innovation	20		
Implementation plan and timing	20		
Order cut-off time for next-day delivery	20		
Warehouse operating days and times	15		
Lot number expiry date management	15		
Comprehensive value-adding services (VAS)	10		
Bonded warehouse	5		
Location	5		
Payment terms	5		
Contract length	5		
Company turnover	5		

On receipt of the completed RFPs, each response was examined thoroughly and marked against the decision table. Based on the rate schedules produced by the 3PLs, Apprise Consulting calculated the total cost for each 3PL. These costs were sent back to the 3PLs for verification.

Based on the results of the decision table, four companies were shortlisted and arrangements made to visit the sites over a two-day period. A second decision table was produced based on these visits, which took into account the above together with the following:

- quality of management;
- timely response to queries;
- company culture;
- warehouse environment and cleanliness.

One of the warehouses visited was very untidy with damaged products at the pick face. First impressions are very important at this stage. By contrast, the successful company ensured that two of their directors were present at the meeting, they responded quickly to all additional questions, and the warehouse was seen to be clean and efficient.

Two companies were shortlisted, and references were taken up from existing clients. Finally, a letter of intent was sent to the successful company. The process began on 17 October 2018 and the letter of intent was sent out on 21 December.

The process ran smoothly because of the comprehensive data produced by the client, and the communication between the 3PLs, the consultant and the client.

The authors have seen a number of companies immediately outsource following a change of management. In these circumstances, there is an adage which says: 'if it ain't broke, don't fix it!'. Companies should go through the processes outlined in Chapter 5 before making these decisions.

Many enterprises have determined that standard inbound and outbound freight transport and warehousing are 'consequential' processes of their business, rather than 'fundamental' or 'core' processes. This has resulted in a large percentage of warehousing and freight transport being outsourced. We do see an inconsistency here with a number of UK retailers operating their own warehousing and transport in-house and outsourcing some of the more complicated services such as reverse logistics.

There are also a number of companies such as Mondelēz that operate both models and are therefore able to benchmark both in-house and third-party services. See the Mondelēz case study in Chapter 7.

In the Tate and Lyle case study in Chapter 5, the following reasons were given by the supply chain team as to why they felt outsourcing was the right choice for them:

- the company's strategic direction – they wanted to focus on core competencies (brand / sales / R&D);
- to transfer complexity;
- to reduce the logistics cost-to-serve;
- to reduce direct overheads – both people and infrastructure;
- to release working capital;
- to access industry expertise and best practice;
- to leverage economies of scale in both multi-user environments and transport networks;
- to access the flexibility to scale up or down;
- to leverage enhanced IT systems.

The advantages of outsourcing – survey results

In the 2018 logistics outsourcing survey carried out by CILT (CILT, 2018), cost reduction and related topics dominate the perceived benefits of outsourcing logistics services. Gaining access to supplier expertise is the next most commonly stated benefit, followed by flexibility and the ability to focus on core competencies.

The top benefits have remained constant over the last seven years of the survey, with cost gradually becoming the number one perceived benefit over expertise and flexibility.

Public sector and charity respondents had a slightly different order of priority in 2018 to the other groups; they and other respondents mentioned the ability to transfer risk to the LSP as a benefit. Access to shared user services and flexibility were also mentioned frequently as benefits.

Table 2.4 shows the advantages broken down by user/supplier.

Table 2.4   CILT outsourcing survey results – the advantages of outsourcing

	Retail and manufacturing	Public sector and charity	Logistics service providers	Consultants and academics
1	Cost reduction Cost-saving opportunities, greater value for money	Saving internal resource Reduced overhead and headcount	Cost reduction Cost-saving opportunities, greater value for money	Cost reduction Cost-saving opportunities, greater value for money
2	Expertise Access to LSP expertise and professionalism	Cost reduction Cost-saving opportunities, greater value for money	Expertise Access to LSP expertise and professionalism	Expertise Access to LSP expertise and professionalism
3	Focus on core More focus on core activities of the business instead of logistics	Transfer of risk Part of risk moves to LSP, reduction of risk for business	Flexibility Increase in ability to respond to changing demand	Flexibility Increase in ability to respond to changing demand
4	Saving internal resource Reduced overhead and headcount	Flexibility Increase in ability to respond to changing demand	Focus on core More focus on core activities of the business instead of logistics	Focus on core More focus on core activities of the business instead of logistics

SOURCE CILT, 2018

Reasons for not outsourcing logistics

With the growth of e-commerce, we are seeing companies spending a great deal more time, money and focus on getting their logistics operations right, with many retaining the fulfilment operation in-house. This can be seen in the John Lewis case study earlier in this chapter.

So what reasons are given for companies to retain their logistics in-house? The following are some of the reasons why companies may be reluctant to outsource:

- logistics being seen as a core competency and too important to outsource;
- the capability and service quality of the LSP resulting in no service improvement;
- a perceived increase in cost;
- lack of faith in the commitment of LSP;
- fear of losing control over the operation;
- different cultures between the companies;
- management of risk;
- internal politics.

Where companies see their own in-house operation as superior to any third-party supplier, having gone through a benchmarking exercise, for example, there is no reason to outsource. It may also be that the products and services provided are unusual or even unique, and unlikely to be supplied or understood by external companies.

A number of companies feel that outsourcing logistics results in a loss of control of the operation and distances the company from its customers. This is one of the main factors cited in the annual CILT annual outsourcing and procurement surveys.

As for cost reduction, LSPs have to make a profit to survive, and therefore in order for costs to reduce the new operation must make significant improvements in terms of efficiency and productivity.

Service improvement is not always a consequence of outsourcing, and therefore some companies are reluctant to enter into outsourcing contracts without a guarantee of increased service levels.

As part of their outsourcing project, Tate and Lyle also examined the advantages of retaining their logistics in-house. These were as follows:

- no need to pay a margin to the LSP;
- costs remain transparent and in direct control of Tate and Lyle;
- workforce commitment, as employees are on the Tate and Lyle payroll;
- 100 per cent retained customer relationship management and engagement;
- no need to build and maintain IT system interfaces;
- zero cost of change;
- no risk of becoming over-dependent upon the LSP ('lock-in');
- key skills and knowledge retained.

Reasons for not outsourcing – CILT survey results

The top reasons mentioned by respondents to the 2018 CILT survey for not outsourcing are shown in Table 2.5.

Cost was high on the list, as well as on the benefit list; in this case it was the additional costs of paying a margin to the LSP and the potential risk of unexpected costs arising throughout the contract that were cited.

The key reason (and therefore barrier) identified by shippers was the potential risk to service or the quality of the offering. This was related to concerns surrounding the loss of a relationship with the final customer, and a loss of control.

Table 2.5   CILT outsourcing survey results – barriers to outsourcing

	Retail and manufacturing	Public sector and charity	Logistics service providers	Consultants and academics
1	Service/quality concerns Reduction in service quality, reliability and risk of loss	Service/quality concerns Reduction in service quality, reliability and risk of loss	Cost Increased cost related to margin, pricing or unexpected/hidden costs	Cost Increased cost related to margin, pricing or unexpected/ hidden costs
2	Cost Increased cost related to margin, pricing or unexpected/ hidden costs	Cost Increased cost related to margin, pricing or unexpected/ hidden costs	Service/quality concerns Reduction in service quality, reliability and risk of loss	Loss of control Perceived or actual loss of control by client
3	Loss of control Perceived or actual loss of control by client	Internal politics/ attitudes Negative attitude to outsourcing among potential clients	Internal politics/ attitudes Negative attitude to outsourcing among potential clients	Service/quality concerns Reduction in service quality, reliability and risk of loss
4	Relationship Issues with SRM including lack of alignment and communication	Lack of knowledge LSP lacking crucial product/ sector/ customer knowledge	Outsourcing inexperience Lack of outsourcing, procurement and analytical expertise on client side	Internal politics/ attitudes Negative attitude to outsourcing among potential clients

SOURCE CILT, 2018

LSPs in contrast saw internal politics and attitudes to outsourcing as a significant barrier (an attitude shared by public sector and charity respondents), and a lack of outsourcing experience on the part of potential clients. Eleven per cent of LSPs mentioned staffing issues, including the quality of their own staff.

IT-related issues and risks were mentioned as a significant barrier by many in the retailer and manufacturer group, but interestingly not to a significant extent by any other group.

Logistics outsourcing models

According to Mello, Stank and Esper (2008), while prescriptive models would suggest most outsourcing decisions are made using top-down, proactive, systematic- and strategic-competency-driven processes, prior researchers have observed that actual decisions are often made using local, reactive, ad-hoc and seemingly limited-strategy-driven processes.

The fact that a number of companies have reversed their decision to outsource over recent years bears this out to a degree.

There are a number of outsourcing models – some of which have been adapted from more established models, whilst others are logistics specific. This section looks at some of the models, and how they can be used to make those difficult outsourcing decisions. They range from fairly simple models such as decision trees to more complicated decision-making processes.

At the end of the chapter we have produced a questionnaire which can assist companies with the process of determining whether outsourcing is the right option for them.

Outsourcing models

One model adapted by Barnes (2008) from Dornier *et al* (1998) looks at the relationship between the strategic importance of the service (whether it provides competitive advantage to the company), and the criticality of the service (what are the consequences if the service is performed badly).

If we take the example of a car manufacturer, outsourcing may be a good opportunity when the service is not of strategic importance – it doesn't provide competitive advantage – yet contributes to improved operational performance (the delivery of finished cars to the dealerships, for example). Late delivery of the car, however, can result in an unhappy customer. Working with Tier 1 suppliers can also come into this category.

If the service is strategically important but doesn't enhance operational performance, then entering a close relationship with a service provider is an option. This could relate to the relationship between the car manufacturer and its Tier 1 suppliers, as discussed above. However, it may be that if suitable in-house expertise exists, then it may be cheaper to produce in-house.

R&D and assembly of the finished car are both strategically important and have an effect on operational performance, and so are more likely to be retained by the company.

A non-core service can be eliminated or, if unable to do so, a transactional relationship with a supplier is suggested. An example here might be the valeting of the cars prior to delivery.

The model is shown in Figure 2.2.

The model in Figure 2.3, loosely based on McIvor's (2000) outsourcing decision tree, looks at core and non-core competencies and leads the reader through a process of determining the importance of the service, the capability within the company and any political or strategic constraints.

Figure 2.2   The Barnes/Dornier decision outsourcing matrix

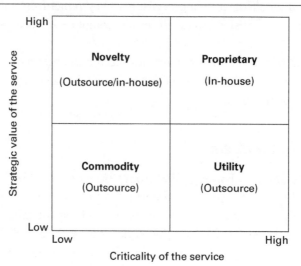

SOURCE Barnes, 2008, adapted from Dornier *et al*, 1998

Figure 2.3 The outsourcing decision tree

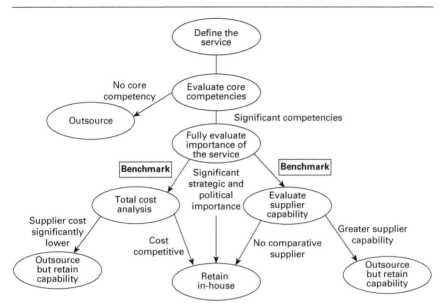

SOURCE adapted from McIvor (2000)

McIvor's model also encourages the company to benchmark its current operation throughout the process to ensure that whatever decision it comes to, the outcome should at least equate to (if not exceed) the current levels of service, and result in cost reduction.

McIvor also produced the following model (Figure 2.4) concentrating on process importance and capability, which builds upon the Vitasek model shown in Figure 2.1.

In Figure 2.5, Kremic, Tuken and Rom's (2006) model highlights the conflicting areas of benefits and risks when it comes to outsourcing. If the company feels that the risks are too high, then they will not consider outsourcing. If the benefits outweigh the risks, they will consider which functions are a potential for outsourcing, and go to the next stage.

At the evaluation stage the company can benchmark against potential suppliers.

The final model (Grubišić Šeba, 2018) shown in Figure 2.6 also utilizes a decision tree, but looks at a number of areas such as core business, cost,

Figure 2.4 McIvor's process and capability analysis

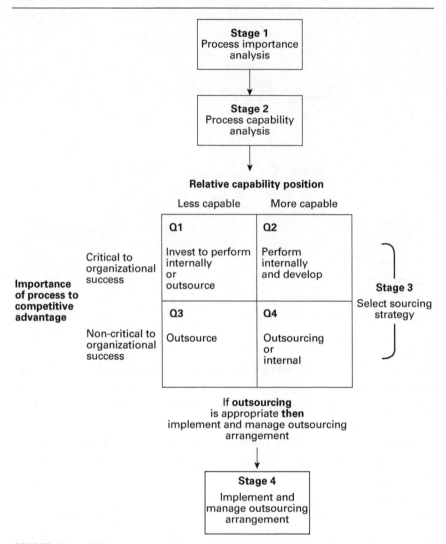

SOURCE McIvor, 2009

competency and flexibility. The model continually asks questions until an acceptable outcome is reached.

As we have demonstrated, there are many models available. However, these only tend to look at a part of the whole process, and in terms of important decisions such as outsourcing, we need a more comprehensive approach.

Figure 2.5   Kremic, Tuken and Rom's benefits vs risks model

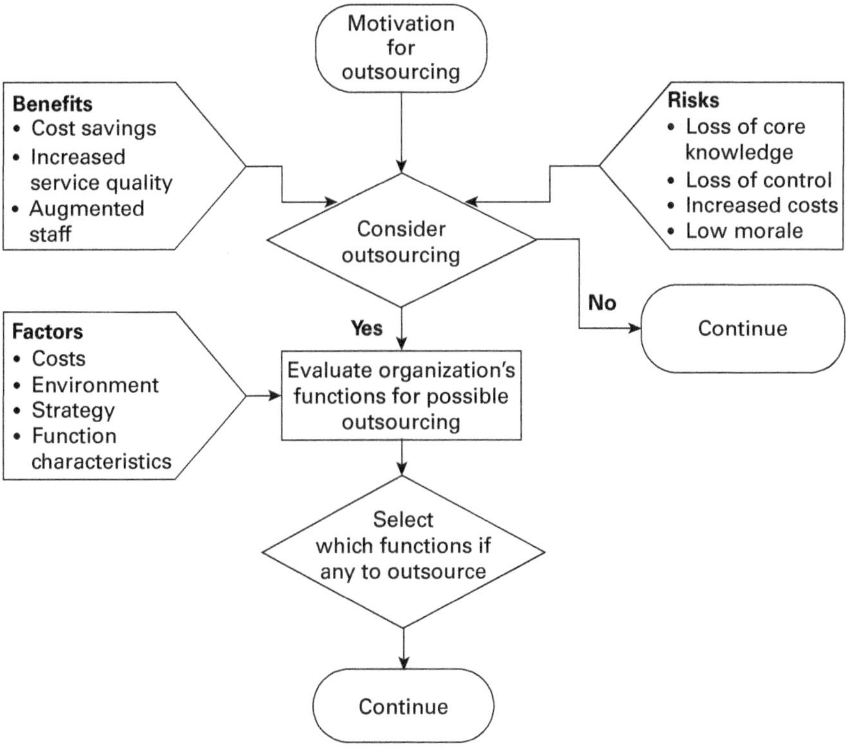

SOURCE adapted from Kremic, Tuken and Rom (2006)

We have produced the following questionnaire to help determine whether a company should outsource or not. At each stage in the questionnaire there are a number of questions which need to be discussed, the answers to which will, in part, determine the next steps.

You won't always be able to give an absolute yes and no answer – however, there is likely to be a leaning one way or the other. If your answer to a question is a genuine 'don't know', then you will need to undertake further work. There may be a requirement to undertake a benchmarking exercise to fully assess the current logistics operation and examine the feasibility of outsourcing.

Figure 2.6 Grubišić Šeba's outsourcing decision tree

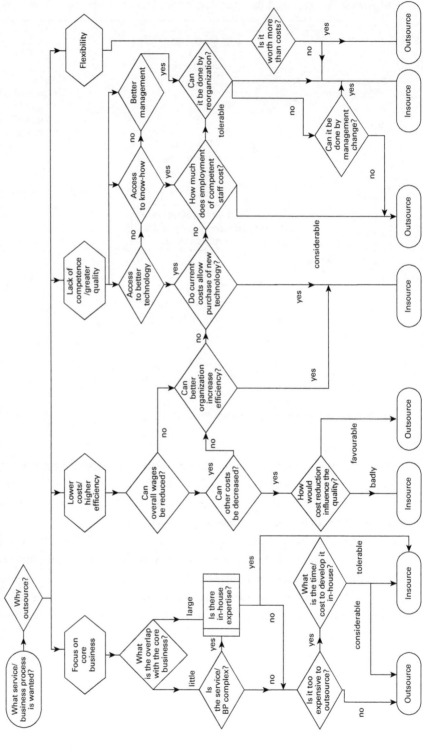

SOURCE: Grubišić Šeba, 2018

Table 2.6 Outsourcing questionnaire

	No	Don't know	Yes
Current situation			
Is logistics a core activity within our business?		R	O
Do we have the expertise (core competence) internally?		R	O
Do we compare favourably against our competitors in logistics terms?	BM	R	O
Does our logistics operation give us differentiation?		R	O
Are we able to leverage economies of scale within the operation?		R	O
Are there internal political reasons for retaining an in-house operation?		R	O
Do we have sufficient capital to fund a logistics operation?		R	O
Are we a risk-averse company?		R	O
Do we worry about losing control of a key activity?		R	O
Does operating our logistics give us greater flexibility?		R	O
Is there the likelihood of a loss of crucial expertise if we outsource?		R	O
Do we have sufficient wider market knowledge?		R	O
Could outsourcing threaten our corporate image?		R	O
Are we able to manage industrial relations issues internally?		R	O
Feasibility of outsourcing			
Is the availability of suitable suppliers a problem?		R	O

(*continued*)

Table 2.6   (Continued)

	No	Don't know	Yes
Is comprehensive market knowledge essential for our business?		R	O
Do we have greater capability than the potential suppliers?		R	O
Are there constraints to outsourcing, such as: • legal, eg staff protected by TUPE? • existing long-term leases? • a unionized environment?		R	O
Is our logistics operation very complicated?		R	O
Are there likely to be technological issues with outsourcing?		R	O
Are there confidentiality and security issues with outsourcing logistics?		R	O
Do we have problems finding suppliers with the right cultural fit?		R	O
Do we have the capability and expertise to undertake value-adding services?		R	O
Is our own performance sufficiently reliable to avoid issues with the LSPs?		R	O
Cost and service			
Are service levels likely to decline if we outsource?	BM	R	O
Are costs likely to increase if we outsource?	BM	R	O

Key:
   O = Outsource
   R = Retain in-house and optimize performance
   BM = Benchmark

Conclusion

Some will say there is no right or wrong answer when it comes to outsourcing, as there are so many variables and criteria which need to be taken into account.

If a company considers its logistics operation fundamental to its success, then it either needs to operate it in-house or take a partnership approach with an experienced and trusted LSP. However, if it believes the logistics services operated do not add significant value, then outsourcing to an LSP could well be the answer. The company will still need to manage the relationship, to ensure that the service to the customer does not fall below the expected standard.

As discussed in the sections on advantages and barriers to outsourcing, some companies see outsourcing as a positive in terms of cost reduction and service improvement, whereas others see increased cost and reduced service levels as an inevitable consequence.

The decision whether or not to outsource can be complicated, and requires a great deal of thought and preparation. Outsourcing logistics is a strategy decision, and cannot be seen as a quick fix. If undertaken, care needs to be taken throughout the entire process.

Chapter 5 leads you through the process from start to finish.

The logistics services marketplace

03

Introduction

On a global scale there are thousands of logistics providers offering third-party logistics (3PL) services, yet there are only a handful of very large 3PLs with the ability, network, systems and infrastructure required to provide a global service. These include companies such as DHL, XPO and Kuehne + Nagel.

This marketplace can also be confusing in terms of the titles given to outsourcing logistics providers. This chapter will provide its own definitions of the main types of players and the roles they play in logistics outsourcing.

This chapter will examine the size of the market as a whole and the percentage of logistics services outsourced. It will also discuss profitability within the sector, considered a barrier to growth and innovation by many. The chapter will look at five key markets including North America, India, Europe, Asia Pacific and China.

The chapter will go on to discuss increasing activity in mergers and acquisitions with a number of investment companies purchasing logistics service providers (LSPs) and companies such as Walmart, Amazon and Alibaba entering the third-party logistics market with strategic acquisitions to enhance their own service offerings.

The size of the global logistics market

According to the 2019 Third-Party Logistics Study (Langley *et al*, 2019), logistics outsourcing continues to grow, especially those logistics services which are more transactional, operational and repetitive. However, there is also a trend appearing regarding the outsourcing of IT services. This coincides with 3PLs introducing greater innovation and technology into their relationships – as Chapter 11 will discuss further.

In the same study, 61 per cent of shippers indicated they were increasing their use of outsourced logistics services, which is the same figure as reported in 2018. In comparison, 86 per cent of 3PL providers agreed their customers had increased their use of outsourced logistics services, which compares to 83 per cent in 2018.

The study goes on to say that total logistics spend as a percentage of sales revenue has remained constant at 11 per cent.

Research by Transparency Market Research (2017) shows the global logistics market, in terms of revenue, is set to expand from US$8.1 trillion in 2016 to US$15.5 trillion by 2024, registering a compound annual growth rate (CAGR) of 7.5 per cent from 2015 to 2024.

A report from consulting firm Armstrong & Associates (2017a) states that total 3PL revenue stood at $680.7 billion in 2010, $802.2 billion in 2016, and is on track to exceed $1.1 trillion in 2022.

Table 3.1 shows CAGR figures by world region. The largest growth comes from the Asia Pacific area. This is likely to continue as companies in this area continue to move from an in-house logistics operation to an outsourced version.

Table 3.1 CAGR and 3PL revenues by world region

Region	2016 global 3PL revenues (US$ billions)	CAGR 2010 to 2016
Africa	26.2	1.6%
Asia Pacific	305.0	5.7%
CIS/Russia	21.7	–3.3%
Europe	172.3	–0.6%
Middle East	40.2	2.4%
North America	199.6	3.8%
South America	37.2	–0.7%
Grand total	802.2	2.8%

SOURCE Copyright © 2017 Armstrong and Associates. Used with permission.

The chart in Figure 3.1 represents global revenue streams of the LSP market in 2017, sorted by major country. As can be seen, the US and China lead the way in terms of LSP revenue.

Utilizing the figures from this chart and combining them with each region's GDP figures, we can see that Europe and North America are operating reasonably efficiently. However, areas such as the CIS, Africa and the Middle East have high logistics costs in relation to GDP.

Figure 3.1   LSP global market size estimates

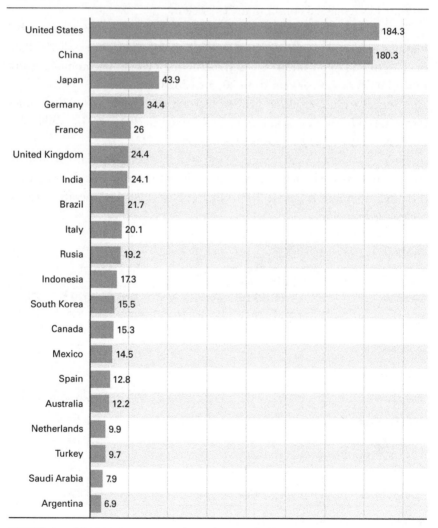

Country	Value
United States	184.3
China	180.3
Japan	43.9
Germany	34.4
France	26
United Kingdom	24.4
India	24.1
Brazil	21.7
Italy	20.1
Rusia	19.2
Indonesia	17.3
South Korea	15.5
Canada	15.3
Mexico	14.5
Spain	12.8
Australia	12.2
Netherlands	9.9
Turkey	9.7
Saudi Arabia	7.9
Argentina	6.9

SOURCE Copyright © 2017 Armstrong and Associates. Used with permission.

Table 3.2   Logistics as a percentage of GDP and LSP revenue by region

Region	2017 GDP	Logistics (GDP %)	2017 logistics cost	LSP revenue %
Africa	2,193.5	15.4%	338.6	7.7%
Asia Pacific	26,776.4	12.7%	3,406.6	9.7%
Commonwealth of Independent States	2,027.8	16%	325.2	7.8%
Europe	18,505.5	9.5%	1,759.9	10.5%
Middle East	3,720.2	13.4%	496.9	8.7%
North America	22,696.1	8.6%	1,950.9	11.3%
South America	3,938.7	12%	473.8	8.8%
	79,858.2		8,751.9	

SOURCE Schwemmer M, Fraunhofer, (2017)

Table 3.3   Contract logistics revenue 2018 to 2023

	2018 € millions	2023 (forecast) € millions
Asia Pacific	78,910	117,993
Europe	68,426	75,253
Middle East & North Africa	3,793	4,805
North America	50,629	56,225
Russia, Caucasus and Central Asia	1,644	1,902
South America	6,066	7,542
Sub-Saharan Africa	2,005	2,754

SOURCE TI, 2019

LSP revenue as a percentage of total logistics costs is also relatively low. This suggests that there is certainly room for greater use of LSPs in these regions.

In a recent report, Transport Intelligence (TI) provide the data in Table 3.3 for contracted logistics services globally, and forecast growth to 2023.

The World Bank Logistics Performance Index

A good indicator of where LSPs can improve logistics operations in specific countries comes from the World Bank Logistics Performance Index (LPI). This can be accessed at the following URL: https://lpi.worldbank.org/international/global.

The LPI Global Rankings are based on six criteria, namely:

1 the efficiency of customs and border management clearance ('Customs');

2 the quality of trade and transport infrastructure ('Infrastructure');

3 the ease of arranging competitively priced shipments ('Ease of arranging shipments');

4 the competence and quality of logistics services – trucking, forwarding, and customs brokerage ('Quality of logistics services');

5 the ability to track and trace consignments ('Tracking and tracing');

6 the frequency with which shipments reach consignees within scheduled or expected delivery times ('Timeliness').

Table 3.4   LPI index – top and bottom countries 2018

	Top 10	Bottom 10
1	Germany	Afghanistan
2	Sweden	Angola
3	Belgium	Burundi
4	Austria	Niger
5	Japan	Sierra Leone
6	The Netherlands	Eritrea
7	Singapore	Libya
8	Denmark	Haiti
9	United Kingdom	Zimbabwe
10	Finland	Central African Republic

SOURCE World Bank LPI

It is understandable that areas with high levels of conflict are more likely to be lagging behind the high-income countries. European countries as well as Japan and Singapore dominate the top ten. The USA comes in at number 14, China at 26 and India at 44.

Individual country analyses

This section will look at individual countries in terms of their potential for outsourcing logistics.

USA

A report from supply chain consultancy Armstrong & Associates (2017b) found that 90 per cent of Domestic Fortune 500 companies worked with at least one 3PL – representing a significant increase from 46 per cent in 2001, when they first started tracking this data.

Armstrong and Associates explain that this increase reflects how shippers continue to outsource logistics functions to 3PLs 'in order to control costs and increase supply chain efficiency', and 'company size continues to be a good predictor of 3PL use. The larger the company, the more likely it will have at least one relationship with a 3PL.'

Figure 3.2 shows the logistics market by segment in 2018.

Table 3.5 shows the leading logistics companies in the United States in 2018, based on North American net revenue in million US dollars.

Armstrong & Associates estimates that US 3PL market net revenues (gross revenues less purchased transportation) grew 12.1 per cent to $86.4 billion, and overall gross revenues increased 15.8 per cent, bringing the total US 3PL market to $213.5 billion in 2018.

India

A recent report by NOVONOUS (2015) states that the 3PL logistics market in India is expected to be worth $301.89 billion by 2020. The Indian logistics market is expected to grow at a CAGR of 12.17 per cent. This is because of the boom from e-commerce companies, and the expansionary policies of fast-moving consumer goods (FMCG) majors.

Research by Mahindra Logiquest (Venkatesh and Vulugundam, 2015) suggests that with the introduction of goods and services tax (GST), instead

Figure 3.2   US logistics market by segment (total gross revenue in $billions), 2018

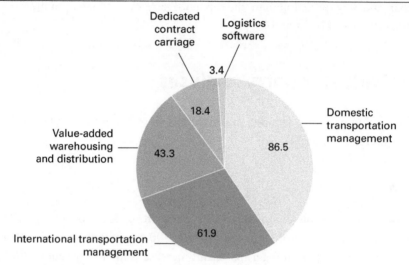

Table 3.5   Top 12 US LSPs by revenue

2018 position	2017 position	Company	Net revenue (millions $)
1	1	XPO Logistics Inc	6,112
2	2	UPS Supply Chain Solutions	4,750
3	3	DHL	3,809
4	6	J B Hunt	2,900
5	4	C H Robinson	2,705
6	7	Ryder Supply Chain Solutions	2,636
7	5	Expeditors	2,620
8	12	Penske Logistics	1,840
9	17	Lineage Logistics	1,837
10	10	NFI	1,700
11	8	FedEx Logistics	1,625
12	11	Kuehne + Nagel Inc	1,579

of maintaining smaller warehouses in every state, companies will be setting up fewer but larger warehouses and will follow a hub and spoke model for freight movement from warehouses to manufacturing plants, distributors and retailers.

There is a significant opportunity for LSPs who can manage pan-Indian routes and deliver accurately and efficiently.

Europe

The European logistics market is worth more than €1 billion, and generates approx. 7 per cent of Europe's GDP. Freight transport equates to 45 per cent of the total market (78 per cent of which is road transportation), with warehousing at approximately 33 per cent. Annual growth is around 2 per cent.

The top seven countries (Germany, the UK, France, Italy, Spain, the Netherlands and Poland) make up 75 per cent of total European logistics spend, with 13 countries accounting for 90 per cent of total logistics spend.

Europe is seen as a fairly mature outsourced logistics market. The top 12 LSPs based on revenue, according to Fraunhofer SCS (Schwemmer, 2017), are shown in Table 3.6.

Table 3.6   Europe's top 12 LSPs by revenue

Company	2017–18 revenue (million €)
Deutsche Post DHL (Group)	25,174
Deutsche Bahn AG	15,160
Maersk A/S	13,300
Kuehne + Nagel International AG	13,053
SNCF SA	10,040
Mediterranean Shipping Company Holding SA	9,500
La Poste (Group)	8,414
CMA-CGM SA	7,500
UPS Europe NV	6,700
The Royal Mail Holdings Plc	6,299
DSV A/Sfer	5,768
Dachser SE	5,280

SOURCE Schwemmer, 2017

Figure 3.3 shows the breakdown of services between outsourced and own-account operations. The chart shows that niche areas and those which require significant investment tend to be outsourced. These include air freight, less than truck load delivery (economies of scale for the LSP), courier and express parcels, and ocean cargo.

Asia Pacific

According to Armstrong (2014), the geographic region with the highest 3PL revenue spend and the highest 3PL growth rates is Asia Pacific, where growth has traditionally been driven by companies outsourcing or offshoring manufacturing to lower-cost countries.

While this trend still continues in Myanmar, Malaysia, Indonesia, Vietnam, Cambodia, and to a lesser extent in China, Thailand, the Philippines and Singapore, increasing domestic consumption, the movement of some manufacturing from China to lower-cost APAC countries and demand for products are driving the need for modern distribution networks in the Asia Pacific region.

The emphasis is shifting away from export trade and ocean or air freight forwarding to intra-regional ground distribution. 3PLs providing value-added warehousing and distribution services in these countries are experiencing significant growth.

Figure 3.3   The logistics market value in Europe in 2016 (€ billion)

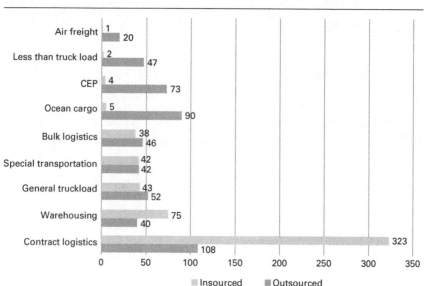

SOURCE Schwemmer, 2017

Buyers in the region are becoming more sophisticated, and they are pressing LSPs to offer more flexible, lower-cost solutions while expecting the 3PLs to continue investing in infrastructure.

China

The Chinese Government's Medium and Long-Term Development Plan of the Logistics Industry (2014–2020) marks the logistics sector out as a national strategic industry. According to the 2019 Third-Party Logistics Study (Langley *et al*, 2019), the demand for logistics has risen steadily and logistics services have become more professional, resulting in third-party logistics growing rapidly in China. The manufacturing industry in China has seen significant transformation and upgrading, which has led to greater requirements for professional logistics services.

Most 3PL providers in China originate from enterprises in traditional transport, warehousing and cargo agency. Some 3PLs are spin-offs from logistics services of manufacturing enterprises, and there are also 3PL firms that were established by merging the logistics resources of several enterprises. In addition, there are some newly established 3PL companies that have been developed in response to customer and market needs.

Table 3.7 China top 12 LSPs by revenue (10,000 CNY)

Company	Revenue (10,000 CNY)
China Cosco Shipping Corporation Limited	17,861,977
Xiamen Xiangyu Co., Ltd	12,197,438
Sinotrans	7,315,751
SF Express	7,109,430
Hebei Logistic Industry Group Co Ltd	4,283,982
Shandong High-speed Logistics Group Co Ltd	3,132,382
JD Logistics	2,636,382
Kailuan (Group) International Logistics Co Ltd	2,246,411
Deppon Express	2,035,011
China Merchants Logistics Group Co Ltd	1,508,239
JC Trans Logistics	1,441,103
Faw Logistics Co Ltd	1,130,000

In terms of ownership, there are a number of state-owned 3PL enterprises that not only have extended logistics networks and ample resources in China, but also explore international markets to become cross-border logistics conglomerates.

The top 12 companies involved in third-party logistics are shown in Table 3.7.

In-house spend vs outsourcing

According to the 2019 Third-Party Logistics Study, 28 per cent of shippers indicated they are planning to insource many of their logistics activities, which is higher than the 26 per cent reported in 2018, but still lower than the 35 per cent reported in 2016. Also, 36 per cent of 3PL providers agree that some of their customers are returning to insourcing, a reduction from the 42 per cent reported in 2018.

While these percentages may seem to conflict, individual shipper responses pertain only to their organization's plans, while the 3PL responses reflect the providers' thoughts about their overall group of customers.

Outsourced logistics spend as a percentage of total spend currently stands at 53 per cent, according to the same study.

In the same study, they found that outsourced freight transport outlay as a percentage of total transport spend has reduced from 55 per cent to 50 per cent, whilst warehousing spend with LSPs has reduced to 34 per cent from 39 per cent.

The players

In terms of outsourcing logistics, there are a myriad of LSPs operating, from owner-drivers through to the mighty conglomerates such as DHL, FedEx and UPS. They all provide some kind of logistics outsourcing service, although at different levels.

With such a large number of players in the market, companies are striving for differentiation. A recent report by TI (2018) states that the larger 3PLs are leveraging their global scale, technological capabilities, financial and human resources to provide a wider service portfolio and an enhanced value proposition.

Figure 3.4 The hierarchy of LSPs

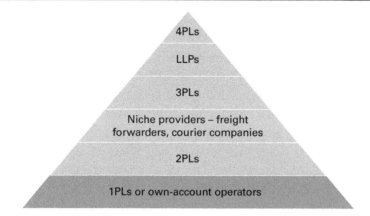

1PLs

Insourcing, own-account or 1PL refers to a company which manages and owns or leases its own warehousing and transportation in the main.

These companies will operate their transport and warehouses either in their entirety or partially, and outsource the rest. It is likely that they will outsource non-core competences such as courier distribution, and may well hire in additional resources such as trucks, drivers and warehouse space at peak periods. If involved in international trade, they may well use a freight forwarder to handle these movements.

The other logistics related services covered in Figure 1.1 are likely to remain in-house.

The different types of LSP

Understanding the differences between all the types of provider can be very confusing and frustrating. Logistics companies will provide services at different levels, and for different aspects of logistics including freight transport, warehousing, reverse logistics and value-adding services.

As shown in Figure 3.4, there is a hierarchy of logistics providers, which is based on the level of service provided to their customers. However, it is not completely straightforward as these types of companies will also work for each other to supplement services either locally or globally.

For example, a 3PL providing a dedicated or shared-user warehouse service to a client may not operate any of its own transport and will therefore subcontract the work. Therefore it could be classed as a 3PL for warehousing, but a lead logistics provider for freight transport if it is contracted to manage the whole logistics process. An example of such a company is Unipart in the UK.

Other examples include freight forwarders and couriers. The confusion here is when some of these companies supplement their core competencies by providing warehousing and transportation services to their client.

The evolution of DHL (a subsidiary of Deutsche Post) albeit through acquisition, is a case in point. DHL is an amalgamation of contract logistics companies such as Excel Logistics and Nedlloyd Districenters, freight forwarders such as Air Express International and Danzas and courier companies such as Securicor and UK Mail.

Container shipping companies also evolved, and many now supply freight forwarding, warehousing and transportation services either directly or through subsidiaries. Typical example is Maersk.

There are significant overlaps in this area which makes accurate definitions nigh on impossible.

Table 3.8 shows the top 20 LSPs globally in 2017/18, according to research by Armstrong and Associates (2017c).

Table 3.8   The top 20 global LSPs

Rank	3PL	Gross revenue (US$ millions)*
1	DHL Supply Chain & Global Forwarding	27,598
2	Kuehne + Nagel	22,574
3	D B Schenker	18,560
4	Nippon Express	16,720
5	C H Robinson	14,869
6	DSV	11,374
7	Sinotrans	9,530
8	XPO Logistics	9,506
9	UPS Supply Chain Solutions	7,981
10	CEVA Logistics	6,994
11	Expeditors	6,921

(continued)

Table 3.8 (Continued)

Rank	3PL	Gross revenue (US$ millions)*
12	DACHSER	6,911
13	J B Hunt (JBI, DCS and ICS)	6,828
14	GEODIS	6,255
15	Hitachi Transport System	5,935
16	Panalpina	5,621
17	Bolloré Logistics	5,012
18	Kintetsu World Express	4,752
19	GEFCO	4,740
20	Toll Group	4,660

NOTE Revenues are 2017 Gross Logistics Revenue (in USD millions) company reported or Armstrong & Associates estimates, and have been converted to US$ using the average annual exchange rate in order to make non-currency related growth comparisons. Updated July 2018. Note that DSV has recently acquired Panalpina, which will put their combined business into fourth place in this list.

2PLs

These companies tend to operate small fleets of freight transportation vehicles, and range from owner-drivers (single vehicle operators) through to multiple vehicles. Some of these companies may well also operate small warehouses.

A 2PL can be defined as an organization that manages and executes a particular logistics function, using its own assets and resources, on behalf of another company.

The advantages of 2PLs are:

- a single point of contact for its section of the operation;
- a single profit.

The disadvantages are:

- they are operators as opposed to strategists;
- they concentrate on asset utilization, not customer value;
- they may be unable to provide all the services required;
- multiple points of contact for the shipper, if shipper has multiple suppliers.

3PLs

In 2008 in the United States, legislation was passed declaring that the legal definition of a 3PL is 'a person who solely receives, holds, or otherwise transports a consumer product in the ordinary course of business but who does not take title to the product'.

A more comprehensive description is 'a relationship between a shipper and third party which, compared with basic services, has more customized offerings, encompasses a broader number of service functions and is characterized by a longer-term, more mutually beneficial relationship' (Murphy and Poist, 2000). This extended definition of a 3PL takes some of the changing conditions into consideration, such as the greater scope of the services required by customers and the enhanced role of the relationship between the parties involved.

As described above, a 3PL is very similar to a 2PL. However, it will have greater resources than a 2PL and is more likely to be involved in some sort of strategy discussion and is expected to be more proactive and innovative.

The advantages of 3PLs are:

- a single point of contact for the client;
- increased resources compared to a 2PL;
- greater geographic coverage compared to a 2PL;
- a single profit margin.

The disadvantages are:

- they may concentrate on asset utilization, not customer value;
- they may be unable to provide all the services required.

Lead Logistics Providers (LLP)

A good definition for an LLP is as follows: 'An organization that manages the full scope of logistics services for a company by aggregating and coordinating the services of multiple LSPs, including itself'. It's an asset-owning company, but also sub-contracts a percentage of the work to other carriers and warehouse operators.

The advantages of LLPs are:

- a single point of contact for the client;
- seamless key performance indicators;
- a wider pool of resources compared to 2PLs and 3PLs;

- increased geographic spread compared to 2PLs and 3PLs;
- some supply chain expertise.

The disadvantages are:

- they may be reliant on partners to provide some of the services;
- there will be several profit margins when using sub-contractors;
- they need to ensure that all owned assets are fully utilized.

Fourth-party logistics providers (4PLs)

According to Accenture, who came up with the name, a 4PL is 'an integrator that assembles the resources, capabilities, and technology of its own organization and other organizations to design, build and run comprehensive supply chain solutions' (Accenture, n. d.).

CSCMP (2013) suggests that a 4PL differs from a 3PL in the following ways;

- a 4PL organization acts as a single interface between the client and multiple LSPs;
- all aspects (ideally) of the client's supply chain are managed by the 4PL organization;
- it is possible for a major third-party logistics provider to form a 4PL organization within its existing structure.

The advantages of 4PLs are:

- the ability to step back from day-to-day operations to see the big picture;
- experienced supply chain staff;
- neutrality and an unbiased service – they are looking to optimize your supply chain rather than their own assets;
- greater access to resources and greater flexibility;
- greater information flow through sophisticated supply chain systems;
- a single point of contact;
- seamless key performance indicators;
- a wider range of possibilities compared to 2PLs, 3PLs and LLPs;
- the ability to select the best 3PLs for the task required;
- the ability to instigate shared user transportation for clients;
- payment by results options, such as gain share schemes;
- a global reach in many circumstances.

Figure 3.5   Accenture's four components of 4PL, as modified by Rushton and Walker

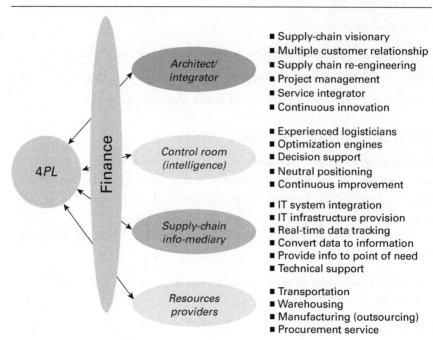

- Supply-chain visionary
- Multiple customer relationship
- Supply chain re-engineering
- Project management
- Service integrator
- Continuous innovation

- Experienced logisticians
- Optimization engines
- Decision support
- Neutral positioning
- Continuous improvement

- IT system integration
- IT infrastructure provision
- Real-time data tracking
- Convert data to information
- Provide info to point of need
- Technical support

- Transportation
- Warehousing
- Manufacturing (outsourcing)
- Procurement service

SOURCE Rushton and Walker, 2007

The disadvantages are:

- they are completely reliant on partners to provide the operational service;
- there will be several profit margins;
- there may be reluctance on the part of 3PLs to work for 4PLs.

Figure 3.5 shows a comprehensive view of a 4PL. Although providing resource is included in the description, the main focus is on vision, innovation, integration, continuous improvement and technology.

A true 4PL has the following attributes:

- it is a non-asset owning company;
- it uses sophisticated IT systems;
- it is a strategist that manages all logistics operations on behalf of companies;
- it can be expected to provide the most cost-effective logistics systems to its clients;

- it is an intermediary between the shipper and the transport companies;
- it develops contracts on behalf of the shipper with an optimum number of transport and warehousing providers.

If we take the initial definition of a 4PL as being non-asset owning, then 4PL contracts such as the recent contract between Opel/Vauxhall and GEFCO are not true 4PL arrangements. This contract covers all inbound and out-bound logistics for Opel/Vauxhall in Europe and Turkey. GEFCO will distribute parts to Opel/Vauxhall assembly plants from supplier sites world-wide. The group will also deliver vehicles to dealers and importers. GEFCO will use its own assets to undertake these deliveries (GEFCO, 2018).

It is the authors' opinion that the large 3PLs, fearing the loss of lucrative 4PL contracts, set up 4PL divisions in order to compete with the 4PL companies already in existence.

Figure 3.6 shows the size of the 4PL market in 2018, and forecasts its growth to 2027.

Figure 3.6   The size of the global 4PL market, 2018 to 2027

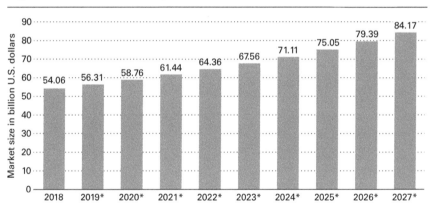

* = forecasted figures
SOURCE Statista, n. d.b

3PL, LLP or 4PL?

The decision to outsource your logistics operations is difficult enough – but then you have to decide which type of organization to place the contract with: 3PL, LLP or 4PL?

The questionnaire that follows is a straightforward 'yes' and 'no' question-naire which will give you the opportunity to decide whether working with a 4PL is right for your company. In order to decide whether a 4PL relationship is suitable for your company, ask yourselves these fundamental questions.

Complete the questionnaire to determine your outsourcing options. Tick the most relevant box for your current operation.

4PL questionnaire

Question	Yes	No
Section 1		
1. Does your organization struggle to manage increasing levels of supply chain complexity?		
2. Do your customers' supply chain demands exceed your organization's capacity to deliver?		
3. Do you wish you had full visibility throughout your supply chain?		
4. Would you like to have access to the technology capabilities to integrate processes and logistics providers across your supply chain?		
5. Can you make better use of your capital currently dedicated to supply chain assets such as staff and IT?		
6. Do you wish you had experienced supply chain managers within the company?		
7. Are you operating warehouses and manufacturing plants globally with little coordination between them?		
8. Are you looking to expand your business globally?		
9. Is neutrality and objectivity fundamental to your choice of logistics provider?		
10. Is your relationship with your suppliers and logistics providers adversarial?		

(continued)

(Continued)

Question	Yes	No
11. Is dealing with a multitude of logistics providers taking up too much management time?		
12. Are you under pressure from your customers to become more environmentally friendly, with an expected target of carbon neutrality?		
13. Are you happy to enter into a longer-term partnership?		
14. Are you happy to share resources with your competitors?		
15. Are you comfortable with having all your 'eggs in one basket'?		
16. Do you want your logistics contracts to be based on a gainshare/cost reduction basis?		
17. Are you looking for more than a task- or functionally-oriented logistics provider?		
Section 2		
a. Do you consider the supply chain critical to your organization's success?		
b. Is supply chain management a core competency within your company?		
c. Is full control of your supply chain very important to you?		
d. Do you undertake regular supply chain reviews in order to improve efficiency and reduce costs?		
e. Do you have full visibility throughout your supply chain?		
f. Is the relationship with your current logistic providers important to you?		

(continued)

(Continued)

Question	Yes	No
g. Do you want full control over your choice of logistics providers?		
h. Does your company have a policy against single supplier sourcing?		
i. Is having internal supply chain and logistics expertise important to you?		
j. Are you risk-averse?		

If you have answered yes to the majority of the questions in Section 1, then it is definitely worth considering 4PL companies. On the other hand, if you answered yes to the majority of questions in Section 2, then a 4PL may not be your preferred option.

Freight forwarders

As discussed in Chapter 1, freight forwarders are involved, in the main, in international trade. Many freight forwarders do not own assets such as trucks and warehouses, similar to 4PLs, although unlike 4PLs they tend not to operate the full range of supply chain services.

Nick Bailey from TI reported that the global freight forwarding market grew by 8.0 per cent in 2017 – a rapid expansion compared with recent years and the biggest annual gain since 2010 (Bailey, 2018).

The forwarding market and its largest players are embracing technology, as they seek to transform their operations from within. The entry of 'tech forwarders' – including digital forwarders and spot market platforms – has driven the largest forwarders to enhance their own technology usage and the capabilities they offer to shippers.

Customer-centricity is also at the top of the agenda, as the world's largest freight forwarders look to drive efficiency and establish new routes to market.

CASE STUDY Choosing an overseas freight forwarder

For UK retailers purchasing from overseas suppliers, there are two considerations when determining the type of contract.

High volume of container movements

Volume dictates whether the retailer deals directly with the container line, the NVOCC or a major freight forwarder. In this case the volume of containers moved enabled the retailer to deal directly with the shipping line. In this example the retailer is buying under the Incoterm Ex-Works.

Shipping a container from supplier to destination is like buying a plane ticket – the cost is based on capacity available and how close to travel you buy. If you have enough volume, you can negotiate annual contracts directly with the container lines on an annual or longer-term basis. A significant volume should get you the best price.

Under normal conditions, buying last-minute can cost a lot more, especially if there is a shortage of vessel capacity; however, shippers (or, in this case, buyers) need someone to have expertise in this area to keep an eye on the market. If shipping companies have excess capacity and the container shipping price drops too far for an extended period, then you might need to re-negotiate a new contract.

Separately, engage a larger freight forwarder (examples include Maersk, Yusen and Expeditors) who have offices within the origin region you are buying product from. They will manage the handoffs between the different points in the supply chain; that is, the process for the vendor to book the container, check the documents, undertake customs clearance at both origin and destination, book and transport into the distribution centre.

The preference is for continuity and continuous good service over continual change of contracts in order to save a few cents. Experienced partners deliver high levels of on-time-in-full service; however, it requires both parties to understand each other's systems, processes and people so that when things go wrong – which they often do – they can work together to find a solution. This will only work well if the two parties have built up an established relationship over time.

If the relationship with the freight forwarder works, continue working with them. Have regular reviews to discuss performance levels and periodically benchmark costs in the market.

Lower volume movements

In this situation, it is worthwhile working with a freight forwarder who manages the negotiation of freight rates with carriers (container lines or NVOCCs – depending on volume) and provides the logistics management.

This is likely to be at a slightly higher cost, but with limited expertise in the organization and the freight forwarder being able to pool volumes from other clients this will give a better result than trying to manage the freight movements in-house.

As with all LSPs, spend time selecting an organization. In terms of freight forwarders, select one which is local enough to understand your needs, works effectively within your organization and understands your business, is represented in the countries you are trading with, and has a cost structure that benchmarks well in the industry.

By John Gurr, supply chain consultant

Other players

There are a number of other players in this space. These include companies such as CollectPlus who were set up to provide last-mile services to e-commerce and retail companies. They utilize the resources of other companies such as Yodel, a sister company, and convenience stores, allowing the customer to collect their orders in a convenient manner.

Parcelly and Doddle are other companies providing last-mile, pick up and drop off (PUDO) services.

We also have companies such as Ocado who see themselves as 'a leading pure-play digital grocer in the UK, a provider of end-to-end e-commerce grocery solutions and an innovative and creative technology company'. They now provide comprehensive logistics services to retailers including Morrisons in the UK, Group Casino in France, Sobeys in Canada and Kroger in the USA.

Amazon has recently purchased Deliveroo for last-mile delivery, whilst in China Alibaba and six large Chinese logistics companies (including SF Express) established a company called Cainiao for delivery of packages in China. They also took a 10 per cent stake in Chinese express delivery company ZTO Express, highlighting the importance of controlling the last mile and to some extent the last yard delivery.

'Amazon is acting increasingly like a 3PL,' according to Evan Armstrong, president of Armstrong & Associates, a logistics industry research and consulting firm (Transport Topics, 2019). Armstrong estimates that Amazon provides logistics services for 12 per cent of business-to-consumer shipments world-wide, and he notes that third-party sellers account for more than half of all units sold through the Amazon platform. Amazon has also recently begun a freight brokerage operation in the North Eastern states of the US.

There are also companies who provide load matching services to shippers and LSPs, and these are now expanding to provide comprehensive transport management systems – a form of 4PL service.

In some literature, we also see companies labelled as fifth-party logistics providers (5PLs) and '7PLs'. According to LogisticsGlossary (n. d.), a 5PL: 'develops and implements, preferably in close consultation with the client, the best possible supply chains or networks. 5PL logistics is often linked to e-business.' It isn't entirely clear, however, exactly how this differs from a 4PL.

A 7PL has been described as a 3PL which also provides 4PL services. In the author's opinion, this basically describes an LLP.

As can be seen in Table 3.8, the top 20 list of global LSPs is made up of companies who can also be classed as couriers, freight forwarders, contract logistics providers and freight transport companies. It is therefore very difficult to categorize these companies, as they provide a number of different logistics services across divisions and across continents.

Maybe we should move away from all the different labels, and classify them all as LSPs.

Trends in the marketplace

Randall Miller from Ernst and Young has identified six industry-specific change drivers (Miller, 2018) that will impact the transport and logistics industry over the next decade.

Global uncertainty

Disruption in the global supply chain cost US$56 billion in 2015 in Europe alone. Economic turbulence, protectionism, and geopolitical instability are forcing transportation and logistics providers to adopt new business models and new alliances.

Urbanization

With the rise of megacities, transport and logistics providers need to cope with the challenges of urban logistics, including congestion, difficulties in loading and unloading, and last-mile delivery.

Digitalization

Digital technologies will transform the industry, with new efficiencies and new visibility. However, technology is a double-edged sword that also creates rising customer expectations and security challenges.

Technology innovation

Business model disruption is coming from established companies and a host of new entrants who are harnessing the latest technology innovations. This will lead to horizontal and vertical integration across the value chain, and networks that are real-time optimized.

Need for new talent

New technologies require new skill sets – including design thinking, data sciences and robotics. Hiring costs will rise, and innovation will be a key competitive factor.

Sustainability and transparency

Stakeholders, government agencies, and consumers are keenly interested in the practices that guide transport and logistics companies, including sustainability, labour conditions, and environmental compliance.

Profitability

Motor Transport in the UK publishes an annual table detailing the average revenue and return on sales of the top 100 logistics companies in the UK by revenue.

As shown in Figure 3.7, the average revenue per company has increased appreciably over the last 10 years, echoing the increase in logistics outsourcing and a number of high-profile acquisitions. However, the return on sales has fluctuated and reduced over that period.

This reduction in profit is seen as a significant barrier to LSPs investing in expensive technology. This, coupled with shorter contract periods, can lead to companies concentrating wholly on day-to-day operations, trying to reduce cost but with very little emphasis on innovation.

This is beginning to change, as shippers recognize that in order to compete with their peers they will need to harness the expertise within these LSPs and work with them to introduce more innovative solutions.

Figure 3.7 Motor Transport's top 100 logistics companies

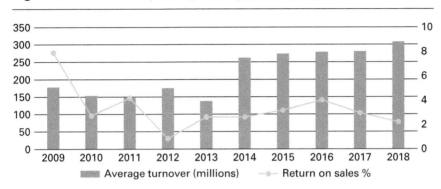

SOURCE Motor Transport Top 100, n. d.

Acquisition

There has been a significant amount of acquisition activity in the logistics provider market sector. The 1990s and 2000s saw many UK and European 3PLs being swallowed up by overseas companies. Names that have disappeared from European roads include Hays Distribution, TDG, Norbert Dentressangle, Christian Salvesen, Swift Transport, Storage and Haulage, Danzas, Lowfield and many others.

Since early 2014, there have been 10 major acquisitions by 3PLs totalling US$18 billion. These are primarily due to 3PLs' need to expand their array of services and extend their geographic footprints in order to drive scale.

In the 2010s we are seeing a number of e-commerce logistics and service providers being purchased by what we would term as traditional LSPs, investment companies and IT companies.

With regard to future trends in logistics, Thomas van Mourik (CEO of Culina Logistics, part of the Mueller Group) in conversation with *SHD* Magazine said that the bigger logistics companies will continue to grow, whilst the smaller companies will be acquired (Adams, 2018). He went on to say that the entry barriers into the logistics market space are nigh-on impossible to overcome, be it cost or complexity. Culina recently purchased the UK 3PL Great Bear to enhance its logistics offering in the UK.

More recently, we have seen DSV buying Panalpina for $4.6 billion. Once the deal is made official, DSV and Panalpina will become one of the world's largest transportation and logistics services providers, with a combined pro forma revenue of more than US$17 billion and more than 60,000 employees.

We are also seeing investment companies such as Emergevest buying up a number of logistics companies including PalletForce, Turners (Soham) Ltd, NFT Distribution and C M Downton.

Eddie Stobart endorsed the advantage of having a UK-wide pallet distribution service when it acquired The Pallet Network (TPN). They have also purchased iForce, a leading company in e-fulfilment.

Kinaxia Logistics has, over the past six years, purchased 11 mid-size haulage companies. Their vision is to build a flexible and efficient, service-focused, haulage and warehousing group through investment in, and partnership with, medium-sized, profitable, growing privately owned companies across the UK. Kinaxia maintains the local identity of companies that join the Group, but implements common systems and processes at an operational level.

Other previous, notable acquisitions included Norbert Dentressangle's purchase of UK companies including Christian Salvesen and TDG, and its subsequent purchase by the American logistics provider XPO.

Examples within e-fulfilment include Stamps.com Inc purchasing Metapack, Rhenus recently purchasing CML and RCS in the UK, and Yusen Logistics purchasing ILG. Acquisitions within the courier market include DHL's recent purchase of UK Mail and FedEx's purchase of TNT.

The Netherlands postal service's own acquisition of TNT in 1993 set a trend, with the German post office purchasing companies such as Danzas, Nedlloyd Districenters, Air Express International, Elan and most notably DHL; Japan Post purchasing Toll Group; and La Poste buying DPD, Parceline and Interlink in the UK.

In Australia, one of the major trends in logistics outsourcing is the rationalization of major players over the last five years. In Australia alone, according to Mal Walker of Logistics Bureau (Walker, 2013), the following companies have either merged or been taken over:

- DHL/Exel/Tibbett and Britten;
- Schenker/Bax;
- Toll/Patricks/Brambles/SembCorp/Finemores;
- Linfox/Mayne/FCL/Westgate.

In India we have recently seen the acquisition of Flipkart and its distribution network by Walmart.

In the US in 2018, according to Evan Armstrong, there were a number of large 3PL mergers and acquisitions. Korea's CJ Logistics acquired DSC Logistics, and Hub Group acquired CaseStack. The Jordan Co, a finance company, purchased Odyssey Logistics and Technology, GlobalTranz and Unitrans Inc (Armstrong, 2019).

Conclusion

In this chapter we have endeavoured to provide definitions for each of the types of LSP currently operating within the market. It is hoped that at some stage, because of the current confusion between 3PLs, 4PLs, LLPs, 5PLs and 7PLs that we will see a consolidation of these services under a single banner – namely 'LSP'.

As discussed, the logistics outsourcing market continues to grow; however, we are also seeing some companies taking their logistics back in-house.

In the 2019 Third-Party Logistics Study (Langley *et al*, 2019), the companies who didn't outsource their logistics provided the following reasons:

- loss of control;
- greater expertise in-house;
- too difficult to integrate their IT systems with the LSPs;
- no perceived cost reduction and/or service improvement.

These reasons are likely to be very similar to those of companies that are now insourcing their logistics services.

The logistics outsourcing market is becoming increasingly global and is being driven by the growth in e-commerce. This has led to a significant number of acquisitions and mergers recently.

Supplier or partner?

04

Introduction

In today's world of extended supply chains, technological innovation and increasing customer service expectations, the success of a company can be determined as much by their ability to harness their suppliers' capabilities as that of their internal staff. The use of ARM-based chips by one of the world's most innovative companies, Apple, to deliver continuous innovation in areas such as low power technology is an example of this.

Innovation is only one area where suppliers can dramatically impact on their customers' success: service performance (both good and bad), security of supply and even price can make or break a customer offering. It's not surprising that Supplier Relationship Management (SRM) is a key element of procurement thinking, with pages of advice available on achieving success in collaborative partnerships (including in Chapter 9 of this book).

But what do we mean by a partnership, as opposed to a supplier relationship? In a world where many companies have a global supplier base that extends into thousands of companies, is it practical to aim for partnerships – or should most of these companies remain as suppliers?

This chapter will explore the spectrum of supplier relationships for logistics services and ask which factors determine the appropriate strategy for different products and services. It will also look at the relationship options from the supplier perspective and the risk of misalignment if this perspective is radically different from the policy being pursued by the purchasing company.

Even the best strategies fail if those implementing them are not aligned to the same direction of travel. All activities in the outsourcing lifecycle (see Chapter 5) should be adapted to suit each type of relationship, and failure to do so will directly impact on an organization's success. While the tools we describe are applicable to the wider procurement of goods and services, our review will focus on examples in the logistics services market and look at activities that support each type of relationship.

Finally, this chapter will examine the most strategic and business-critical supplier relationships, and ask how collaboration can be made to work in the logistics market and how partnerships can deliver success.

Paper clip or computer chip – market categorization

As supply strategy and SRM make their way up the management priority list, senior managers are aware that their supplier relationships have the potential to make or break their companies – and not just because of purchase price. However, as more services are outsourced and supply chains become more complex and global, how do companies decide on where to focus their effort in this area?

One of the key models employed by procurement departments to evaluate their supply base is the Kraljic Model. First developed by Peter Kraljic in 1983 and published in *Harvard Business Review*, this model is a very useful framework to assess supply markets.

Under the supply positioning part of the model, the goods and services bought by an organization are classified against two key criteria: supply risk and profit impact. Essentially the model is asking, 'How easy is to replace this product or service with an alternative?' and 'What impact can this product or service have on my organization's profitability?'

Supply positioning identifies four different categories of purchases. The distinguishing characteristics of each are shown in Figure 4.1. The appropriate purchasing and supplier management strategies for each category, together with examples in the logistics services market, are discussed in more detail below.

Many examples given are for products and services outside the logistics industry, as these are often easier to categorize. The chapter also includes examples from the logistics services industry.

Non-critical items or services

Sometimes called Routine items, these are purchases for which there are alternative suppliers, a ready supply of the goods or service, and it is possible to specify the item or service unambiguously.

As the spend or savings potential for these items is relatively low, they should be bought efficiently through bundling of items or services together.

Figure 4.1   Supply market categorization: typical features applicable to logistics services

Bottleneck	**Strategic**
Unique or special requirements	Service of strategic importance and
Little or no choice of supplier	critical to business success
Risk to business continuity	Service complex and cannot be 'traded'
Relatively low spend on service	Cost or profit impact significant
Non-critical or Routine	**Leverage**
Standard service specification	Standard market traded goods or services
Several potential suppliers	Commodity trading
Service suitable for tariff pricing	Cost or profit impact significant
Relatively low cost or profit impact	

Complexity/uniqueness — High / Low (vertical axis)

Relative spend or savings potential — Low / High (horizontal axis)

The ability to specify requirements, coupled with alternative suppliers, enables reverse auctions and other transactional purchasing methods. 'Minimize effort' should be the aim for this category: across purchasing, accounts payable processes and contract management.

Examples of Non-critical or Routine purchases in the logistics services market include many transport services where there is a choice of suppliers. Full truck load or palletized, ambient transport services are examples of this, and are increasingly bought through freight exchange sites, intelligent freight matching services or reverse auctions. The spot hire of palletized warehousing services by companies such as Stowga also fall into this category.

Research by the Chartered Institute of Logistics and Transport (CILT) Outsourcing and Procurement Forum and Huddersfield Business School in 2017 showed a pattern of short contract lengths, tariff-based contracts and procurement processes led or with heavy involvement of procurement departments for transport services (Dani, 2018). This was akin to a 'commoditization' of transport services, and contrasted with longer contracts and fewer tariff-based contracts for warehouse services.

CASE STUDY   Non-critical example – the humble paper clip

It is obvious to the reader that a paper clip is a product with many alternatives and little risk to business continuity or market success.

Efficient purchasing is a priority for this type of purchase: in this case, a typical strategy is the bundling of all office stationery under a single contract that is periodically tendered, with the supplier managing stock levels and replenishment. Few people would argue that this purchase requires a close relationship or partnership!

Strategic goods or services

At the other end of the spectrum, there may be purchases that not only impact significantly on an organization's profit, but also on their market position and competitive edge: these are the Strategic purchases. Examples of Strategic purchases are the relationships that the world's leading airlines have with Boeing, IBM with Microsoft in the 1980s, and Apple with ARM Holdings for the development of the ARM chip that now powers billions of mobile and communication devices (Sparkes, 2014).

In these examples, the innovation, enhancements, exclusive developments or even supply prioritization of the supplier can have a direct impact on the end customer's offering to their own customers, while the feedback of end-customer requirements and provision of a marketplace for innovation is critical to the supplier's business.

Strategic services: UK grocery e-fulfilment and Ocado

Ocado was founded in the UK in January 2000, and launched its services with a partnership with Waitrose for product sourcing and fulfilment in January 2002. This partnership agreement comes to an end in 2021, but Ocado, through its heavy investment in robotics and IT, is now positioning itself as a technology provider, and has developed new partnerships as the e-fulfilment partner for Morrisons and, in 2019, Marks and Spencer.

By accessing Ocado's systems and technology for e-fulfilment, these retailers are able to make up for an earlier lack of development of this critical and growing route to market.

In the logistics and supply chain market, examples of Strategic services include national warehousing and distribution contracts, full e-fulfilment contracts and global or regional logistics contracts. The way in which these products and services are tendered, selected, negotiated, contracted and managed are critical to the successful partnership, and are discussed further in Chapter 5 and Chapter 9.

Some people ask whether logistics services should ever be classified as Strategic; compared to product-related or innovation-based relationships. While that may be true for businesses such as Apple, for other businesses their main fulfilment operation, e-fulfilment solution or other services will certainly be Strategic services. There is also a challenge as to whether these services, if Strategic, are core to a business and whether this determines if they should be outsourced. This is discussed in Chapter 2.

There are no prizes for having a large number of Strategic purchases: these contracts require a significant level of time and investment on both sides.

Some businesses might not have any Strategic services in the logistics market.

If your directors have not met the supplier, it is probably not a Strategic purchase.

Bottleneck services

These are services where there is little market choice (perhaps because of legacy technology, geography or complex specifications) and there is a potentially significant supply risk for the purchaser.

An example of this type of purchase might be engineering components that are classified as obsolete and unsupported by the supplier, but are still in use. Another example could be a specific raw material grown only in limited areas and at risk from crop failure. For these purchases, the focus should be on securing supply and finding alternatives in order to reduce business risk. Challenging complex and bespoke specifications is also a key strategy for Bottleneck purchases.

Many logistics services have the potential to fall into the Bottleneck category. These include the carriage of dangerous goods, temperature-controlled movements in some markets, the transportation of different or unusual freight, particular shipping lanes with little competition and groupage/LTL routes. This quotation from a manager in a chemicals business during Huddersfield Business School's research into transport services illustrates the point:

'No, I don't see a trend to commoditization [in transport] – we are a chemical manufacturer and when we contract with companies that do chemical transportation, they first have to have a licence to carry chemicals.'

Sometimes purchasers may not be aware of alternative suppliers in the marketplace. Others may not have considered alternative modes or routes to create choice and reduce supply risk; in this case, the strategy should be to seek out new suppliers, simplify requirements and consider new modes.

An example of this is the movement of round timber in Scotland, where certain routes have been transferred from road to short sea.

Suppliers, in contrast, may specialize in or aim to create Bottleneck marketplace services to avoid the low margins typical of a Non-critical marketplace. Examples of this are logistics companies that service industries such as the film industry or art dealerships which require specialist vehicles and handling, or those that specialize in consolidation and groupage services in a particular region.

Where alternative modes or alternative suppliers cannot be identified for Bottleneck services, the priority is to secure supply.

Leverage purchases

The final category identified by Kraljic is that of Leverage products or services. Often these are commodities where a strong market exists, but the performance of the purchasing organization in buying well can have a significant impact on profitability. Investing in market research and knowledge together with hedging are all techniques in this area of the matrix.

Leverage examples in the logistics services market could include cross-border movements and international shipping; fuel purchase is an obvious example for the third-party logistics (3PL) companies themselves.

By selecting the paper clip and the computer chip as examples (with apologies to paper clip suppliers), the contrast between Routine and Strategic purchasing strategies is stark. However, in practice most contracts between suppliers and customers will not be at these two extremes.

Customers and suppliers may also differ in their view of the relationship. For example, a supplier may attempt to build the high-level engagement and governance associated with Strategic purchases with a customer that has identified the purchase as Routine, and is trying to minimize effort!

Category-based strategies for logistics services

Once the categorization has been completed, the next steps are to ensure that there is a strategy and action plan in place for each service or group of services. Overall the objectives are:

- to ensure that the business-critical services and objectives of the strategic purchases are secured;
- to protect supply by reducing dependency on Bottleneck suppliers;
- to develop the market insights necessary to deliver the profit impact on Leverage services;
- to buy and manage Non-critical services as efficiently as possible.

Examples of the application of these overall objectives to logistics services purchasing are shown in Table 4.1. This demonstrates that the actions and

Table 4.1 Strategies and actions for managing logistics services by supply categorization

Bottleneck	Strategic
Few/no alternative suppliers or service.	High strategic importance, high barriers to change, long-term contracts
Examples: specialist logistics services, long-term warehousing with a high degree of integration, some groupage services.	Examples: dedicated strategic warehousing/fulfilment, e-fulfilment partner, regional suppliers.
Strategies:	Strategies:
<ul><li>find and develop alternative suppliers;</li><li>challenge or simplify the specification for the service;</li><li>secure continuity of supply (eg risk management at warehouses, disaster recovery and IT security);</li><li>ensure the tender/procurement process is appropriate for this category.</li></ul>	<ul><li>minimize suppliers in this category;</li><li>invest in SRM (see Chapter 9);</li><li>maintain top-to-top senior manager relationships;</li><li>align objectives and incentives;</li><li>spend time and effort selecting the right partner and putting a bespoke contract in place;</li><li>invest in project and risk management on both sides for joint implementations;</li><li>set up robust KPIs and performance management with regular reviews;</li><li>think about the long term: how you plan to renegotiate and benchmark, how you plan to exit the relationship if it's not working;</li><li>check that you remain an attractive customer and are core to your supplier's business.</li></ul>

(continued)

Table 4.1 (Continued)

Non-critical or Routine	Leverage
Choice of suppliers and substitution of product/service possible.	Significant financial impact of choice and substitution of product/service possible.
Examples: full truck load transport, shared and tactical warehousing, bought pallets, parcel services, some groupage.	Examples: traded commodities, fuel, deep sea shipping.
Strategies:	Strategies:
• bundle services together to reduce effort (eg one supplier for several routes);	• carry out market research to inform purchase;
• utilize e-sourcing tools and catalogues;	• tender regularly to obtain commercial benefit;
• standardize KPIs and reporting;	• if this is bought as part of a service, ensure your supplier has expertise (eg if you have a fuel mechanism in a services contract).
• use standard terms and conditions;	
• use short-term contracts and tariff-based fees;	
• maintain competition;	
• switch supplier if service is poor;	
• make the invoicing and payment process efficient (eg consider self-billing/ERP management of transactions).	

strategies for each category are very different, and few can be delivered by purchasing alone. In the Strategic category, there needs to be complete alignment internally and externally regarding the objectives and strategy for the service.

Categorization and risk management

Many logistics services can be categorized differently at different points through the life of the contract. In some cases, there could be several potential suppliers at the time of tendering, but the choice and implementation of the chosen supplier, where investment and barriers to change are high, moves the purchase into the Bottleneck or Strategic categories for the life of the contract.

This is the case for national, regional or product specific warehousing and distribution services where business processes change, capital investment and interface development between customer and supplier lock in the relationship for three to five years, or even longer. Recognizing this is important: it should be addressed in the contract, and relationship management techniques should be employed for the ongoing relationship. This is discussed further in Chapter 9.

Although purchasing organizations will need to manage many of their Routine purchase relationships, while minimizing effort and buying efficiently, they should not overlook the risk of neglecting specification and vendor assurance activities for these purchases.

The examples where this has happened are numerous and are often a consequence of extended supply chains: the horse meat scandal in the Non-critical purchase of meat for ready meals in Western Europe in 2013, and the risk to reputational damage from child labour and increasing focus on worker welfare in globally outsourced products are two such examples.

Finally, it is important to note that categorizations and purchase strategies change with time and need to be regularly reviewed. Suppliers may not continue to innovate and offer market-leading solutions; customers may decide that this market segment is no longer a strategic focus and new risks enter the marketplace. A strong purchasing organization will review the categorization of its product and service purchases at least annually, and will share action plans across the organization.

Meanwhile, back at the supplier...

As part of any purchase categorization process, the viewpoint of the supplier must not be overlooked. This is particularly important for Strategic and Bottleneck purchases where once the deal is done, the buyer can be effectively 'locked in' and the balance of power can rest with the supplier.

Steele and Court's 1996 Supplier Preferencing analysis evaluates customers from the vantage point of the supplier. Customers are evaluated against two criteria: their attractiveness (to the supplier), and the relative value of the contract.

A customer's attractiveness to a supplier will vary based on the service being supplied, and will be different for different suppliers. The following are common factors that will influence the perceived attractiveness of a customer to a supplier:

- brand name;
- customer references (this is further affected by whether or not the customer authorizes their use as a reference);
- market fit with the supplier's priorities;
- volume of orders;
- business growth;
- profitability/financial stability;
- length of contract;
- payment behaviour (both payment terms and adherence to those terms);
- behaviour across all the touchpoints between the two organizations;
- organizational culture;
- cost to serve (minimum order size, delivery costs, lead time, service credits);
- the supplier's willingness to learn and adapt by working with the customer;
- tendering behaviour (is previous good service valued? is procurement behaviour open and transparent?);
- performance bonuses;
- future opportunities.

In the logistics marketplace, transport companies seek shippers whose flows are synergistic with their other customers: any shipper exporting goods from the UK to the continent will benefit from large flows of physical goods moving into the UK and suppliers chasing backhaul opportunities.

When customer attractiveness is plotted against supplier power, the potential scenarios may be identified as shown in Figure 4.2.

This analysis is an over-simplification as it does not take into account the relative market strength of the supplier, the threat of alternatives or changes over time.

It is important to note that many suppliers will not undergo this type of formal review, and employees of the supplier may not behave as predicted in this model; however, the employees and managers in a supplier business are likely to instinctively adjust their behaviour based on their judgement of the relative worth of different customers.

It is vital that purchasing organizations try to put themselves in the mind of their suppliers, particularly for Bottleneck and Strategic services. If securing supply in a potentially supply limited market, a performance bonus may be necessary to drive up attractiveness. If you are a relatively small company, with limited brand value, any failure to pay on time or behave well is likely to jeopardize the relationship you need with your Strategic suppliers.

Figure 4.2   Supplier preferencing analysis

	Development	Core
High	May be a new or growing account, with the potential to deliver growth or new opportunities to the supplier. Worth nurturing by supplier as it could develop into new core business. Risk of becoming a nuisance account if predicted growth or opportunities do not materialize.	Business account is attractive and in the core market areas the supplier wishes to pursue. A priority for the supplier to give good service and retain and develop the account.
	Nuisance	**Exploitable**
Low	An unattractive and low-value account. Customer likely to be neglected and receive poor service.	An unattractive account but relatively high-value. Risk of exploitation (such as over-charging) by the supplier, particularly where alternatives are not available.

(Vertical axis: Attractiveness, Low to High. Horizontal axis: Relative spend or savings potential, Low to High.)

Ask yourself whether you are well matched with your potential Strategic suppliers: is your business likely to be attractive enough to become core business within their company? This is often an area overlooked in out-sourcing logistics services: outsource to an organization radically different in size to your own, and you may not get the attention you need.

If there is a mismatch for Routine purchases, then you simply shop around and find a new supplier who does give you good service. A mismatch for Bottleneck and Strategic services requires a longer-term action plan.

How should the procurement process adjust to these markets? It is important that your whole procurement policy fits with your assessment of the marketplace carried out above. Companies need to recognize that their procurement process is the first step in establishing the relationship. An adversarial stance at this stage could forever damage a Strategic relationship.

Consistency and an aligned action plan

A purchasing strategy that includes market and supplier categorization, and identifies risks and actions, will never succeed fully if not shared across the organization. The relationship that operational personnel develop with a

Strategic supplier (where they might meet weekly and have joint projects) is likely to be different from that of a buyer working across many different contracts; however, there needs to be a consistency of approach between all personnel interfacing with the supplier.

If, for example, a logistics service has been identified as a Non-critical or Routine purchase (such as full vehicle, ambient, cross-border transport), operational personnel should have an effective KPI and management reporting process set up with suppliers that are consistent across many suppliers or routes and not bespoke. Relationship building activities should be focused on Strategic services and not employed for Routine services.

Where the categorization work has identified supply risks or risks of exploitation, it is particularly important that this is shared with Operations and a joint action plan established. If a buyer is trying to reduce dependency on a Bottleneck transport supplier through trialling a new LSP, the company's operations team need to understand this rationale and support the initiative.

The way in which relationships should be managed is discussed further in Chapter 11.

Collaboration

How does the categorization discussed in this chapter relate to collaboration between businesses? First, we need to define collaboration:

Collaboration: two or more entities working together towards shared goals.

The crucial difference between collaboration and the activities described under, for example, a Strategic relationship, is that collaboration is not restricted to companies with a customer/supplier relationship, whereas the market and supplier categorization tools are focused on this type of relationship.

Collaboration is likely to be a vital strategy to achieve success in a Strategic purchase, where it is carried out between the purchasing organization and a supplier; however, it can also be carried out between companies with a different type of relationship – even between competitors. Competitive collaboration has been used to save empty running in the transport industry, although whether these initiatives have the long-term impact of world-class LSP networks is questionable.

Progressive industry commentators have proposed the idea of peer shipments – where drug manufacturers collaborate on shipments to reduce costs and avoid the prospect of paying to ship a lot of vacant space. This requires a great deal of organization, change management and trust.

An example of this is a supply chain course at the University of Warwick which brings together delegates from AstraZeneca, Syngenta and GlaxoSmithKline.

Conclusion

The Kraljic matrix approach provides shippers with a useful tool for identifying the right strategy to apply to outsourcing different logistics services. The insights gained by this exercise need to be applied not only to the way the service is procured, but also how the contract is managed throughout its life. All personnel within a shipping company need to understand and support the strategy if it is to succeed.

The perspective of the LSP must not be overlooked, and shippers need to ensure they are working with LSPs for which their business is attractive long term and that payment performance and other factors do not undermine important relationships.

The concepts explored in this chapter are fundamental to the choices that shippers need to make when outsourcing a service. This approach should run through the entire logistics services outsourcing lifecycle; this topic is tackled in the next chapter.

The outsourcing 05
lifecycle

Introduction

All companies outsourcing logistics services should go through a similar cycle of deciding which services they need, finding and selecting suppliers, managing the contract and reviewing performance. The main steps are summarized in Figure 5.1.

Different authors split this cycle into varying numbers of steps; the Chartered Institute of Procurement and Supply (CIPS) has a 13-step process and detailed advice on each, whereas there is more grouping in our version. This chapter will explore each stage of this cycle, and discuss the important activities and considerations for each.

The description of this cycle could expand to a full book on its own, and readers are encouraged to use additional sources such as CIPS for further help and information on general procurement processes. Our description and recommendations will be focused on logistics services.

The outsourcing process is shown as a cycle, rather than a straight line, to emphasize that this process should not be a one-off event, but instead a repeated pattern where each sub-process feeds into the next one. The learning and experiences from one outsourcing cycle, both good and bad, should be inputs into the next cycle.

Similarly, the learning and experience of one sub-process should feed into the activities of the next sub-process. An example of this is where your market research on a transport service under Step 1 demonstrates that this is a specialist Bottleneck service with only one reliable supplier, and you therefore abandon previous plans to hold an e-auction for the service.

Occasionally information at a later stage of the cycle requires previous assumptions and decisions to be revisited.

The time spent on each phase of the cycle will be determined by the relative importance of the service being outsourced, and the resource that is available to manage the process. The results of the categorization activities

Figure 5.1   The outsourcing lifecycle

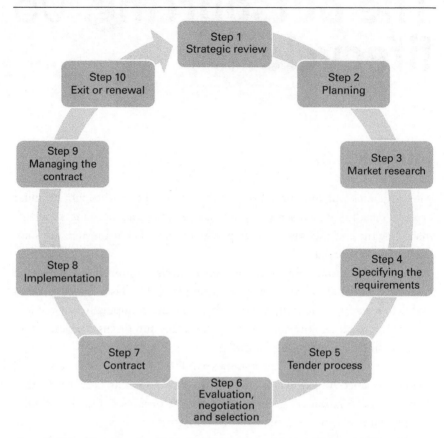

described in Chapter 4 will be critical in prioritizing resource allocation, as well as which services are bundled into one cycle and which are bought separately.

The overall time spent, and cross-department resource needed, to outsource a Strategic service such as a partnership for a national e-fulfilment service will be much greater than for a simple A-to-B freight transport service. For this type of Strategic service, the time spent on Step 1 will be crucial to the overall successful outcome of the process.

Many companies embark on the tendering stages of an outsourcing cycle without spending enough time in the early part of the cycle considering options and priorities for the process, and how their requirements might have changed since the last time the service was tendered. This limits the scope and opportunities of later activity.

The cycle – step by step

Step 1: Strategic review

Finding the right logistics partner is critical to the smooth operation of a supply chain; however, as described in Chapter 4, some services are more critical than others to longer-term business performance. Before diving into a tender process or asking for quotes, it is vital that buyers and logistics managers ask themselves what the business requirements of this service are – both now and in the future.

For some services, this step is the time to ask the fundamental questions we addressed in Chapter 2:

- Is this service a core competence of our business? Does it provide us with a competitive edge?
- Should this service be outsourced/continue to be outsourced?
- Has anything changed since we last reviewed our logistics operation?

We are not suggesting that these questions should be debated each time logistics services are tendered, but rather that the reasons for whether to outsource logistics or retain in-house should be understood by all the relevant stakeholders and challenged if and when circumstances change.

Similarly, the category management analysis described in Chapter 4 should be refreshed as part of this Step 1 process. It should not be assumed that categorization carried out several years previously is still valid: markets change, and previously unique or market disruptive technologies become Routine purchases with time.

Also included in this step should be a high-level specification and market review to understand:

- What are we buying? Is it a standard service or bespoke? Is it complex or easy to specify?
- Can we identify alternative suppliers?
- Do the alternative suppliers have the capability to supply?

Other questions that are worth asking at this stage are shown in Table 5.1.

There are several models that are useful to use during this review in order to further develop market understanding and to order thinking. Three key models frequently employed by procurement teams are SWOT analysis, Porter's Five Forces model and PESTLE analysis.

Table 5.1 Questions for shippers to explore in Step 1

	Service type		
All	**Strategic**	**Bottleneck**	**Non-critical or Routine**
• Have I outsourced this service before? What was the outcome?	• Where does the 'knowhow' for the current operation lie – with my organization or the current supplier?	• Is there an opportunity to challenge and simplify the specification of this service before tendering, in order to increase the number of potential suppliers?	• Can I bundle together different routes or services in one process?
• What is the performance of the current supplier or internal team for this service?	• How do I align my objectives for this outsourced service with those of my proposed partner?		• Am I locked into contracts for related services that could be bundled together in the future?
• What are the primary objectives for outsourcing this service (eg reduced costs, improved service, reduced risk)?	• What are the risks to the business from changing supplier or outsourcing for the first time?		• How can I reduce the administrative burden of buying this service?
• How has this service changed over the last few years? How might it change in the future?	• If the risks are significant, how do I mitigate them?	• How can I ensure supply continuity?	• Can I consider self-billing options?
• What flexibility do I need from this service in the future?	• How long will I need to contract these services to get my desired outcome?	• How can I protect myself against supplier demands for price rises through the life of the contract?	• Are my volumes high enough to enable reverse auctions or other marketplace bidding?
• Is there a competitive market for these services?	• If the contract is for a significant time period, how will I agree price changes during the life of the contract?		
• Is there technology available in the marketplace that I should be benefiting from? Am I likely to achieve this through outsourcing?	• Who will provide the business-critical IT solutions?		
• What type of service am I buying: Routine, Bottleneck, Strategic or Leverage?	• Does my business or my current supplier have critical skills, an innovative approach or a commercial advantage in the delivery of this service?		
• Will the supplier have to invest significantly to provide these services; if so, what contractual commitment am I likely to have to give?			
• What length of contract am I aiming for, and why?			

SWOT analysis will need little introduction for many readers, as it is a key business management tool that examines the Strengths, Weaknesses, Opportunities and Threats facing a business or activity. It is useful in this context for summarizing the output of a strategic outsourcing review and for ensuring key risks and opportunities are not overlooked.

Michael Porter looked at the balance of the different forces at play within any market; reviewing these forces for the logistics services being procured or outsourced is a useful exercise and prompts thinking on how the market dynamics may change.

In Table 5.2 examples are given for a review of Porter's Five Forces for a logistics services provider (LSP); although this exercise is more usually done by buyers during Step 1, by showing examples for an LSP more of the analysis is relevant to the logistics market.

PESTLE analysis provides a framework for the review of an outsourcing opportunity or service against six macro-economic factors:

- political factors;
- economic factors;
- social factors;
- technological factors;
- legal factors;
- environmental factors.

An example of a change in the forces in a market is the potential impact of Brexit on the export of goods by road from the Irish Republic to continental Europe, the majority of which must pass through the UK 'landbridge'. The threat of border delays and costs related to Brexit has prompted the Irish government to support exporters in developing alternative short sea routes, and to explore alternative logistics partners with customs expertise and accreditation.

Another example is the combined effect of Ultra Low Emission Zones, congestion charges and changes to employment and tax legislation for self-employed drivers in the UK, which is prompting many van-based delivery services to re-examine their solution for delivering to sites in central London.

While a review to this depth may be inappropriate for all services, it is useful to use these models as checklists to identify factors and market forces that may otherwise be overlooked.

Sometimes it will not be possible to answer the questions posed in Table 5.1 or establish what supplier capability exists in the marketplace without carrying

Table 5.2 Example of Porter's Five Forces applied to an LSP

Force	Explanation	Logistics industry examples from an LSP's perspective
Competitive rivalry among existing competitors	This describes the degree of competition a company faces in their chosen market. This will change with time. A high degree of competition will give buyers choices.	Strong competition in road transport has driven down margins in many markets. Many LSPs choose to focus on local or specialist services with less competition.
Bargaining power of suppliers	This describes the balance of power between a company and its suppliers.	All LSPs are vulnerable to fuel price fluctuations. The largest, global LSPs will have significant power in the supplier market for property, vehicles, equipment and many other goods and services vs their smaller rivals.
Bargaining power of buyers	This describes the balance of power between a company and its customers (the buyers of its goods and services).	Strong buyer power exists in markets such as FMCG, ambient, palletized full truck load road freight with high volumes and many potential suppliers. Weak buyer power exists for carriage of dangerous goods, specialist services, regional services and long-term contracts with high switching costs.
Threat of substitute services	This examines whether the service provided could be replaced by another service, eliminated entirely or done in a different way	For LSPs, substitute services could include: • mode change, eg replacement of road freight with short sea or rail modes; • insourcing by the shipper; • change of supply chain by the shipper.

(continued)

Table 5.2 (Continued)

Force	Explanation	Logistics industry examples from an LSP's perspective
Threat of new entry	This is about whether it is easy for new competitors to enter the marketplace. How high are the barriers to entry?	For LSPs providing relatively simple transport or warehousing services, barriers are low and new entrants are common. For sophisticated, specialist or high-volume services barriers are high: capital, IT, know-how, property requirements and their associated risks all deter new entrants. Many LSPs enter new markets only when they can do so either with an existing customer or by acquisition.

out a Request for Information (RFI) step. This process is described under Step 3, but can be carried out as part of Step 1.

For Routine purchases, a strategic review can be carried out by the procurement team working with the operational managers who control this service. Bottleneck services, such as embedded factory support logistics or specialist transport services, may require cross-department approaches to find alternatives and challenge specifications to reduce risk and secure supply.

For Strategic services, it is necessary to involve senior managers and managers from other functions such as finance/HR/marketing in the strategic review process, as these are business-critical decisions. These senior managers will need to be involved in the procurement process including selection and relationship management, so early engagement is crucial.

Step 2: Planning

At the end of Step 1, there should be an aligned business view as to whether a service should be outsourced (or continue to be outsourced) and what the key deliverables of the service are. The current marketplace needs to be understood and the potential risks of the outsourcing or procurement process highlighted.

The more critical or complex the service being tendered, the more important it is that there is careful planning before a timetable or approach is committed to. The questions that should be asked at this stage are as follows.

Creating the specification and collecting the data

- Do we have accurate data and alignment on the service specification today, or will achieving this be a significant activity requiring time and resource to pull it together?

Contracts

- Will we be buying based on our standard terms and conditions, or national or international frameworks (see Chapter 6), or will there be a contract negotiation stage?

- Do we have a standard contract we can use, or is drafting a contract an activity we need to allow for (both in terms of time and cost)? See the second case study at the end of this chapter.

- For Strategic services, do we have a clear idea of contract management and strategic alignment clauses, or will these have to be defined?

Designing the procurement project plan

- What will the procurement process be, how long is it likely to take, and will it require external support and/or IT platforms?

- Do we need to include time to work with shortlisted suppliers to define business processes or solutions (as may be the case for Strategic purchases)?

- Will the process include multiple bidding stages and/or auctions?

- Do we have comprehensive information on the market so that we can go straight to Request for Proposal (RFP), or do we need to run an RFI stage first?

- What is the likely time that prospective suppliers will require to create a proposal/make a bid?

- Will we need to factor in time for site visits during the process for the suppliers to see our operation?
- Do we need to allow for audit visits to the supplier premises?
- What does the lead time between procurement and implementation need to be?

Agreeing a communications plan

- Who are the stakeholders at the incumbent LSP, internally and externally?
- What are the sensitivities that should be managed?
- What communications are required for each stakeholder group, and do any of these have legal obligations associated with them?

Designing the implementation plan

- Will the supplier have to invest in equipment or facilities with a significant timescale implication? What are those timescales?
- Are there interfaces or IT developments required before go-live?
- Are we going to have a handover period between the contracts?
- How can we de-risk any implementation?
- What ramp-up period, if any, should we allow for?

Resource

- What resource is needed on our side for the procurement process and the implementation of the contract? Do we have the necessary resource internally, or do we need to bring it in?
- What resource would we expect to see on the supplier's side? How can we ensure this is provided?

For a significant service, particularly Strategic services, there should be a project plan created and a project team assigned to the project before the procurement process starts. If going through the questions above demonstrates that there is not enough time to conduct a process properly, serious consideration should be given to extending the existing contracts rather than skipping some of these processes.

Step 3: Market research

A degree of market research and market understanding will have been necessary to complete Steps 1 and 2. For new services or changing marketplaces, this research at the strategic review stage may be extensive and require an RFI. Where this is not necessary, there will still be the need to conduct research before embarking on a full tender or other procurement process.

Any negotiation training emphasizes the need for preparation, and Step 3 is part of this. The objectives of these activities include:

- identifying suitable suppliers;
- generating interest and awareness in the marketplace;
- gathering information on the market alternatives to inform the specification;
- researching price or cost drivers.

The research can be conducted through visiting exhibitions, meetings or calls with suppliers, web searches and using industry publications to provide supplier lists. Some useful publications and links are provided in Appendix VII. Experienced buyers and operational managers will have been carrying out such research on a continuous basis, months or years before a tender, but it is useful to take stock and review what information is missing or needs updating at this stage.

There is no standard format for an RFI, as the questions asked will depend on the service being procured and the gaps in information identified. However, some questions should be broad and open enough to allow suppliers the freedom to respond with ideas that may inform the rest of the process.

Table 5.3 provides an example of an RFI for food-related export freight transport and warehousing services. This needs to be accompanied by a high-level view of the actual logistics requirements and volume of traffic together with a non-disclosure or confidentiality agreement. A Word version of this template can be downloaded from the How to Logistics website.

One of the key objectives of any RFI, or other contact with potential suppliers, should be to generate interest in the future tender process. Behaviour towards the suppliers therefore needs to be professional, open and positive to ensure that they are not put off taking part in any future process.

Table 5.3   Sample RFI for export freight services

Supplier's company name	
Address	
Main contact - Name	
Email	
Telephone number	
Annual revenue	
Main logistics services offered by your company	Please specify whether you provide full truck load, less than truck load or parcel services:
Specialist services	Please specify any specialist services you provide for food and food-related goods:
Temperature capability	Frozen (yes/no): Chilled (yes/no): Ambient (yes/no):
Export markets serviced by your company	Please list the countries here and the routes you use (eg ports and sailing routes):
Markets where you, or your partners, can provide warehousing services	Please list the countries here, and the temperature regimes of the warehousing:
Transit times and scheduled services	For the following markets, please provide your standard transit times and the days of the week you run this service:

(*continued*)

Table 5.3   (Continued)

	Market 1	Service	Market 2	Service	Market 3	Service
Customs capability	Please give details of the customs-related services you can provide:					
Accreditations - please provide details of the accreditations you have	Authorized Economic Operator					
	British Retail Consortium Food Safety Certification – Storage & Distribution Standard					
	ISO 9001:2015 Quality Control & Management					
	ISO 14001 Environmental Management Systems					
	OHSAS 18001 Health and Safety certification					
	Licensed bonded warehouse details					
Reference customers						
Other comments	Please use this area to provide any further details you believe are relevant:					

Step 4: Specifying requirements

Regardless of whether a logistics service is Routine or Strategic, any quotation you receive from potential suppliers will be more accurate, and is likely to be more competitive, if the specification and data you provide regarding the service are complete and credible. Tenders with vague specifications and poor or missing data damage the buyer's reputation and increase the perceived risk for new suppliers.

A good specification of requirements is needed to level the playing field between existing and potential suppliers; bad or missing data exposes the purchaser to future variations in pricing, as it forces suppliers to make assumptions.

This does not mean that LSPs expect you to be able to accurately forecast future volume or changes to your business, but sharing data on existing activity and your assumptions on how it might change will allow them to quote more accurately and will set a framework for future discussions on variations to plan.

Table 5.4 shows typical data that suppliers would expect to see for different types of logistics services. In addition to this information, buyers should provide the following:

- specific key performance indicators (KPIs) for the services;
- standards of performance for each KPI;
- reporting requirements (in terms of information required, frequency and format);
- mandatory process requirements (such as inbound stock checks or signed PODs);
- system interfaces or mandatory systems to be used.

In some cases, the purchasing organization will want input from the supplier on the final specification of processes and services; the supplier may have more experience of the service than the purchasing organization. The areas open for discussion should be made clear in the RFP process. Where variations to specification are agreed through the process, these should be clearly documented and shared with all parties.

Any answers to questions posed by one LSP have to be circulated to all the other LSPs to ensure consistency.

A comprehensive questionnaire can be found in Appendix VI.

Table 5.4   Data required for warehousing and transport services

Warehousing	Road transport
• format of goods in and goods out (pallets, cases, items, containers);	• format of goods carried;
• movements in/out per week;	• delivery/collection addresses;
• vehicle movement forecast: inbound and outbound;	• transport order file for representative period;
• forecast stock levels;	• seasonality;
• number of SKUs;	• special requirements;
• order size;	• load size;
• hit rate;	• lead time for orders;
• lines per order;	• order transmission process;
• percentage pick;	• IT requirements including tracking/ POD submission;
• required processes;	• temperature regime;
• hold/release requirements;	• fuel mechanism (if any)
• seasonality across the year;	• any accreditation requirements.
• uplift for peak hours/peak days;	
• temperature requirements	
• customer service requirements;	
• return processing;	
• IT requirements including interfaces;	
• value of goods/stock;	
• insurance requirements;	
• risk management requirements.	

Step 5: Tender process

As described in Chapter 4, the appropriate tender process will vary depending on the type of service being procured, the experience the procurement team has of tendering this service and the marketplace. In some cases, particularly for Bottleneck services, this step will consist of negotiations with a single supplier supported by benchmarking of cost elements, rather than a tender.

Table 5.5 describes the potential tender processes appropriate for each of the Kraljic-based service categorizations.

Table 5.5   Tender process options based on Kraljic categorizations

Bottleneck:	Strategic:
• RFI to confirm or seek alternative specification or suppliers; • potential negotiation with single supplier to secure supply.	• RFI to establish supplier capability and market; • multi-stage RFP or ITT including shortlisted supplier input to solution; • complex pricing models; • extensive vendor assurance/ referencing.
Routine:	**Leverage:**
• identify suppliers through RFI if needed; • specification as issued by buying organization; • RFQ or ITT process with identified criteria and multiple suppliers; • tariff-based pricing/bidding; • opportunity for e-sourcing and reverse auctions; • services bundled.	• extensive market research but unlikely via RFI; • e-auctions and trading.

If an RFI has not been carried out in an earlier stage of the procurement cycle, it may be sensible to use one at this stage in order to ensure that as many suitable suppliers are involved in the process as possible. Alternatively, this stage could start with a pre-qualification process, to ensure that only suppliers with the requisite business resilience, skills and experience are taken into the pricing stage of a tender.

Most logistics services will be procured through one of the following processes:

- **Request for Quotation (RFQ)** – this is the simplest form, in which the services and volumes are described and quotations for the service are provided, typically in a competitive environment. It is used for many transport services, shared user services and the simpler warehousing contracts.

- **Request for Proposal (RFP)** – this process is used when the specification is not so defined, and greater supplier input is required in the form of a proposal. The requirements are more open to allow the LSP to use their experience and expertise to help the shipper define the solution. Sometimes this form of procurement is used when the shipper does not have the expertise, or perhaps the time, to define the solution.

- **Invitation to Tender (ITT)** – used where services are complex but well described. They include a great deal of detail on the specification, volumes and standards of performance. ITTs are common in construction projects, but also used for complex logistics services where the shipper has done significant pre-work and knows what they want.

Although the above definitions apply, many companies use these terms interchangeably, particularly RFP and RFQ, and the rest of this chapter will do so.

In each case, it is important to remember that evaluation of best value (rather than best price) will require the process to capture a supplier's experience, capability, approach and risk profile as well as pricing.

As mentioned before, competition is a critical component for a successful RFP process and buyers must establish this before embarking on the process. Two suppliers may be enough to establish competition, if both are realistic options.

To ensure the most competition, the RFP must be well designed and buyers need to keep in mind the time and effort LSPs spend responding to tenders. Like all companies, LSPs must prioritize business development opportunities and weigh up each opportunity against the effort and likelihood of success.

A 2012 report by BravoSolution for CIPS entitled 'To Bid or Not to Bid: 5 Best Practices for Asking RFP Questions' (Badasha, 2012) recommended the following tips for a successful RFP:

- Think small and focused – only ask the most relevant questions.
- Include key terms and conditions in the RFP – score the suppliers' response to them.
- Explain questions – to ensure that only relevant supplier details are collated (rather than a long list of experience or qualifications that are not relevant).
- Give suppliers the correct answers – this means that buyers should detail exactly what they need, where they know it. If you have a preferred fuel mechanism, then describe it, rather than asking an open question on this topic.

- Collate a library of best questions – for services such as transport which you tender frequently, learn which questions work best rather than starting from scratch. This is not the same as recycling general RFP questions that are not relevant!

'[C]ondensing what you want to know from suppliers is a challenge for many companies,' according to Ian Dawson, author of the report and e-sourcing consultant at BravoSolution. 'The ultimate goal of every RFP should be to entice all relevant suppliers to submit a bid, which drives higher competition and a better savings opportunity for the buying organization.'

Tender management

For many companies, tender management will be done by sending out specifications and pricing templates (unless LSPs are invited to provide their own pricing template) to suppliers by email, and receiving back clarification questions and submissions by email. For any tender it is important that tender management provides the following:

- transparency;
- an audit trail of communications and decisions;
- availability of all documents and supplier submissions to the whole selection team;
- circulation of all replies to supplier questions to all respondents;
- control of all communication with suppliers for this process through a single person or communication channel (normally this would be the buyer or an external consultant brought in to manage the process);
- a clear timetable for bidders;
- honest and timely feedback to all bidders.

Larger organizations typically use e-sourcing portals to manage tenders. These have the advantage of structuring responses to the format determined by the purchaser and having one system where all communication is captured. These portals may be combined with bidding or e-auction portals for some tenders.

Whether a portal is used or not, critical for eventual selection will be the structure of the pricing template.

Structuring pricing for RFPs

In constructing an RFP, thought must be given to the structure of the pricing requested, as well as the way prices and other factors will be evaluated. It is tempting to leave the suppliers to bid in the format they choose, but this will make evaluation extremely difficult. On the other hand, being too prescriptive can stifle innovation, and a different pricing strategy can potentially be more competitive and advantageous.

Different logistics services have different pricing options. These are discussed at length in Chapter 6, which includes a table on the most common pricing structures and examples of tariff types for different logistics services. An important part of Steps 3 and 4 will be to determine the right pricing structure for your tender; you then need to ensure all bidders use the same template to input pricing so that you can compare prices and ensure best value.

As discussed above, the LSPs may have alternative pricing mechanisms they wish to propose. Where you believe there could be value in exploring this, the LSP should be given the opportunity to outline this mechanism as an alternative to the pricing template provided. However, they should also provide pricing against your mechanism.

Price evaluation

For logistics services it is important that the price for each service element or route is not reviewed in isolation, but multiplied by the volume of units that price relates to; a supplier may appear competitive until each price is weighted. This methodology is illustrated in the simplified examples following, in which Supplier 1 and Supplier 2 have each provided pallet matrices for the geographies specified in a customer's tender.

Price per pallet – Supplier 1

Number of pallets	1	2–5	6–10	11–16	17+
Region A	£50	£45	£35	£30	£28
Region B	£55	£50	£35	£30	£25
Region C	£70	£65	£55	£50	£45

Price per pallet – Supplier 2

Number of pallets	1	2–5	6–10	11–16	17+
Region A	£70	£65	£45	£30	£24
Region B	£60	£55	£48	£32	£24
Region C	£75	£65	£60	£45	£40

Initially, Supplier 1's prices look more competitive. However, when multiplied by the profile of volume for the customer's business, it is evident that Supplier 2 is the lower-cost option.

Customer volumes

Number of pallets	1	2–5	6–10	11–16	17+
Region A	0	50	60	3,000	20,000
Region B	10	150	200	800	7,000
Region C	100	200	500	1,000	5,000

Total annual cost – Supplier 1

Number of pallets	1	2–5	6–10	11–16	17+
Region A	£0	£2,250	£2,100	£90,000	£560,000
Region B	£550	£7,500	£7,000	£24,000	£175,000
Region C	£7,000	£13,000	£27,500	£50,000	£225,000
Subtotal	£7,550	£22,750	£36,600	£164,000	£960,000
				Total*	£1,190,900

* ie, this is the sum of the subtotals.

Total annual cost – Supplier 2

Number of pallets	1	2–5	6–10	11–16	17+
Region A	£0	£3,250	£2,700	£90,000	£480,000
Region B	£600	£8,250	£9,600	£25,600	£168,000
Region C	£7,500	£13,000	£30,000	£45,000	£200,000
Subtotal	£8,100	£24,500	£42,300	£160,600	£848,000
				Total*	**£1,083,500**

* ie, this is the sum of the subtotals.

The same methodology should be used for warehousing and other services to identify total cost for each supplier and priorities for negotiation. Chapter 6 includes a discussion on alternative warehouse tariffs and how they should be analysed.

Enough data should be provided to the LSPs to produce an annual cost for the whole operation.

E-auctions or reverse tenders

Where the specification is well understood in the marketplace, where the service and procuring company are attractive to suppliers and where there are several suppliers bidding for the services, an e-auction or reverse tender may deliver significant savings. This is particularly common for Routine and Leverage services such as large, full-vehicle transport contracts, palletized transport or parcel services. Volumes and spend must be significant in order to attract bidders.

Under this process, routes or lanes are posted on the e-auction site and suppliers can bid for this work. There are various techniques the buyer can employ to maximize the likelihood of a beneficial outcome, including target price, visibility of the winning bid and closed bids for some routes. Many companies buy management and analytical services to optimize the value from the e-auction.

Critical to successful e-auctions for logistics services is pre-qualification or another process to ensure that bidders in the e-auction process have the capacity, capability and longevity to provide the required service levels at the required peak volume.

Price adjustment mechanisms

As well as setting out the template for pricing, buyers should also be clear on what price review mechanisms are available over the life of the contract, as this will influence the pricing policies of the bidders. For Routine purchases, the simplest approach is to have short-term contracts and no price adjustments through the life of the contract to ensure that pricing is only set through a competitive process. However, to avoid the burden of frequent re-tendering, price adjustment mechanisms may be necessary.

Transport companies in many sectors may require protection against fuel inflation and request a fuel mechanism within the contract. Fuel can be up to 30 per cent of the overall road freight transport cost. If the RFI or sector experience indicates this is the case, then it is important to include the following within your pricing template:

- the base fuel price bidders are using for their pricing (this can be provided by the buyer or LSP);

- the percentage of the cost of the service that is related to fuel (this should be provided by the LSPs);

- the fuel mechanism you expect to be using should be included within your draft contract (see Chapter 6 for an example of a fuel mechanism).

For longer-term contracts, and in markets with high labour costs, LSPs may also try to have an inflation-based mechanism for wage inflation.

Some price adjustment for contracts over two years is likely to be necessary, and buyers should give consideration as to whether this is best handled through an annual review, automatic mechanism or negotiation. The treatment of price adjustment in contracts is discussed further in Chapter 6.

CASE STUDY   Buying complex outsourcing solutions

A discussion group run by the Chartered Institute of Logistics and Transport (CILT) Outsourcing and Procurement Forum explored how to purchase complex services (often Strategic), and whether traditional purchasing processes can deliver the right partner in this category.

Through discussion it was recognized that most processes follow the funnel shown in Figure 5.2. The challenge is how to ensure that most time in the procurement process is used in engaging in a deeper more detailed level with the finalists, rather than being taken up with selecting a shortlist of suppliers. When the process solution is part of the supplier's offering, how can this be handled in a competitive way?

Figure 5.2   The supplier selection funnel

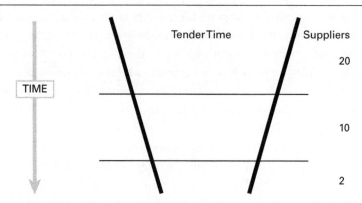

Risk: the more time spent in discussion with many parties, the less time there is for detailed discussions with finalists

The output of the discussion can be summarized as follows:

- Pre-select suppliers by technical expertise and referencing knowledge/track record.
- Electronic RFIs provide a common platform for responses.
- Personal knowledge of capability is also valuable.
- Understand the complexity and key elements of your service.
- Understand whether the expertise in the service and processes sits with yourself or the suppliers – allow enough time for detailed discussion and solution design with final suppliers where they have the expertise.
- Data-driven tenders provide the base for comparison of a 'virtual solution', but this may not reflect the real world.
- There needs to be a reality check in the process – this requires engagement from both parties.
- Both sides need to communicate and understand the risks, and agree that these are reasonable.
- Clients need to check the delivery of the agreed service and specification after implementation – and potentially at agreed intervals throughout the contract.
- Service processes should develop and improve over time – the mechanism and resource for this needs to be agreed and provided by both sides.
- People change over time – performance and supplier capability must not be too dependent on individuals and must be based in the operation, not in business development.

Step 6: Evaluation, negotiation and selection

The selection of the successful service provider or providers will require the following:

- a set of criteria on which the decision will be based; these should have been agreed at the specification stage and ideally shared with the bidders;
- expert evaluation of the technical elements of the bids;
- consistent cost evaluation;
- an agreed process for making the decision; including meeting shortlisted bidders and getting internal sign-off for the decision;
- a selection panel or group of people empowered to make the decision; as a minimum this should consist of the buyer and an operations manager;
- the support of senior management in both procurement and operations in the purchasing company; these senior stakeholders should be involved from the earliest stages, agree the process, and provide support during implementation.

Criteria

As mentioned above, the criteria that are used at this stage of the process should have been agreed during the previous two steps. Criteria will vary widely depending on the service being procured: for example, a fresh seafood exporter will place more emphasis on transit time and reliability than a powdered milk supplier. The criteria in Table 5.6 are examples of criteria that can be used to support the selection of a logistics service provider.

Some criteria will be mandatory and unnegotiable – if a supplier is not capable of meeting these criteria, you should not consider them. Be wary of making too many criteria mandatory: you may find that your best-performing suppliers in other areas cannot meet conditions you have unnecessarily set as mandatory, or that suppliers select themselves out of the process when they see them.

The list of selection criteria is designed to cover a wide range of businesses – select the criteria that are important to you, and not an entire list!

Other criteria will need to be balanced against their relative importance using weighting: each criteria is scored, and the score is multiplied by a weighting factor. An example decision table for warehousing services is

Table 5.6 Selection criteria for general logistics services

Criteria	Source	Comments
Price	RFP	Are they competitive? How does the price compare across different routes or elements of the services? When you weight this with volume, are they still competitive?
Value and price credibility	Historic pricing/ market research/ competitor pricing spread	Has the specification delivered a tight and credible spread of pricing? Does it match expectations? Is it likely to be sustainable? Does it represent value?
Experience of supplying this service	Market research/RFP response/ interview response/ references	How credible is their experience of operating in this marketplace? Do they work for your competitors?
Synergies in logistics market	As above	Are they part of, or operating, a relevant network of transport movement, hubs or shared services?
Locations	RFI/RFP	Are the geographies in which they have capability a match for your business? How will they manage new areas or areas with low volume?
Size relative to purchasing organization	RFI/RFP	What is the size of their relevant operations in relation to the business you are awarding?
Dependency	RFI/RFP	Are they dependent on one or more customers? What would happen if this customer removed the business (particularly relevant for shared warehousing services and transport networks)?
Growth potential	RFI/RFP/ interview response, references	Do they have the capability to match your growth forecasts? What evidence is there of this?

(continued)

Table 5.6 (Continued)

Criteria	Source	Comments
Use of subcontractors/ partners	RFI, RFP/ interview response/ references	How do they manage the performance and risk of their subcontractors? What proportion of the service are they planning to outsource?
Personal relationship/fit	Interview/ meetings	Have you met them? Are they responsive and easy to deal with? Is there a cultural fit? This is a crucial element for Strategic services.
Alignment	RFP/interview/ market research	Are the objectives of the supplier aligned to your own? Is your segment/ service a core or a development area for them? Are you an attractive client *for this service*?
Technical credibility and resilience of the proposal	RFP/interview/ benchmarking/ expert review	Are the assets proposed sufficient? Is there enough flexibility and resilience built in for peak demand/growth/failures? Have they suggested improvements or changes to your specification? For Strategic services, it is worth getting an expert review of this.
Continuous improvement	RFI/RFP/ references	Do they have a track record of making improvements during the life of a contract? What structure have they put in place to support this?
Innovation	RFI/RFP/ references	Does the company have a track record of innovation (over and above continuous improvement)? Only include as a criterion if truly important for your service. If important, is it properly resourced?
Other customers served	RFI/RFP/ references	Do they have a credible list of customers? Do you know any of them?
Financial status	P&L/company accounts	Is the business stable? Is there a parent company?
Quality systems and accreditations	RFI/RFP	What quality management systems and relevant accreditations to they have? Only review the ones that are relevant to your business.

(*continued*)

Table 5.6   (Continued)

Criteria	Source	Comments
Terms and conditions	Pre-contract discussion	Have they accepted your contract/terms? Are they insuring the goods for a sufficient value?
KPI acceptance	RFP	Will they provide management reports and KPI reporting? Do their suggested KPIs match your requirements?
HR capability	RFP response/interview	Is this a unionized environment, or will there be a transfer of staff? Will there be redundancies? Does the company have the resources, experience and approach to manage these issues well?
IT capability	RFP response/IT analysis of response/references	Does the supplier have the internal or external capability to deliver the IT aspects of the services, including timely implementation of any interfaces and changes to systems?

provided in Table 5.7. The weighting does not need to be shared with the suppliers, except in public sector procurement, but doing so is good practice and allows the supplier to understand the relative importance of aspects of your specification.

The technical credibility of the proposed solution may require expert evaluation. This is particularly true for complex warehousing and fulfilment services requiring new assets or changes to IT. The evaluation of IT solutions is covered in Chapter 10; warehousing and fulfilment technology needs to be evaluated with equal care.

LSPs may try to minimize assets (cranes, racking solutions, vehicles, yard space) in order to be competitive. Best value to the shipper may be a solution with greater resilience, flexibility or capacity rather than the lowest cost solution. However only detailed review, combined with engagement with the LSPs, will ensure this value judgement can be made.

Process

The selection process should be fit for purpose in relation to the services being procured. However, all processes should include personnel from procurement and from operations so that a value for money and risk-based approach can be taken.

For almost all services there should be a face-to-face meeting with the supplier(s) as part of the procurement process; small services (such as individual transport routes) should be bundled into groups to facilitate this and to enable efficient management on both sides.

The exception to this is when automated or semi-automated freight matching services are used: here the risk is typically lower, the relationship transactional and the freight matching service is providing some form of due diligence or pre-qualification on the transport provider. These services are discussed more fully in Chapter 1 and Chapter 11.

For Strategic and Bottleneck services, and for many Non-critical or Routine bundled services, the selection process should include visits to the suppliers' sites. Audits of the suppliers' processes and facilities may also be appropriate (see Appendix I).

These site visits manage risk, start building the relationship and support evidence gathering on the RFP submission. The LSP's future Operations Manager for the proposed contract should be present, in addition to the LSP's business development team: the LSP will find it more difficult to over-promise, and cultural fit can also be determined.

Strategic services will require a multi-stage selection process with detailed negotiations, discussions on process and the design of solutions with a very small number of shortlisted suppliers.

The involvement of senior managers on both sides in the decision making is critical for Strategic services and is part of the alignment of objectives that these services require. Even Bottleneck and Routine service award decisions should be signed off by senior managers to ensure that support is available if escalation by rejected parties or resource issues on implementation are later encountered.

Negotiation

The evaluation of the bids will have identified the strengths and weaknesses of each proposal; negotiation offers an opportunity to improve upon initial bids or to tackle uncompetitive or weak parts of the offering.

Negotiation advice, training and support is widely available from organizations such as CIPS and applicable to logistics services as much as any other goods or services. It is important to have personnel on both sides who have been trained and are skilled in negotiation; however, the most important lesson from such training is 'Preparation, Preparation, Preparation'.

Table 5.7 Example decision table for a regional distribution centre

Service/Benefit	Weight	Company A		Company B		Company C		Company D		Company E	
		Score	Total	Score	Total	Score	Total	Score	Total	Score	Total
Total cost	25	3	75	2.8	70	1.8	45	4.5	112.5	5	125
Proof of continuous improvement culture	25	3	75	2.3	57.5	4.8	120	4.8	120	1.5	37.5
On-site pick and pack experience	20	2.5	62.5	1.8	45	4.8	120	4.8	120	2.8	70
Staff flexibility	20	4	100	3.8	95	4.5	112.5	4.3	107.5	2.3	57.5
System ability to deal with multiple clients	20	2.8	70	4.5	112.5	4	100	3.5	87.5	1.5	37.5
Management team we are comfortable working with	20	2.8	70	3.5	87.5	4	100	3.8	95	3.3	82.5
Dedicated senior contract management	15	3.5	87.5	2.8	70	2.5	62.5	3.5	87.5	5	125
End-to-end supply chain management capability	15	2.8	70	3.8	95	4	100	3.3	82.5	2.3	57.5
WMS capability	15	4	100	3.8	95	4.3	107.5	4.3	107.5	1.3	32.5

Criterion	Weight										
Current use of scan technology within the warehouse	15	3.3	82.5	2.8	70	4.3	107.5	3.5	87.5	1	25
Pool of capable management talent	15	3.5	87.5	3	75	4	100	3.8	95	1.3	32.5
Capacity to expand	15	3.8	95	4.3	107.5	2.5	62.5	4	100	3	75
Proposed service levels	15	2.8	70	3.8	95	4	100	3.5	87.5	3.5	87.5
Suitability of space	15	2.8	70	4.5	112.5	3.5	87.5	3.8	95	3	75
Implementation costs	10	1	25	4	100	3	75	3.8	95	5	125
Payment terms	10	3	75	3	75	4.8	120	3	75	3	75
Existing supplier/ understanding of culture	10	2.3	57.5	4	100	3	75	2.8	70	4.8	120
Implementation timescale	10	3.8	95	3.5	87.5	3.8	95	4.3	107.5	1.5	37.5
Other customer synergy	10	3	75	3.3	82.5	4.8	120	3.8	95	2	50
Total score	**300**		**1,442.5**		**1,632.5**		**1,810**		**1,827.5**		**1,327.5**

Documentation and communication

People move on and suppliers sometimes disappoint; it is therefore important for scoring of selection criteria, and the rationale for any decisions, to be documented and retained within the procurement organization.

Timely and appropriate feedback to both successful and unsuccessful suppliers should be prioritized – failure to provide feedback to unsuccessful suppliers who have invested significantly in the process will reduce their willingness to participate in future exercises. This undermines the competitive set, and potentially the quality of proposals, for the next RFP.

Step 7: Contract

For many logistics services, the contract stage will be straightforward; this is particularly true for Routine services purchased under standard terms and conditions or national or international frameworks. It is also true for services where the contractual terms were made a condition of the tender and were provided at the RFP stage.

For complex, long-term and Strategic services with property or investment considerations and/or IT development requirements, the contract negotiation and agreement stage are critical to protecting the interests of both parties and set the foundation for the future relationship, governance and eventual exit or renewal. This process can be extremely time-consuming, even when a draft contract has been supplied by the shipper.

For this type of process, all parties need to bear in mind that excessively aggressive, one-sided or protracted contract negotiations or terms can impact negatively on a Strategic relationship right at its start. The aim of this process should be to align the objectives of the two companies.

The main elements and considerations of contracts for logistics services are covered in Chapter 6 – although particularly relevant for Step 7, these influence many of the procurement lifecycle stages.

Step 8: Implementation

A shared implementation plan and action list should be drawn up by both parties, even for the implementation of Routine services. However, the scope and depth of such plans will vary based on the criticality and risk associated with the service, and may range from a short list of communication steps to a complex plan over several months where specialist equipment or new processes are required.

Even the simplest plan should include the following:

- a Gantt chart with milestones;
- giving notice to any incumbent suppliers;
- exchanging precise ship-from and ship-to details, including access restrictions;
- agreeing how orders are transmitted to the new supplier;
- agreeing the service level agreements (SLAs) that define the standards expected in the contract, eg transit times, collection on time performance or acceptable stock losses (for warehousing contracts);
- management reporting requirements (if not laid out in RFP), including KPI reporting that the supplier should provide;
- setting up the supplier in your accounts system;
- checking accreditation and insurance, and other risk mitigation actions;
- agreeing account management and operational contacts;
- agreeing frequency of meetings during the first three months and subsequently;
- loading and transit trials, if required.

For complex warehouse services with building development, equipment installation and IT interfaces, a full project team with a project manager, project sponsor and steering team should be set up, and the implementation plan needs to include:

- design sign-off;
- building, equipment or development lead times;
- delivery milestones;
- supplier commissioning and testing;
- user acceptance testing;
- staff training;
- potential Transfer of Undertakings Protection of Employment (TUPE) transfer or other consultation timelines;
- performance learning curves;
- ramp-down at existing suppliers or facilities;
- adapting KPIs and Standard Operating Procedures for the implementation and ramp-up phase;
- a Plan B: an alternative timeline or solution if milestones are not achieved.

Where companies are transferring from one operation or supplier to another, rather than implementing a new service, they have two main options:

1 'Big Bang' implementation, where all services and operations are transferred in one go. For example, closing the current warehouse on the Friday night, transferring over the weekend and opening the LSP warehouse on the Monday.

2 Phased implementation, where services are transferred gradually to the new operator and the client pays the costs of two or more facilities for a period.

There are several risks involved with the 'Big Bang' approach, and for critical services this should be avoided if possible.

Table 5.8 Big Bang versus phased implementation for transferring logistics services

Option	Big Bang	Phased approach
Advantages	The shortest period of bearing the cost of two or more facilities. Clarity for customers on provision of service. A clear point of TUPE transfer (if relevant). No splitting of orders. It may be the only option if the operation is carried out in same building or with the same assets.	Lower risk to service. If issues emerge at the new operation, it can slow down the switch. Time for staff training. It allows for a learning curve.
Disadvantages	High risk, high impact if it fails. No alternative if issues emerge after transfer. It's hard to train staff on new systems and processes. It's harder to plan for a learning curve.	The cost of running dual facilities/operations. It's hard to transfer assets. You may need to split orders. Potential confusion. Less impetus to solve issues at the new operation. Split stock leads to higher stock levels.

Elsewhere in this book we discuss the importance of aligning objectives between the shipper and LSP. This alignment will need to adapt through the life of a contract, and shippers should consider incentivizing outgoing LSPs for performance areas such as minimizing stock loss and protecting service during the transfer.

There are several other potential pitfalls when it comes to implementing a new contract, both from the shipper and LSP perspectives. The root causes of the implementation problems provided in Table 5.9 are adapted from the list created by Rushton and Walker (2007) on this topic.

Many of these issues are discussed further in Chapter 8 on risk management. Chapter 8 also includes a discussion of a recent high-profile implementation failure for KFC in the UK.

IT implementations can be a significant challenge with the risk of new processes, control systems or interfaces not working properly. Some suppliers fail to ensure their IT development teams are fully aware of process requirements during the tender phase, leading to unrealistic resourcing and poor implementation plans.

User acceptance testing must be properly resourced by professionals with the necessary experience to test rigorously. This needs to include interfaces with other systems. IT issues and options related to outsourcing are discussed in depth in Chapter 10, and include implementation recommendations.

Table 5.9 Root causes of implementation problems

Client-initiated problems	Supplier-initiated problems
• Unrealistic goals at start-up.	• Failure to manage expectations/ changes to project scope.
• Poor decision-making mechanisms.	• Not having executive support.
• Not accepting any responsibility in the implementation process.	• Not dedicating the implementation team to a single project.
• Not allowing operatives enough training time.	• An inexperienced project management team.
• Misinterpretation of the service agreements and associated metrics.	• Inadequate training.
• Poor specification of requirements.	• Not developing agreed start-up and steady-state metrics.
• Not recognizing or providing for the cost of implementation.	• Cost pressure due to underestimation.

SOURCE: after Rushton and Walker, 2007

Both parties also need to understand that their relationship is being built during the implementation phase, and a lack of honesty, alignment or joint risk management during this phase will have repercussions through the life of the contract.

Finally, as with any implementation plan, the shipper needs to have a credible Plan B: an alternative timescale, go-live date or way of halting the implementation if milestones are missed in the implementation plan. Activating a Plan B may be costly in both financial and reputational terms for the senior managers and companies involved on both sides – but the alternative is a potentially catastrophic loss of service and/or reputation.

Step 9: Managing the contract

Once the implementation plan has been achieved and the service is operational, it is easy to breathe a sigh of relief and move on to the next project. After implementation, it is appropriate that the operational teams on both sides take on the management of the contract. However, as with any relationship, it is important to get into good habits at an early stage and to adjust where necessary.

Contract governance is important for all services, and critical for Bottleneck and Strategic services. The management reporting and meeting schedule that was agreed in the contract and implementation phases should be adhered to. For Routine services, all meetings don't need to be face-to-face, but some form of quarterly review of performance, challenges and sharing of plans is important.

The regular reviews should include a review of the KPIs set for the contract and whether these meet the agreed or specified levels. If these are not met, actions need to be taken. If both sides agree that KPIs are not at the right level or defined properly, a new agreement on these should be negotiated.

The worst governance behaviour is to undermine contracts by taking no action on long-term failure to meet KPIs. Such actions may not all be on the LSP's side; if the shipper's operation is the root cause, this should be tackled, not ignored.

Volumes and activity should also be compared to tender expectations. Where there are issues these should be discussed, and a joint action plan agreed.

Gavin Williams, Business Development Director of XPO, speaking at a CILT outsourcing and procurement event in 2016, had these recommendations for good governance of a contract:

- one common goal, measured the same;

- performance dashboards in place and accessible to all;

- balance the governance agenda – today's agenda versus strategic direct; formal and informal dialogue;

- ensure contractual change is a natural fabric of the governance process;

- relationship mapping – top to bottom, broad and wide.

But he also emphasized that good governance ALWAYS comes down to good people, and concluded with the following statement:

> 'Poor performance happens, be it over a short or long term. What is important is that the appropriate governance is in place to identify root cause, support its resolution, and use the issue to enhance, not damage, the relationship.'

CIPS defines three levels of contract and relationship management of increasing depth and strategic importance: contract management, supplier management and supplier relationship management. Chapter 9 defines these levels and discusses supplier relationship management in detail for the most complex and strategically important relationships.

Performance management is covered in Chapter 7. Both these topics are critical to the successful management of an outsourced contract, and should not be neglected.

Step 10: Managing exit or renewal

In the early stages of the cycle it is easy to ignore the end of a contract, but the actions taken in Steps 1–9 will lay the foundations for managing an exit or a renewal. Even the most successful supplier relationships come to an end eventually, when the service is no longer required or the companies involved change focus or direction. Some contracts end when a new management team takes over.

It is better to recognize this at the start of the process and make plans accordingly, particularly as the buying organization. It is also worth recognizing that personnel on both sides of the relationship may have moved on by the end of the contract – so the more that can be clarified and documented, the better.

In Chapter 6 the need for a contract that prepares for exit or termination is discussed: clauses to regulate notice periods, access to data, stock, staff transfers, intellectual property and other matters are needed to govern this process. The contract is the one document that is normally retained by both

Table 5.10   Termination considerations

All services	Warehouse services	Transport services
• A clear review of contractual obligations and rights before initiating exit, including redundancy. • A communications plan with staff at both companies and externally. • A TUPE consultation or equivalent. • Check with operational staff on additional services carried out by LSP that may not be documented.	• Clarity on any rent obligation/ dilapidations. • Regular stock checks during exit; with stock transfers to customer managed and stock losses (above an allowance) charged for. • A plan for managing final orders if stock not available. • A phased order transfer plan. • A cut-off date after which new orders will not be taken. • An asset list agreed as part of exit plan, with clear ownership agreed and transfer managed where needed. • Clarity on leased assets and whether there is any obligation on purchasing organization for remaining lease term. • Clarity on redundancy liability, if any, for purchasing organization.	• Clarity on any branded vehicles or assets with contractual commitment. • A phased order transfer plan.

parties, so in addition to these clauses, the more the specification, assumptions and service requirements are documented in here, the better. It will make renewal or a new tender much easier for your successors!

A key decision at this stage of the cycle is whether to renew or tender again. Clearly there is overlap between Stage 10 and the type of review carried out in Stage 1 in order for this decision to be made. However, the amount of analysis will vary depending on the service.

Although renewal is often a tempting option, this may lead to critical issues with the contract, such as changes to requirements and gaps in performance not being addressed by either party. Sadly, it is often only the discipline of an RFP process and the risk of losing a contract that leads to movement or step changes in performance by both sides.

Most companies with well-developed procurement departments have rules on how often a contract may be renewed, and a maximum duration without an RFP for this process. In the public sector these rules are likely to be particularly rigid. However, before a full RFP is run for Bottleneck or Strategic services, the purchasing organization must be confident that there are alternative, credible suppliers in the marketplace.

Managing an exit

The end of a contract needs to be managed in the same way as an implementation project, with a plan and a project manager. If the services are being carried out by a new supplier, then the implementation recommendations under Step 8 need to be considered. These also apply if the service is being brought back in-house.

If the services are no longer required, the exit still needs to be properly managed in order to minimize costs and reputational damage.

For open-book contracts there may be a liability for the purchaser for redundancy and other termination costs. These need to be reviewed carefully before a decision is taken and in conjunction with the contract: the costs involved may be significant.

Table 5.10 provides guidance on actions required as part of a termination.

Case studies

The following two case studies by Mark Rowlatt show how two companies approached an outsourcing process, and the long-term results and learnings from each process.

CASE STUDY   Outsourcing process – Tate & Lyle Sugars

Tate & Lyle is one of the leading refiners, traders and suppliers of sugar into the UK market serving both the retail and industrial sectors.

Tate & Lyle had not changed its physical route to market, logistics network and modus operandi associated with its retail (packed products) for many years. They were working with a plethora of transport companies (in excess of 30), and a number of regional warehouse keepers.

Service levels were low, and logistics cost to serve considered to be high and compounded by the multitude of contact points that were challenging to control. Given the increased expectations of multiple grocers requiring the adherence to time-sensitive delivery windows at their regional distribution centres and punitive fines imposed for on-time-in-full non-conformance, there was a clear need to act.

Outsourcing process – key elements

Project investment was secured from the Tate & Lyle operating board to engage a firm of specialist logistics consultants to undertake a robust, situation analysis to focus on order composition, inventory mapping and customer SLAs. They were required to produce and model a number of options to simplify and optimize the physical network and logistics operations.

An initial list of 18 potential LSPs were identified. The process of reducing the LSPs down to a final two companies was as follows:

1 expression of interest email sent to each LSP;

2 non-disclosure agreement sign-off;

3 formal ITT issued;

4 responses examined;

5 contract due diligence undertaken on two potential LSPs;

6 final negotiations with both LSPs.

The process resulted in two highly viable contractors being shortlisted. This ultimately became a choice of one of the LSPs to establish and operate a national distribution centre to cater for all multi-product lines and less than full truck load orders.

The transport solution was orientated around a core fleet of dedicated vehicles, internal groupage and pallet network deliveries. This segmentation was to be supported by separately engaging four transport companies to handle all full truck load orders on a regional basis direct to customer from Tate and Lyle's warehouse at the refinery in East London.

Key to the process and the successful outcome was the recognition that several specific criteria would need to be considered and evaluated, that were ultimately brought together in the form of a scorecard. The project steering committee members, having agreed on the criteria and given weight (level of importance) to each, used the scorecard to provide input and score the formal presentations and proposals that the final two competing LSPs delivered including the supporting documentation and warehouse visits.

The criteria judged were as follows, and the weighting and scores can be found at the end of this case study:

- solution cost;
- solution design;
- LSP organization capability and orientation – size and scale;
- financial stability;
- sector knowledge (food and retail) and existing customers leading to potential synergy;
- systems capability – warehouse management system and transport management system, and ability to interface;
- futureproofing – risk and resilience;
- cultural fit;
- implementation plan – robust / overall timeline / risk mitigation;
- quality accreditations;
- environmental accreditations;
- contracts and commercials (fit for purpose/minor points of contention);
- warehouse infrastructure – location, design and quality;
- warehouse location;
- multi-user leverage;
- experience of TUPE.

Of the above, there were two criteria that proved to be most pivotal, but also the hardest to measure objectively and factually: futureproofing, and cultural fit.

Futureproofing was felt to be a de-risked threat, as the warehouse location proposed by the LSP was at the time of the contract award considered to be a strategic node in the LSP's overall UK network.

In respect of cultural fit, the overall contracting process and level of engagement with individuals working at a variety of levels within the LSP's organization complemented by an appreciation of core values and behaviours had a strong resonance with Tate & Lyle.

You can never tell

Tate & Lyle awarded the contract to the LSP who scored highest on the scorecard. The LSP was awarded a three-year contract and within six months service levels had improved significantly from 93 per cent on-time-in-full (OTIF) to more than 98.75 per cent, with overall logistics cost to serve reducing by approximately 15 per cent year on year.

However, at the end of the three years the contract was not renewed – primarily due to the two pivotal criteria deviating from expectation. In terms of futureproofing, the LSP decided not to renew its lease on the warehouse facility in which the Tate & Lyle operation was housed. An alternative site was proposed, but was considered by Tate and Lyle to be a step backwards given its location.

In terms of cultural fit, the 3PL also suffered a significant loss of business with its largest client and had embarked on a strategy predicated by small business acquisition to help sustain turnover. Focus at senior level therefore became more focused on internal integration, as opposed to external customer relationship management.

Having kept in contact with the other shortlisted LSP throughout the period, they were contacted and after various discussions and negotiations a contract was agreed with this company.

Learning points

- Establish clear objectives to drive the outsourcing proposition, for example: cost out / service enhancement / capability build / futureproofing.

- Obtain board level buy-in and senior sponsorship to ensure appropriate x-functional engagement.

- Utilizing the expertise of consultants to support the entire process can be hugely advantageous in terms of providing modelling capability, industry and sector knowledge, benchmarks and an unbiased professional view.

- Build a relationship with the LSP and keep communicating at a senior level – explore how the LSP's business and priorities are changing.

- Remain open minded throughout – there will undoubtedly be many twists and turns along the way.

- Ensure effective and regular communication, particularly with internal stakeholders in order to prepare for change, and also to manage expectations particularly during the post go-live period, when execution will be under the microscope.

Table 5.11   Tate & Lyle – weighted scorecard

Criteria	Weighting (1 = low, 5 = high)	LSP score 1 = poor, 10 = excellent	Weight x score	Possible total
Solution cost	5	8	40	50
Solution design	5	10	50	50
Financial stability	5	9	45	50
Systems capability – WMS, TMS, interface	5	9	45	50
Cultural fit	5	9	45	50
Contracts and commercials	5	9	45	50
Sector knowledge (food and retail)	4	9	36	40
Implementation plan	4	9	36	40
Warehouse infrastructure	4	9	36	40
Experience of TUPE	4	9	36	40
3PL organization capability and orientation	3	9	27	30
Futureproofing – risk and resilience	3	7	21	30
Quality accreditations	3	7	21	30
Warehouse location	3	9	27	30
Environmental accreditations	2	6	12	20
Multi-user leverage	2	4	8	20
Total	**62**		**530**	**620**

Total per cent for LSP = 85.5 per cent of possible maximum score.

CASE STUDY   Outsourcing process – Company X

Company X is a consumer goods business, manufacturing and selling a wide array of fast-moving consumer goods (FMCG) into multiple markets and channels. The organization's model is predicated around manufacturing items under licence and brand ownership. In the EMEA region, Company X outsources the provision of logistics services using three separate platforms, with two operations in the Benelux and one in the UK.

The focus for this case study is the UK domestic logistics operation.

Some years ago, Company X, on entering the UK market, selected a privately-owned transport and warehousing contractor to distribute its products. A step change event occurred in 2016 when, due to the need to react quickly to a contractual dispute, the services for other divisions were also moved at pace to the same LSP.

This action effectively created a challenging scenario, with all of Company X's UK inventory holding and physical order fulfilment requirements residing with a relatively small and privately-owned company. There was a heavy turnover bias towards Company X. At the time it was a challenging environment to gain advantage from investment, and to sustain important ISO quality-related standards and accreditations.

To address this situation, Company X made an approach to the LSP marketplace with the clear objective of de-risking and futureproofing its logistics operations by working with a market-leading LSP.

Outsourcing process – key elements

Investment was secured to manage and support the overarching process. Support for the outsourcing project was segmented, utilizing a mix of freelance contractors and logistics consultants deployed at various stages as follows:

1 Deep-dive situation analysis and tender (vendor engagement and tender response evaluation) – carried out by a freelance contractor engaged for 12 months.

2 The contracting phase – carried out by logistics consultants with specialist knowledge.

3 Implementation and post go-live – managed by an interim contractor engaged for six months with a strong change management skill set.

An initial list of nine potential LSPs was identified, which, after the tender and due diligence phases, was reduced to the three LSPs who had produced viable propositions. All three were initially included in a final contract negotiation stage.

Two of the LSPs offered a solution based on running Company X's logistics operations from new-build warehouse facilities, and one provider offered an established shared-user warehouse.

A specific challenge in terms of the overall business case to justify the switch from the incumbent LSP centred around the fact that the current contract was being performed at relatively low cost, and at an acceptable level of service given the dedicated focus driven by the importance of the business to the LSP.

Not surprisingly, the estimated annual cost to serve working with a new partner exceeded the existing spend, but the pressing need to futureproof and secure proven expertise and better quality infrastructure ultimately compelled Company X to commit to contracting with one of the two shortlisted LSPs who proposed to accommodate the operation at a new-build distribution centre.

The multiplier effects of slippage

Whilst the decision by Company X to work with three specialist consultants undoubtedly created a number of challenges at the handover stages in the overall process, the one single aspect of the project that created a negative multiplier effect was the contracting phase.

Company X delegated the creation of the contract to a consultant, but also relied on internal legal counsel based in the US to govern the variations and play an integral role in the negotiation process.

Exacerbated by a number of tough rounds of negotiation, the actual contract was finally signed off some three months behind schedule, which ultimately meant that the operational go-live date was postponed by an equivalent period from April to July.

This had two further detrimental consequences – the first being the challenge of ensuring a smooth transition and implementation during the vacation months of July and August with staff absences, both at management and operational level. Secondly, instead of being the second client to be moved into the new multi-user facility, they had to defer to another new client. Introducing all three clients in such a short space of time provided the LSP with a number of challenges to stabilize the overall operation.

As a result, the service to Company X was only adjudged to have reached an acceptable level, measured by an OTIF KPI, at the beginning of the following year: six months post go-live.

Learning points

- Rather than deciding to build a contract from within, it would have been better to have asked the LSP to have presented their standard contract as the base for negotiations. This would have saved time and money. (Note though that this may not always be beneficial to the shipper, as a LSP's standard terms are likely to favour them.)

- Engaging three specialist consultants created issues in terms of hand-off through the phases. Appointing a single consultant or interim hire would have enabled continuity across the key stages of solution evaluation, contract negotiation, implementation planning and post go-live support.

- Whilst a significant improvement was gained by moving to a newly built distribution centre, further discussions could have taken place to explore alternative options in terms of warehouse location with the other competing LSPs to provide a more robust benchmark. Back to the adage 'all that glistens is not always gold'.

Conclusion

The steps needed to outsource or re-tender and award logistics services are a continual cycle, and should not be considered as either a one off event or a linear sequence of events. Decisions and actions taken at one step of the cycle impact not only on subsequent stages, but also the next cycle.

The time and resources that need to be employed at each step are related not only to the spend or savings potential of the purchase, but also the category of services required, as discussed in Chapter 4.

Far too many companies launch into a procurement event without spending enough time and management effort reviewing the services they require, whether they should be outsourced, and how the market has developed since they last tendered.

For Routine services the methodology of competitive tendering and selection are well defined and will be repeated regularly. However, when procuring complex Strategic logistics services, shippers need to ensure there is sufficient time in the process to explore potential solutions with the shortlisted bidders and to conduct extensive due diligence and cultural fit.

Once an award is made, then professional and detailed implementation plans will be required for all services if there is to be no supply interruption. Again, realistic planning is key, and sufficient time and resources need to be deployed on IT systems and integration, staff communication and training and the management of TUPE transfers if relevant.

After implementation, both sides must ensure good contract governance is in place, with regular reviews against the KPIs for the contract including physical meetings for key personnel.

Third-party logistics contracts and pricing mechanisms

06

**BY NIGEL KOTANI OF EXCELLO LAW
AND JO GODSMARK**

Introduction

'I don't have a contract with my best customer', and 'We don't have a contract with that supplier' are often heard in the logistics industry, particularly in the road transport sector. But these statements are neither true nor desirable for successful logistics outsourcing.

Any service, even the movement of one load from A to B, will necessitate the supply of a quotation and an acceptance from the buyer – and at that point a contract is made. One party will have accepted the others' terms and conditions, even if they did so unknowingly and/or in the mistaken belief that their own terms and conditions applied.

It is always better to know the contractual conditions on which you are operating, rather than finding them out when things have gone wrong. This chapter will explore the main elements of logistics contracts, both national and international framework and bespoke contracts, and why they are important. Common pitfalls and decisions that need to be made are discussed.

Price and price mechanisms are core to any logistics contract and this chapter will include definitions, options and examples for charging mechanisms for logistics services.

Contract fundamentals

Reduced to its fundamental basics, the main provisions that go into a logistics contract fall into three broad categories:

- the service that the logistics service provider (LSP) is to provide, specified in considerable detail as to items such as service levels, timeframes, locations and technical requirements;
- what the shipper pays and when;
- terms and conditions (T&Cs) covering areas such as limitation of liability, obligations on the shipper, rights, remedies and duration.

Logistics contracts fall into two broad categories: simple contracts which incorporate or rely on a national or international framework, and bespoke contracts. For a shipper requiring infrequent transport services, and accordingly ordering only occasional spot deliveries, simple contracts are enough. For a high street retailer with 500 stores and using a single LSP for all its transport needs, a bespoke contract is a necessity.

Arguably the most problematic legal issue faced when negotiating a logistics contract is that the profit margins of LSPs are insufficient to enable them to cover the losses of shippers if something goes wrong.

Losses in logistics contracts fall into two broad categories:

- Direct losses, primarily comprising loss of or damage to goods, such as caused by a warehouse catching fire or a ship sinking. As detailed later, the LSP's liability for these losses is generally limited by contract to a level that is lower than the value of the goods, meaning that in practice the shipper often insures against such losses.

- Indirect or consequential losses, primarily comprising loss of sales or profits and damage to reputation, such as caused by empty shelves or angry customers. For the reasons stated above, LSPs' liability for such losses is invariably excluded entirely by contract. This is a problem, as insurance for such losses is either unobtainable or prohibitively expensive.

International and national frameworks

Logistics framework contracts essentially cover the T&Cs, leaving the shipper and the LSP free to focus on agreeing and documenting between them the items in the other two categories, namely the service the LSP is to provide and what the shipper is to pay.

The agreement between them on these items will generally be very simple, and will accordingly often be documented in the form of email exchanges, purchase orders or sales orders, though it can equally just be arranged by phone, especially if the parties know each other well. Either way, with the elements of agreement, consideration and intent to create legal relations all clearly present, their arrangement will constitute a legally-binding contract.

The national frameworks which apply in the UK are standard terms produced and recommended by trade bodies. These include the British International Freight Association (BIFA), the Road Haulage Association (RHA), the Freight Transport Association (FTA) and the United Kingdom Warehousing Association (UKWA).

Generally, these frameworks are incorporated by reference, with an LSP's sales order, for example, stating in its small print that the LSP operates on RHA standard terms. As one would expect of terms produced by trade bodies, these national frameworks tend to favour LSPs rather than shippers.

There are many international frameworks which apply to cross-border shipping, including the Montreal Convention (covering air carriage), the Hague-Visby Rules (ship carriage), Convention concerning International Carriage by Rail (COTIF) and the Convention on the Contract for the International Carriage of Goods by Road (CMR). Which one applies depends on the form of transport being used, and whether the countries in question are parties to the relevant treaty.

The frameworks in question are not incorporated by contract, but simply apply by operation of law. If taking goods by sea from the UK to France, for example, the Hague-Visby Rules will apply irrespective of whether the LSP and shipper want them to or are even aware that they do.

It is worth noting that Incoterms are an international framework for trade terms in relation to goods, covering matters such as which party pays for the carriage and duties, and at what point risk in the goods passes between the parties. They are not a framework that sets out the terms and conditions for the carriage service itself.

Whilst the precise details vary between different frameworks, the main T&C areas which they tend to cover are the following:

- **LSP rights:** these can include provisions such as the LSP having the right to choose the precise route or having the right to use sub-contractors (and whether, if the LSP does use subcontractors, it appoints them as principal or as the shipper's agent).

- **LSP protections**: these include items such as the LSP having a lien over the shipper's goods, and a right to store and dispose of them in the event of non-payment by the shipper or non-acceptance of the goods by the recipient. Other provisions in this category include the right of an LSP to refuse to carry certain types of goods, such as dangerous goods, unless expressly agreed at the time the order is placed, and the LSP having a right to claim compensation against a shipper if its goods contaminate other goods carried or stored by the LSP.

- **Shipper obligations**: these include obligations on the shipper to properly package the goods, to pay all relevant duties on the goods, to load and unload the goods (though this will often be expressly varied to make it the LSP's duty), to insure the goods (should the shipper require cover, which it generally will) and to pay demurrage in the event that it causes delay.

- **Technical details**: these are predominantly found in the international frameworks in order to ensure cross-border compatibility, and include matters such as the type and contents of the documentation to be used in respect of the goods being transported.

- **Rights of termination**: these are predominantly found in national frameworks which relate to warehousing.

- **Limitations of liability**: these can include causes of damage (such as exclusion of losses caused by war), time limits for bringing claims and limitations on damages (see later in this chapter for more detailed information).

- **Jurisdiction**: this determines the forum in which disputes are heard, which in national frameworks will usually be the courts, often with the possibility of an alternative dispute resolution process, but which in international matters can be considerably more complex. For example, if a Norwegian LSP has arranged transport to the US on a Liberian ship of a cargo of Japanese silk on behalf of a UK shipper, and it is damaged by acid leaking from car batteries loaded in China, but which were manufactured in Vietnam by a Korean company, in which country does the shipper issue legal proceedings if everyone is denying liability?

Liability under national and international frameworks for loss of or damage to goods is often limited to a low amount. Under RHA T&Cs, for example, it is currently capped at £1,300 per tonne, which is fine if one is transporting coal, but not much use if it is mobile phones.

Unhelpfully for shippers, in international frameworks, and even some national ones, liability caps are often incomprehensible by virtue of being expressed by reference to obscure international values, such as to 2 Special Drawing Rights per kilo under BIFA or to 25 francs per kilo in CMR (with a franc being 'the gold franc weighing 10/31 of a gramme and being of millesimal fineness 900' according to the Convention).

In terms of liability for delay and other indirect losses it is even lower, with FTA for example capping them at the carriage charges.

The UKWA terms and conditions of storage cap liability for all types of loss at £100 per tonne, which will certainly necessitate the shipper to take out its own stock insurance.

The national frameworks generally permit the shipper and LSP to expressly vary some of the provisions. With dangerous goods, for example, the restriction on carrying them 'unless otherwise agreed' clearly permits the parties to expressly agree for them to be carried. Another common variation is an agreement that the LSP takes advantage of economies of scale and relationships with insurers by arranging insurance cover, but with the cost passed on to the shipper. These express provisions are typically set out in the same email or purchase / sales note which contain the details of what's being shipped, where and at what price.

Within international frameworks, because they apply by operation of law and not by agreement between the parties, there is much less scope for variations to be agreed between the parties, though there is generally no restriction on agreeing supplemental provisions.

Returning to the challenge raised at the very beginning of this chapter, which arises from LSPs' profit margins being insufficient to cover the potential losses to shippers:

- Direct losses are usually covered by insurance, either with the shipper obtaining it, or with the parties agreeing that the LSP should obtain it and pass the cost on to the shipper.

- Indirect losses will almost certainly not be covered, either because liability is expressly excluded or because it is limited to a very low amount. Whilst, as detailed above, shippers and LSPs are free to expressly vary many of the provisions in the frameworks, because of this fundamental problem of the shipper's losses generally exceeding the LSP's profit margins it will be almost impossible for a shipper to persuade an LSP to accept liability for indirect losses which exceed those set out in the relevant national or international framework.

The unavailability or impracticality of insurance make this a real problem for shippers, as the losses they suffer from damage to reputation can be as great as the damage to goods, but with nothing like the same levels of protection available.

The only real option (the word 'remedy' not really being appropriate) that shippers have when an LSP which is operating under a national or international framework causes indirect loss by, for example, delaying the delivery of goods, is to accept whatever cap the relevant framework imposes for indirect losses and just not use that LSP again (or, on a warehousing contract, terminate the contract on notice and move to a different warehouse).

Bespoke contracts

Having dealt with T&Cs in the international and national frameworks section, it makes sense to continue that theme before moving on to what service the LSP is providing in a bespoke contract. Payment is covered later in this chapter.

T&Cs in bespoke contracts will cover essentially the same areas as the national and international frameworks, but generally in more detail and with greater variations. Indeed, there is so much overlap between the T&C sections in bespoke agreements and the national frameworks that it is possible for even bespoke contracts to focus on the main basics of price and service and incorporate one of the national frameworks by reference to cover any issues not expressly covered elsewhere.

For example, a bespoke contract might state that 'RHA Conditions of Carriage 2009 will apply to the extent that they are not inconsistent with the terms of this agreement'. Whilst there is no inherent problem with that approach, it is only advisable if the parties have a good working knowledge of what's in, and what's not covered by, the RHA Conditions of Carriage 2009.

In practice though, there are benefits of having the T&C provisions specifically negotiated and set out in full in a bespoke contract – not least the fact that having all the relevant T&C provisions in a single document rather than in two is more convenient and reduces the scope for ambiguity and inconsistency. This is, by some distance, the most common approach.

Typically, the type of T&C provisions that a bespoke logistics contract is likely to cover (and this is not intended to be an exhaustive list or to cover the relevant item comprehensively) include the following:

- **Exclusivity of use:** for example, is the shipper proposing to use a single LSP for all its transport needs within a specific geographical area, or is the LSP one of several service providers that might be used?

- **Guaranteed volumes:** is the shipper willing to guarantee the LSP certain levels of use for the duration of the contract? Even if not, provisions requiring the shipper to regularly provide the LSP with non-binding estimates in advance of its likely volume needs might be appropriate.

- **Duration of contract:** is it going to be a fixed-term contract, or will it be indefinite but terminable on a period of notice? If it's the latter, what is the notice period, and is it the same for both shipper and LSP?

- **Rights of renewal:** some bespoke contracts will grant the shipper a one-off unilateral right to extend the contract for a specified period, usually a year. If so, this might require further discussions on pricing during that period (see later in this chapter for more details). Alternatively, contracts often contain a provision (legally unenforceable) requiring the parties to discuss a possible contract extension at a specified time before the expiry of the contract.

- **Performance measurement:** this is a significant part of any bespoke contract, and arguably one of the main reasons for having a bespoke contract at all, covering key performance indicators (KPIs), regular measuring and reporting of performance against KPIs, and rewards and penalties for achieving or failing to achieve KPI targets (see later in this chapter and in Chapter 7 for more details).

- **Provision of specialist equipment:** this could be items such as specialist warehousing or handling equipment, and the provisions will cover matters such as who pays for (and owns) it, who maintains it and what happens to it at the end of the contract.

- **Use of livery:** on an extensive transport contract this might include the right for the shipper to have its logo and livery on the LSP's trailers, thus providing additional advertising. The shipper would additionally want to include provisions about the lorries being kept clean and driven considerately: a shipper won't be overly concerned if its goods are in an LSP-branded lorry that is filthy on the outside and being driven inconsiderately, but it won't be happy if the trailer is painted with its logo.

- **Contract variation:** it is inevitable during a long and complex contract that one or other of the parties comes up with an idea for changing the way a part of the service is provided, or for extending the scope of the services. Contract variation provisions establish a framework for negotiating, pricing and agreeing variations of this nature.

- **Information technology (IT):** modern logistics services, in both the transport and warehousing sectors, are extremely high-tech and software-driven.

Bespoke logistics contracts will contain licensing provisions concerning the use and integration by the shipper and the LSP of each other's IT systems, including all the rights and protections, such as protection of personal data, one would expect to find in any software licence. See Chapter 10 for more on the considerations relating to IT.

- **Intellectual property (IP) rights**: if the LSP is to use the shipper's IP in any way, then the types of protection that one would find in any IP licence agreement will need to be included in the contract. IP provisions might also cover ownership of any new IP that is created by either party during the performance of the contract (such as ownership of any new code written to ensure that the two parties' IT systems are compatible), with the position in law in the absence of provisions to the contrary being that whoever produces the IP owns it.

- **Contract monitoring**: these provisions might, for example, require representatives of the LSP and shipper to meet on a monthly basis to discuss concerns and performance, and for more senior representatives to meet half-yearly.

- **Transfer of Undertakings, Protection of Employment (TUPE) protection**: TUPE transfers arise by operation of law, not by agreement between the parties, and indeed many of the early TUPE legal cases concerned employees claiming that their employment had transferred between parties who both disputed that it had. It is therefore essential for shippers to include protections which cover the eventuality of employees of the LSP transferring under TUPE to the shipper or to a replacement LSP when the contract ends.

- **Rights of inspection**: this will depend on the pricing mechanism (see section below) but with certain types of pricing mechanism, such as open-book contracts, it will be essential for the shipper to be able to inspect and audit the LSP's records.

- **Limitations of liability**: as with the national and international frameworks, the fundamental problem that the profit margins of LSPs are insufficient to enable them to cover the losses of shippers if something goes wrong means that liability for direct losses (see above) is likely to be very limited, and all liability for indirect losses excluded.

- **Insurance obligations**: because of the limitations of liability, a shipper may want to include provisions requiring the LSP, at its own cost, to obtain insurance cover up to a certain limit for loss of or damage to products, and potentially for public and employer's liability.

- **Benchmarking:** bespoke contracts can include provisions requiring a benchmarking exercise to be conducted during the course of the contract to compare the prices, standards and performance levels of the LSP against those of other LSPs carrying out similar contracts. This can lead to changes in the pricing and performance levels under the contract.

- **Early termination:** this would include termination in the event of insolvency of either party, but would also need to include a right for the shipper to terminate for material breach by the LSP or for its consistent failure to achieve certain KPI targets.

- **Orderly handover:** this covers termination both by the contract coming to an end and by it being terminated early. It will include items such as the delivery of stock still in the possession of the LSP, the ongoing provision of information by the LSP to the shipper and the shipper's ongoing access to the LSP's records.

Revisiting once again the issue of the fundamental challenge arising from LSPs' profit margins being too low to enable them to cover the shipper's losses, direct losses can be covered by express provisions detailing the required insurance cover and who is going to procure it.

Indirect losses remain a challenge and ultimately one where the contract can only supply limited protection. In terms of protection against indirect losses, there are three options.

Avoiding them in the first place

Far and away the best way to protect against indirect losses is by trying to avoid them occurring in the first place. The best way to do that is by a) going through the procurement process properly to make sure that the shipper chooses the best LSP for its needs in the first place and that the LSP is fully informed as to what is needed; and b) through ongoing performance monitoring and management of the contract, combined with frequent and open dialogue and joint reviews.

The first of these falls outside the scope of an analysis of logistics contracts, but very much within the scope of the rest of this book. The second is certainly something that can be covered in contracts (see above in respect of contract monitoring).

However, ultimately it is still down to the shipper and LSP to ensure that they carry through with those obligations, and that they don't simply remain as clauses in a contract that has been hidden away in a drawer and the contents of which have been forgotten.

Penalties for poor performance

A secondary remedy for indirect losses is imposing penalties or reduced payments on the LSP for poor performance. This is covered in more detail in the section later in this chapter on pricing mechanisms, but it should be noted that penalties are a very indirect and imprecise remedy for indirect losses.

For example, it is relatively easy to quantify the cost to the shipper of the permanent loss of a container of £250,000 of goods but much harder to quantify the cost to the shipper of a week's delay to the delivery of that container. It is even harder to quantify those losses when the parties are attempting to do so in advance, in generic contractual terms (e.g. '£X per day of delay per container'), rather than after the event.

In addition, even if the indirect losses could be quantified in advance in generic terms by the parties, the fundamental problem of LSPs' low profit margins and shippers' high indirect losses means that ultimately no sensible shipper is going to accept penalties which even come close to reflecting the shipper's real losses, meaning that in practice penalties tend to be more of a disincentive than a genuine remedy.

Finally, there are legal issues with the enforceability of penalties generally, which are too complex and technical for these pages.

Early termination

The final remedy for indirect losses is ultimately for the shipper to have the right of early termination for material breach and/or consistent failure to achieve targets (see previously in this chapter). There is no question that this would only be enforced as a last resort, and that doing so would have serious consequences for the shipper. It is also questionable whether it is really a remedy at all, given that it is designed to prevent future damage and won't in any way compensate for past damage.

Nevertheless, it is an essential right for the shipper to have, along with provisions for an orderly handover. The good news is that the type of complete breakdown that might cause a shipper to terminate a contract early tends to happen early on in the contract, when it is likely to be much easier to quickly take back control or to take on a replacement LSP.

Turning to the issue of what the LSP supplies under the contract, typically this will comprise a list of services to be provided by the LSP, perhaps contained in a separate document such as Standard Operating Procedures (SOPs) which includes detailed provisions as to how such services are to be delivered, within what parameters and to what standard.

If a detailed and thorough tender process has been conducted, then the specification on the basis of which the LSP submitted its tender will either comprise the list of services to be provided under the contract together with the SOP, or else will be the starting point for the preparation of such a list and SOP.

The list of services and SOP will be drafted and negotiated between the LSP and the shipper's logistics manager or consultant, rather than by a lawyer, though they might be reviewed by the lawyer, especially as they may often be closely linked to the pricing mechanisms. For that reason, despite being of central importance to the contract and of far more immediate relevance to the shipper and the LSP than the T&C provisions, they are dealt with relatively briefly here.

Pricing mechanisms

The structure of the pricing agreement between the parties sets the tone for the relationship and the degree to which the shipper has insight into, and therefore some responsibility for, the LSP's costs. The pricing mechanism should be appropriate for the type of service and relationship being contracted (see Chapter 4): open-book, bespoke mechanisms are complex and time-consuming to manage and should be kept to a minimum.

The terms relating to pricing mechanisms can be confusing. and are sometimes used incorrectly. The common terms for warehousing and transport services are shown in Table 6.1.

Table 6.1 Logistics services pricing mechanisms

Term	Summary	Applications
Open-book	The LSP shares the costs of delivering all or part of the services and agrees a management fee or mark-up on top of these costs with the shipper. The costs are auditable by the shipper. Most of the cost risk sits with the shipper.	Complex, long term distribution centre or fulfilment centre contracts with property or other high fixed costs. It can also be used for dedicated transport contracts, Strategic or Bottleneck services.

(continued)

Table 6.1 (Continued)

Term	Summary	Applications
Closed-book	The LSP quotes a rate for the service for an agreed duration, often through a tender process. The shipper has no rights to audit or have visibility of the profit margin of the LSP. Most of the cost risk for delivering the service sits with the LSP.	Routine services and shared or network services such as most road transport, pallet hire and short-term storage and shared warehousing contracts.
Hybrid	A price mechanism that incorporates elements of both open- and closed-book approaches.	Longer term warehousing or fulfilment centre contracts. Transport contracts with specialist or dedicated equipment. Transport contracts with fuel mechanisms.
Tariff	The price for an element of the service, eg price per route, per kg or per pallet. Normally used in closed-book relationships.	Routine services and shared or network services, such as most road transport, pallet hire and short-term storage and shared warehousing contracts.
Transactional	Another term for closed-book, tariff price mechanisms	As per closed-book
Fixed price	An alternative to open-book mechanisms to protect the LSP, particularly from exposure to changing volumes. The shipper will agree to pay a fixed cost or minimum fee for part of the services; often used in warehousing contracts to secure space.	Warehousing contracts. Transport contracts with specialist or dedicated assets.
Variable pricing	A term used to describe volume-based elements of pricing mechanisms for which an agreed tariff is paid. The opposite of fixed pricing.	Warehousing contracts. Most transport contracts.

(continued)

Table 6.1   (Continued)

Term	Summary	Applications
Fixed plus variable	A type of hybrid pricing whereby the shipper pays for a minimum volume or capacity as a fixed cost and pays for additional volume on a tariff basis.	Longer-term commitments for space or assets. An example would be contracting for 5,000 pallet spaces of storage at a fixed cost per week and additional spaces, or handling costs on a tariff basis.
Activity-based costing (ABC)	Originally an accounting method for allocating overhead, this methodology can be used to extract the costs of activity from an open-book budget. These 'equivalent tariffs' can then be compared to market tariffs.	Warehousing or complex, dedicated fulfilment contracts.
Percentage of sales	A mechanism whereby the LSP charges a percentage of the shipper's sales revenue.	Warehousing or logistics contracts.
Gainshare	A reward mechanism that shares the savings from an improvement project between the LSP and shipper or rewards the LSP for fulfilling a range of objectives.	Warehousing or other Bottleneck or Strategic services.

NOTE The table lists the common mechanisms used and their applications

The pricing mechanism should be determined by the buyer before the RFP so that the LSPs understand this when pricing the services. Some flexibility in the process, however, should allow LSPs to suggest adjustments to the mechanism where they feel it to be beneficial.

The criteria used to determine the appropriate pricing mechanism will include:

- the complexity of the services;
- the category of the service (Routine services should be on a tariff mechanism, Bottleneck and Strategic services may be open-book or hybrid);
- the risk profile of the services and who controls the risk;
- the proportion of fixed costs in the service;

- whether there is a shared-user or shared network element of the service – if so, tariff mechanisms are more appropriate to avoid the difficulty of apportioning shared resources between contracts;
- the objectives of the service: additional objectives above basic service, such as innovation or change management, will require resource.

Closed-book, open-book and cost-plus contracts

In closed-book contracts, charges are based on the activities carried out by the LSP. The charges will include an element for overhead contribution and profit margin. Customers get fixed prices for given volumes which may be index-linked, and have no visibility of the LSP's actual costs or profit.

The LSP's earnings will increase in line with volumes and activity. Conversely, if volumes and activity reduce, so will the LSP's revenue. LSPs will often look to cushion some of the fluctuations in volume by imposing minimum storage and throughput levels.

This type of charging has its advantages and disadvantages. The main advantage is that costs are closely related to sales in terms of order throughput. Storage costs are based on the number of items stored, and therefore can highlight when stock levels are higher than expected.

The main disadvantage is that it is more difficult to budget, as costs will vary month by month depending on activities within the warehouse. With contracts requiring a large amount of investment and commitment by the LSP, they may either price in a lot of risk or refuse to enter into an agreement on a purely closed-book basis. Finally, rate reviews are typically carried out annually and therefore do not reflect any efficiency improvement as it occurs.

A full open-book contract is based on total transparency between supplier and customer. The client can see exactly what costs the third party is incurring and is able to discuss these costs and potential cost-reduction strategies.

It is common in these types of contract to agree a management fee that is determined by performance. A base fee will be agreed, together with set targets. If the targets are achieved, the management fee will be paid in full. If exceeded, the management fee can be increased; if the LSP falls short due to poor performance, it could forfeit some of its management fee.

This type of charging allows shared risk, for the shipper to become involved in the process and for them to help identify areas where its own performance can influence the overall cost. However, they have the disadvantage that the LSP has less direct incentive to find efficiency savings and reduce costs. They are harder to benchmark and place an increased burden on the shipper to review costs and seek efficiency improvements; this can have the effect of reducing the role of the LSP as the expert provider.

Open-book contracts enable shippers to audit costs, and they should do so at regular intervals during the contract term. However, many shippers do not avail themselves of this right and thus undermine their own contracts.

One form of open-book contracts are cost-plus contracts: these are similar to open-book, but in most cases the 'plus' element is based on a percentage of cost added on in the form of a management fee. This can lead to the perverse situation where the higher the costs incurred on the contract, the higher the profit earned by the third party. Solutions to this are discussed later in the chapter.

One disadvantage of any form of open-book or cost-plus contract is that the shipper and LSP must determine what is an acceptable level of overhead and profit for the LSP to receive. What is a 'reasonable' level is a common question in the events run by the Chartered Institute of Logistics and Transport Outsourcing and Procurement Forum.

Before asking this question, shippers should ask what the overhead and profit should cover:

- Is there a separate central office overhead charge elsewhere in the open-book budget?
- If part of the management fee is covering overhead, is there clarity on what it covers?
- Is the LSP facing any risk?
- Is the LSP having to fund any innovation or central team support from this fund?

Management fees should be part of a tender process, but as emphasized before, shippers must be clear what they want from a contract. If low overhead and profit on a contract mean lack of investment in improving service or reducing cost, then that may be a short-term win for the LSP.

Hybrid mechanisms

When faced with long-term, high-investment, high-risk contracts, there are advantages in designing a mechanism that retains elements of both closed-book and activity-based costing for some elements of the services. This allows benchmarking of these service elements and incentivizes the LSP

Figure 6.1 Hybrid/activity-based costing contracts can deliver the best of both worlds

Cost items	Characteristics		Mechanism	Examples
Fixed costs	Costs of the operation which are independent of volumes Identified costs based on invoices (no allocations)		Pay at cost: • Only change by agreement based on provable cost changes • Long-term where appropriate	• Rent • Rates • Utilities • General management • Equipment
Variable costs	Costs of the operation which are directly dependent on the activity of the operation		• Variable charge with agreed productivity • Annual productivity targets	• Direct labour • Some equipment
Fixed management fee	Fixed amount not linked to contract cost base Allocations		• Agreed costs	• Centrally allocated costs, eg IT support, insurances • Management overhead • Profit margin

Fair return linked to risk

SOURCE Davis, 2011

to become more efficient, while accepting that some other areas of the contract need to be paid for on a fixed or open-book basis.

Management consultants AT Kearney (Davis, 2011) advocate this approach, as illustrated in Figure 6.1.

Note that the management fee in the structure shown is fixed and not a percentage of total cost. This solves the inherent disincentive to reduce costs when the management fee is agreed on a percentage of cost basis. Price mechanisms of this type are complex and require investment on both sides at negotiation, contract and contract management stages to work properly.

AT Kearney describe the benefits and drawbacks of this type of hybrid and activity-based costing approach in Table 6.2.

Tariff structures

A tariff-based pricing structure is one with fixed prices for different activities. The most common logistics tariffs are detailed in Table 6.3. Where goods are not palletized, the 'per pallet' quantity should be substituted with an equivalent unit (price per item, price per kg, price per m^3).

Table 6.2   Benefits and drawbacks of a hybrid system

Characteristics	Benefits	Drawbacks
Cost and transparency of service	• You only pay for the service used. • It enables benchmarking across providers. • It facilitates identification of cost savings. • It facilitates budget control for the contract manager.	• It requires time to develop a structure for transparency. • It requires changing the mindset of LSPs.
Risk sharing	• Neither party carries the whole risk. • Lower provider risk results in a lower management fee. • It promotes effective and open partnership.	• The shipper risk is higher than in a rates contract.
Continuous improvement	• The shipper and LSP jointly and actively look for cost and service benefits. • It enables a competitive advantage in achieving improvements beyond market level.	• It requires time and resources to develop and maintain. • It requires changing the mindset of LSPs
Supportive marketing/sales tool	• It facilitates accurate internal cost allocation for the shipper. • It enables accurate pricing quotes for alternative order profiles.	
Strategy focus	• There is more time for strategic management due to less time spent on operational tasks. • A partnership enables use of LSP expertise for strategic decisions.	• There is potential to become dependent on the LSP through too much trust.
Contract fit	• You can use a constant contract structure across the supply chain.	• Cost control is more difficult for a shared-use LSP.

SOURCE Davis, 2011

Table 6.3 Common logistics tariff structures

Service area	Service	Tariff options
Warehousing	Storage	Price per pallet per week or part thereof.
		Price per occupied metre squared/metre cubed
		Price per kg
	Handling	Receipt, handling and despatch charge (per pallet in and out)
		Separate charge for pallets in and pallets out (more suitable if format changed)
		Separate rate for pallet in and carton out
		Rate per carton in-handled (loose-loaded)
	Picking	Price per case or unit picked
		Price per line picked
		Price per order picked
	Administration	Price per order or order line
		Hourly charge
	Value-adding services, eg labelling, re-packing	Price per item or other volume
		Hourly charge
Road transport	Full truck load (FTL)	Fixed cost per route specified (eg £250 per trip)
		Fixed price per postcode/region grouping (eg £350 per trip for a group of postal areas)
		Cost per initial delivery plus cost per additional drop
	Less than truck load (LTL)	Fixed cost per route specified
		Number of pallets/region price matrix
		Price per kg/m³ or other units

(continued)

Table 6.3 (Continued)

Service area	Service	Tariff options
	Pallet networks, pallet distribution	Price per pallet (for regional grouping) depending on size – quarter, half or full pallet
	Parcels	Cost per carton/item Cost per kg/m³
Multimodal route (sea/road or rail/road)	Full vehicle/container transport	Fixed cost price per route
Sea freight	Full container load (FCL)	Cost per container – 20', 30', 40' 45', 45' highcube.
	Less than container load (LCL)	Cost per kg/m³.
Air freight	Full load	Cost per charter.
Air freight	Groupage	Cost per kg/m³.

Care must be taken when evaluating storage charges and the treatment of part-weeks and stock levels. See the following box for examples of this.

Tariffs for storage

There are a number of different ways for LSPs to calculate storage charges, and care needs to be taken in evaluating the tariff offered and the resultant charges. The main tariff variants are:

- average pallets in stock per week;
- peak pallets in stock per week;
- pallets per week or part thereof – calculated as 'opening stock plus inbound stock';
- pallets per week or part thereof – calculated as 'opening stock plus net stock movements'.

Table 6.4 shows an example of stock movements during a week in a warehouse.

For the four tariff options listed above, the pallet number used for the storage calculation would be:

- pallets of stock charged = average stock = 125 pallets;
- pallets of stock charged = peak stock = 200 pallets;
- pallets of stock charged = 100 + 300 = 400 pallets;
- pallets of stock charged = 100 + 300 – 330 = 70 pallets.

Tariffs based on charging for part-weeks, as in the last two bullets above, have significant impact on the storage costs for fast-moving goods. Both shippers and LSPs need to look at storage and handling costs together to estimate cost or revenue – and shippers are advised to calculate annual costs based on forecast.

For non-palletized goods, the same principles apply, but the units need to be agreed between the parties.

Table 6.4   Example stock movements

Number of pallets/ day	Mon	Tues	Wed	Thurs	Friday	Sat	Sun	Total
Opening stock	100	175	200	190	70	70	70	
Intake	100	100	50	10	20	20	0	**300**
Dispatch	25	75	60	130	20	20	0	**330**

Fuel and other price-adjustment mechanisms

For pure Routine purchases, the shipper could tender annually or bi-annually and allow no price variation between tenders. This is typically the case on international full vehicle movements. However, for many services, including many Routine transport services, longer-term contracts are beneficial, and the contract will need to cover how price adjustments are agreed.

The most common adjustment mechanism in logistics contracts is a fuel mechanism. As discussed in Chapter 5, fuel can account for up to 30 per cent of the overall cost of road transport and is subject to major fluctuations in price. Road transport margins are typically too low to absorb the risk of fuel price variations, and in many markets LSPs insist on protection in this area.

In setting a fuel-based mechanism, it is important that the contract states:

- the national (or international) fuel price index to be used (eg, the FTA index in the UK);
- the base fuel price at the start of the contract (on which the agreed rates were based);
- the percentage of the rate that is attributed to fuel.

To prevent the mechanism triggering too frequently, fuel mechanisms should either have some band of price change where the supplier absorbs the cost, or a periodic review of price changes. If set at a time of high fuel costs, fuel mechanisms should, ideally, deal with fuel prices going down as well as up.

Worked example

Company A agrees the following fuel mechanism with Supplier B on an agreed route price of £400 per trip:

- Base price of fuel at time of tender: £0.94 per litre.
- Supplier B's percentage of costs related to fuel = 30 per cent.
- Fuel mechanism agreed to apply over £0.95 and below £0.93 per litre, with a reference price of £0.94.
- Fuel rises to £1.00 per litre.
- Percentage fuel increase = 100 x (£1.00 – £0.95)/0.94 = 5.32 per cent.
- Fuel surcharge = 5.32 per cent x 30 per cent x £400 = £6.38.

Although fuel is the most common price adjustment mechanism in logistics contracts, other inflationary adjustments should also be considered, particularly for longer contracts. These could be dealt with through an annual review based on specified cost indices (eg FTA/RHA cost tables). With increasing regulation, driver shortages and wage inflation in many countries, LSPs may advocate some form of labour cost mechanism. If adopted, this should be set out in the contract in a similar way to a fuel mechanism.

Deep sea shipping contracts will be subject to fixed inflationary terms for some elements and mandatory cost increases for others, such as port charges.

Pricing mechanism and benchmarking

One advantage of setting up at least part of a pricing mechanism under tariff, or tariff proxies such as activity-based costing, is that it enables companies to benchmark against price quotations.

Although the cost elements of an open-book contract may, and in fact should, be benchmarked against industry wage rates and other costs, this will not demonstrate whether the LSP is operating efficiently (for example, wages may be in line with industry norms, but the productivity may be low). Attempts can be made to benchmark productivity for certain activities, but if the shipper can benchmark prices instead, they can get closer to an overall comparison of cost and efficiency. Benchmarking is discussed further in Chapter 7.

Gainshare and aligning objectives

The core job of an LSP is to store, ship and deliver goods, and the main reward mechanisms on logistics contracts will be for transacting these activities. However, shippers will have quality standards that need to be met and may have wider objectives for the contract, such as improving efficiency or the development of new services.

As part of the pricing negotiations and structure, shippers need to ask themselves whether the contract award is enough for the LSP to provide the resource and have the motivation to deliver improvements and/or innovations. Although many shippers accept that additional funding may be needed to meet their objectives, they are wary of simply providing this through a general increase in tariffs or simply paying for additional resource.

One of the ways that users commonly use to try and do this is through the imposition of penalties against the provider for failure to achieve KPIs. Although this approach is understandable from a user's perspective, it doesn't create an environment that is conducive to a constructive partnership. Far from motivating the provider to genuinely enhance the user's business by improving the quality of its service, it risks motivating the provider to provide the most basic service that it can get away with (at the lowest cost) whilst avoiding incurring any penalties.

Countless studies have shown that humans respond better to the promise of reward than to the threat of negative consequences; LSPs are organizations of people, and are no different.

Gainshare mechanisms

One of the most common tools to align objectives between the shipper and an LSP, and to incentivize the LSP, is a gainshare mechanism. A gainshare mechanism rewards the LSP against one or more objectives, typically cost saving or efficiency projects with quantifiable benefits.

Shippers and LSPs agreeing a gainshare scheme need to decide upon several points:

- What are the SMART (Specific, Measurable, Achievable, Relevant, and Timed) objectives that will form the scheme?
- What level of reward will the scheme deliver? Is this likely to be motivating? See the David Lowther interview in Chapter 9 for a view on this.

- Is there a base service level that must be achieved before any payment is made through the scheme? This can be a way of avoiding over-focusing on the initiatives in the scheme rather than general good service against the contract KPIs.

- Will the reward consist only of a share of monies saved through initiatives that are part of the scheme, or are additional monies available?

- If the scheme provides a share of profit generated or cost savings achieved, how long will this benefit be shared for, if the savings continue for several years?

- If the savings require an investment by either or both parties, how will this be handled?

- If the gainshare scheme rewards the LSP for ideas they generate and implement, how will you decide the source of the idea? In practice it might be better to reward the implementation of all agreed good ideas, to avoid endless discussions on credit for an idea.

A simple gainshare example is as follows.

Shipper A agrees a productivity project with its main warehouse provider. The aim of the project is to improve picking efficiency and to reduce customer complaints and returns through the introduction of both new voice-picking technology and increased management focus.

The following gainshare agreement is put into place:

- 50/50 share of net savings for two years;

- 100 per cent to the shipper thereafter;

- additional annual IT costs for voice picking charged to the project as part of net saving calculation for two years and thereafter to the warehouse budget.

The project delivers net savings of £10,000 in the first year, £30,000 in the second year and £20,000 in the third year. The LSP receives a gainshare payment of £5,000 in the first year, £10,000 in the second year and nothing for this project in the third year.

However, the additional costs for the voice picking technology were charged to the warehouse open-book budget in Year 3.

Alignment of objectives

As detailed earlier in this chapter, by far the best way of aligning the objectives of the shipper and the LSP is by aligning the LSP's reward mechanism under the contract with the aims of the shipper.

Where the shipper's objectives are service-related or more complex than can be delivered in a simple gainshare arrangement, it may be worth introducing a more complex reward mechanism based on a basket of objectives. The example at the end of this section illustrates this approach. Such arrangements require management, and need to be designed with care.

On a more generic level, it is important for shippers to treat outsourcing as a collaborative enterprise and to avoid negotiating too aggressively, particularly on price and penalties. What might appear to be short-term advantages in negotiation can easily translate into long-term disadvantages during performance. Shippers will benefit by keeping their logistics manager or logistics consultant closely involved throughout the contract negotiation, and not just during the tender process.

One of the most difficult balancing acts which shippers face generically is in tapping into LSPs' specialist knowledge while still trying to keep control of the process and costs. Regardless of all the theories about incentivizing LSPs in order to benefit from their specialist knowledge, in practice many shippers outsourcing for the first time may really just want exactly the same service as before, but for a lower price and with no disruption in the transition of the service from shipper to LSP.

A first-time shipper needs to be honest with itself as to whether it really does want innovation from its LSP or whether it simply wants an identical service provided more cheaply. If it's the latter, then the shipper is best off negotiating a restrictive contract in which the LSP is forced to operate within strict parameters to ensure that the service provided by the LSP is as close as possible to that to which the shipper is accustomed.

Further down the line, as the relationship develops and both sides understand and trust each other more, it becomes easier for the shipper to accept the possibility of change, which is the point at which the LSP can genuinely start to provide added value through its specialist knowledge, though in practice doing so inside a restrictive contract will be difficult.

One of the biggest and most common mistakes that shippers make, when it comes to contract renewal, is to take a restrictive contract used previously for the initial appointment and simply recycle it for the renewal. If the decision is made to renew an existing contract rather than to appoint a new LSP, it is important for the shipper to reassess its objectives and incentives in the light of their current business priorities. If the relationship has now evolved to one where the shipper wants to benefit from the LSP's specialist knowledge, then both parties will benefit from a new contract that contains the type of price incentive mechanisms detailed below. However, such mechanisms require effort on both sides to develop and administer, and should be used in a targeted manner on specific contracts.

CASE STUDY   Aligning objectives: example reward mechanism

The following example shows how KPIs can be used as a positive motivational tool to incentivize an LSP to provide a service which is completely tailored to the needs of the individual user. In this case study, the shipper is a manufacturer of fragile, expensive crockery.

The suggested KPIs are for illustrative purposes only and are not fully SMART as they do not have a timescale against them.

In this scenario, the outsourcing contract is an open-book arrangement where the LSP's costs are reimbursed and it is paid a management fee, but whereby the outsourcing contract provides that the LSP can receive a performance-related bonus of up to £100,000. The KPIs selected by the crockery manufacturer are as follows:

- minimal damage to goods;
- minimal stock loss;
- orders despatched on time;
- pick accuracy;
- cost reduction (from previous year).

The next step is for the user to ascribe a different weighting to each of those KPIs, depending on the relative importance of each KPI to the user. The aggregate of all the weightings should come to 100.

Weightings ascribed to each KPI

KPI	Weighting
Minimal damage to goods	25
Minimal stock loss	25
Orders dispatched on time	10
Pick accuracy	25
Cost reduction (year-on-year)	15
Total	**100**

In the final step of the creation of the contract, alongside each KPI and its weighting is added a sliding scale of KPI targets, from 100 per cent for top performance against that KPI to 0 per cent for achieving the basic required service against that KPI. This produces the following matrix.

KPI targets

KPI	Weight	100%	75%	50%	25%	0%
Minimal damage to goods	25	<0.1%	0.1%– 0.15%	0.15%– 0.2%	0.2%– 0.25%	>0.25%
Minimal stock loss	25	<0.05%	0.05%– 0.075%	0.075%– 0.1%	0.1%– 0.15%	>0.15%
Orders dispatched on time	10	>99%	98.5%– 99%	98%– 98.5%	97.5%– 98%	<97.5%
Pick accuracy	25	>99.5%	99%– 99.5%	98.5%– 99%	98%– 98.5%	<98%
Cost reduction	15	>10%	8%–10%	6%–8%	4%–6%	0–4%
Total	**100**					

Once the contract is being performed, the actual performance of each KPI is measured.

For the purposes of this case study, let's assume that the following results have been achieved:

- minimal damage to goods: 0.26 per cent;
- minimal stock loss: 0.07 per cent;
- orders despatched on time: 99.1 per cent;
- pick accuracy: 98.2 per cent;
- cost reduction: 7.9 per cent.

At this stage, the actual results (which appear below in bold) are applied to the matrix, as shown.

Example performance against targets

KPI	Weight	100%	75%	50%	25%	0%	Result
Minimal damage to goods	25	<0.1%	0.1%–0.15%	0.15%–0.2%	0.2%–0.25%	>0.25%	0
Minimal stock loss	25	<0.05%	0.05%–0.075%	0.075%–0.1%	0.1%–0.15%	>0.15%	18.75
Orders despatched on time	10	>99%	98.5%–99%	98%–98.5%	97.5%–98%	<97.5%	10
Pick accuracy	25	>99.5%	99%–99.5%	98.5%–99%	98%–98.5%	<98%	6.25
Cost reduction	15	>10%	8%–10%	6%–8%	4%–6%	0–4%	7.5
Total	**100**						**42.5**

Note: The shaded cells are the figures being used to calculate the final figure of 42.5.

The percentage for the column in which each KPI achieved lies is then applied against its weighting. Taking 'Stock loss' as an example, the actual result of 0.07 per cent lies in the 0.05–0.075 per cent range, which is in the 75 per cent column of the 'Stock loss' row. 75 per cent is therefore applied to the 'Stock loss' weighting of 25, to produce the figure of 18.75 (75 per cent of 25).

Applying the actual results to each of the other KPIs in the matrix therefore gives the totals in the Result column.

As the maximum possible score is 100 (the aggregate of the various weightings), the provider in this case has therefore achieved a score of 42.5 out of 100; that is, 42.5 per cent. Applying this figure against the maximum possible performance-related bonus of £100,000, the provider therefore receives an actual performance-related bonus of £42,500.

A matrix of this nature is complex, but provides enormous flexibility. The shipper can choose its own basket of KPIs, with an appropriate weighting for each and, subject to negotiation with the provider, choose which values to give to each result.

A well-drafted contract can even give the user the flexibility to change the KPIs and/or their weighting from year to year throughout the duration of the contract. Certainly, it is a vastly superior tool for motivating and incentivizing an LSP to provide a service directly tailored to the needs of the shipper than the negative and blunt instrument of penalties for failure to achieve targets.

The ultimate alignment methodology is Vested® Outsourcing, which is described in Chapter 9.

Conclusion

This chapter has discussed the different forms of logistics contracts, from national or international frameworks to bespoke agreements. It has reviewed the most important elements in them such as limitation of liability, obligations on the shipper, rights, remedies, duration and reward.

The importance of a contract for setting out the expectations of the shipper, including the levels of service, should not be underestimated. A good contract aligns the objectives of the shipper and LSP, and in bespoke contracts, gainshare and broader reward mechanisms can take this further. However, these forms of complex agreement should be for established and strategic partnerships where the opportunities justify the investment in time.

In contractual negotiations it can be tempting for both sides to see the process as a zero-sum game that needs to be won. This is not the way to enter a long-term, mutually beneficial relationship. Instead, both parties should focus on their broader objectives and ensure that the contract supports these objectives.

Performance measurement and management

07

Introduction

This chapter will examine the importance of performance measurement and management in logistics outsourcing relationships. It will discuss potential gaps between the shippers' expectations and the logistics service providers' (LSPs') actual and perceived service, and go on to suggest which types of key performance indicators (KPIs) need to be measured, monitored and reviewed on a regular basis.

Performance models such as Balanced Scorecard will be examined, as will specific benchmarking tools. Results from the recent Warehousing Education and Research Council (WERC) DC Measures survey (WERC, 2019) are also included, which outline the 12 most popular warehouse/distribution centre (DC) metrics. The report goes on to provide best-in-class performances across a number of warehouse-related KPIs.

The chapter will also provide examples of freight transport and supply chain KPIs that can be used in service level agreements.

Finally, the chapter includes a case study from Mondelēz which provides an insight into the KPIs used by companies to measure DC performance, how Mondelēz have engendered a win–win situation and how they benchmark their own operations with that of their LSPs.

Why is performance measurement and management important?

Performance measurement is the process of quantifying the efficiency and effectiveness of an action or service. In other words, it helps an organization assess the performance of its own processes and/or its suppliers. Performance measurement needs to evolve into performance management, in which the data is collected, measured and acted upon.

All contractual relationships should have some form of performance measurement. If it is a basic contract for the movement of a single container from China to the UK on an ad-hoc basis, for example, then basic contract management and an on-time delivery target will suffice. If on the other hand it involves the management of a dedicated warehouse operation, then there is a requirement for a comprehensive supplier relationship management programme. These concepts will be discussed in Chapter 9.

Too many times we see companies with measures in place, but no action taken if the performance level is below that which is expected. There is no point in having a service level agreement (SLA) if the levels agreed are not measured, monitored and acted upon.

In order to ensure that logistics services are maintained and improved, companies need to continually measure the performance of its suppliers. This is done through the use of KPIs. A KPI is a metric which is focused on a key element of business, departmental, or team performance.

Companies measure performance because they need to:

- ensure customer satisfaction through the agreed service delivery and, if possible, improvement;
- ensure that there is a culture of continuous improvement within the operation;
- discover potential issues before they become major problems;
- train staff in the right areas;
- reward staff and suppliers where appropriate.

Measuring and acting upon the performance of an LSP can lead to the following positive or negative results:

- service improvement;
- contract renewal;

- contract cancellation;

- bonus payments;

- penalties.

Unless logistics companies measure their performance against customer expectations and continually improve on that performance, they are not only in danger of losing customers, but may also incur additional costs or lose out on potential bonuses (see the Mondelēz case study later in this chapter).

CASE STUDY   Nedlloyd Districenters

Nedlloyd Districenters had a contract with a leading housewares producer. During the first week in his position as customer services manager, the author was confronted by the customer with a list of issues relating to incorrect and late deliveries. Up to that point no record had been kept of the failed deliveries by the LSP. There had been very few review meetings up to that point.

The customer services manager, alongside agreeing to investigate the issues, instigated a system of performance measurement and recording in line with the original SLA, in readiness for the next meeting. The customer again complained of poor service, and pointed out a number of issues, similar to those from the previous review meeting.

This time the customer services manager had all the facts, and was able to knowledgeably discuss where the problems lay. It turned out that many of the issues were not the fault of the LSP, but that of the customer and the customer's customers. In fact, the LSP was performing ahead of the targets set in the SLA.

Customers tend to concentrate on the negatives without taking into account the positive aspects of contract performance. A responsible LSP will use customer feedback to determine both the actual performance and root causes of any failures.

This example highlights the need for both parties to both record and investigate issues before entering into a confrontational situation. The relationship improved significantly after this experience.

If companies don't measure the performance of their LSPs accurately, they will not be able to introduce sanctions if the service is below par or reward the company if above par.

In order to ensure that logistics service providers deliver the service their customers demand, they need to comprehensively understand both their customers' requirements and the limitations they have within their own operation.

'Performance' is a broad term that covers both overall economic and operational aspects. Slack, Chambers and Johnston (2001) offer the following description of high-performance operations that most companies strive to accomplish:

- High-quality operations don't waste time or effort having to re-do things, nor are their customers inconvenienced by flawed service.
- Fast operations ensure a quick turnaround of orders.
- Dependable operations can be relied on to deliver exactly as planned. This eliminates wasteful disruption and allows the other micro-operations to operate efficiently.
- Flexible operations adapt to changing circumstances quickly and without disrupting the rest of the operation.
- Low-cost operations lead to higher profits, as well as allowing the company to sell their services at a competitive price.

One of the main things to understand is that in terms of performance measures, an LSP needs to:

- monitor performance against the criteria that are important to their customers (for example, delivery of the Perfect Order);
- monitor performance against the criteria that are important to the LSP as supplier (for example, managing costs).

As can be seen in Figure 7.1, different parties within the relationship have different ideas as to what is important in terms of performance measurement. The figure depicts which KPIs are important to a retailer and which are important to the LSP. Note that the LSP KPIs are very operationally focused.

The retailer in this example is not only concentrating on total cost, but also on the individual cost centres, including freight, warehouse, store, sales channel and inventory. The LSP, although measuring cost, is concentrating on the operational aspects within the warehouse and how they affect its management fee.

A 'Vested®' approach as discussed in Chapter 9 tends to concentrate on the bigger picture and driving shared value, and therefore many of the LSP's measures will become performance indicators (PIs) as opposed to KPIs.

Figure 7.1 Conflicting KPIs

Retail customer	Service provider
• Cost as percentage of sales	• Logistics costs – absolute
• Fixed cost/variable cost split and year-on-year change	• Cost per line, per item, per order
• Year-on-year cost increase vs year-on-year sales increase	• Units/cases per operator hour
• Inventory value change vs sales value change year-on-year	• Management fee/incentive – gained or lost
• Freight costs as a percentage of cost of goods sold	• Percentage pick accuracy
• Cost as a percentage of sales – new stores vs LFL (like-for-like) stores	• Service level – delivery to schedule
• Waste costs – products, late delivery	• Direct/indirect hours
• Segmented cost to serve, eg product, store format, channel	• Cost per pallet stored – core/seasonal flex
• On-shelf availability/lost sales opportunity	• Lost time/cost
• Environmental impact	• Additional revenue generated
Consumer-/Investor-centric ⟵⟶	Operation-centric

The following model by Parasuraman, Zeithaml and Berry (1985) outlines the gaps that can appear in terms of shipper expectations and the LSP's perceived level of service.

As shown in Figure 7.2, there are five distinct gaps in terms of service provision and perception.

- Gap 1 occurs when the LSP has a different view to that of the shipper in terms of the expected quality of service. This is usually where the LSP has underestimated the level of service that will satisfy the marketplace expectations.

- Gap 2 occurs when the management team draws up a different set of targets from those initially discussed with the client.

- Gap 3 is where the actual service provided differs significantly from the service levels included in the SLA. This can be either underachievement or overachievement against goals and targets. It is this area which tends to get the most focus, but may not be the biggest gap.

- Gap 4 is where the LSP portrays and markets itself as being better than it actually is in terms of service.

- Gap 5 is where the shipper has an issue where the expected service is very different to what is perceived to be happening. The Nedlloyd Districenters example mentioned earlier is a typical example of this.

Figure 7.2   The service quality gap model (SERVQUAL)

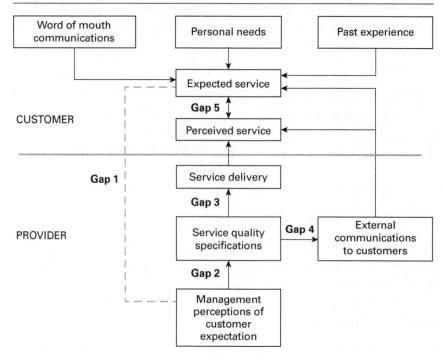

SOURCE Parasuraman, Zeithaml and Berry (1985)

Frost and Kumar (2000) have developed an internal service quality model. The model (Figure 7.3) evaluates the dimensions and their relationships which determine service quality gaps among internal customers (front-line staff) and internal suppliers (support staff) within a service organization.

The gaps are as follows:

- Internal gap 1: a difference in support staff's perception of front-line staff's expectations.

- Internal gap 2: a difference between service quality specifications and the service actually delivered, resulting in an internal service performance gap.

- Internal gap 3: a difference between front-line staff's expectations and perceptions of support staff's service quality. This is the gap which focuses on the front-line staff.

Figure 7.3   Model of internal service quality gaps

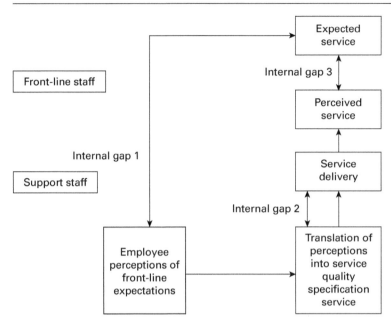

SOURCE Frost and Kumar, 2000

These service gaps can be seen in LSPs with business development teams either overpromising to shippers, or overestimating the capabilities of their own organization.

When combining the two models, we see a number of potential areas for both misunderstanding and potential future conflict.

Therefore, when meeting with the LSP during the Invitation to Tender (ITT) process it is recommended that the procurement and logistics team should meet with the operational staff within the LSP to ensure that their requirements can be met, and that the LSP has experience of providing these services.

How to choose the right performance measures

Each company will have different priorities, a different customer base and a different method of operation. In order to choose the most appropriate measure, companies need to undertake the following process:

- understand the business and its strategy;
- decide on objectives;
- understand which KPIs are likely to assist in meeting the objectives and drive the business forward;
- ensure the KPIs are aligned with other KPIs within the company;
- nominate KPI owners;
- ensure that everyone works towards and buys into achieving the targets;
- if targets aren't achieved, analyse the reasons why and either introduce processes to enable achievement or revise the KPI;
- if the target KPI isn't relevant, replace it;
- if the KPI is too easily attainable, increase the target.

According to Sanchís-Pedregosa *et al* (2011):

> 'Determining the objectives that are to be achieved by outsourcing logistics services is a fundamental building-block for measuring achieved performance. Cost reduction, customer satisfaction and delivery on-time-in-full are seen as the main requirements of a logistics outsourcing operation'.

These measures can be broken down further as follows:

- to make timely deliveries;
- to operate at low cost;
- to meet customer special requests;
- to offer shorter delivery lead times;
- to be flexible and responsive;
- to support other departments' logistical needs;
- to maximize the value added to products/services.

Sanchís-Pedregosa *et al*'s (2011) study of numerous articles on logistics out-sourcing found that there are a number of financially-related measures and non-financially-related measures used in measuring LSP performance. These measures are as follows:

Non-financial:

- value creation;
- innovative ideas;
- perceived quality;

- valuation of mistakes and damage;
- information availability;
- employee morale;
- flexibility;
- reduced delivery times;
- improved service;
- inventory control;
- productivity.

Financial:

- cash flow;
- sales revenue;
- improved capital performance;
- cost savings;
- capital goods reduction.

The most cited performance measure in their research was cost savings.

The first task, therefore, in any performance measurement system is to understand the vision of the company and which services/operations can assist in achieving the company's goals.

Too often companies will produce key performance measures which they are comfortable with and which are easily achievable, but are not aligned to the company's vision and are rarely of interest to senior managers. Departments end up with too many measures which detract from the day-to-day running of the operation.

The measures you choose need to be SMART. That is, they need to be:

- Specific. Objectives should specify what they want to achieve. Are they clear and unambiguous?
- Measurable. Can we put a value on the KPI? For example: how much, how long, how many.
- Achievable. Are the targets you set achievable and attainable?
- Relevant. Are the measures relevant to the overall goal and strategy of the company?
- Timely. Are the timescales realistic, and how often do you measure?

You need to ensure that the data collected is accurate.

Moseley (2004) suggests that when introducing KPIs, you should:

- use terminology that both companies and the staff understand and is meaningful to them;
- understand what your staff need to do to improve service or reduce costs as identified by the KPIs;
- try to use common industry KPIs so that you can benchmark your own operation against your peers, or an in-house operation (as shown in the Mondelēz case study later in this chapter);
- review the data regularly and look for specific trends;
- not overreact to any particular data point;
- only introduce measures you know you can implement, measure and improve;
- only introduce cost-effective metrics; that is ensure that it doesn't cost you more to manage a metric than the likely savings you will make;
- be seen to be using the data; there is nothing more frustrating than collecting data which isn't used.

Adding to the above, a good metric helps to change behaviour in an organization. Ask what will change because of this measurement? If nothing, then measure something else!

As shown in Figure 7.4, there are many levels of management and each has its own area of responsibility.

Covey (1989) introduces the concept of 'stewardship delegation', which is focused on results rather than methods. It suggests that leaders should be given responsibility to lead at their own level and be accountable. If each area is correctly managed, there is no need for senior management to intervene on the detail. A KPI at team leader level, such as cases picked per hour, is completely unsuitable as an executive-level KPI.

This can also be related to the relationship between shipper and LSP. Outsourcing is, at its most effective level, stewardship delegation, and relies on your trust in the fact that your service provider can provide the service effectively.

One potential model to follow when putting KPIs together is the Balanced Scorecard by Kaplan and Norton (1996). Kaplan and Norton believe that you cannot judge the performance of a company solely through financial measures, and suggest three other areas which also require a company's attention.

Figure 7.4 Warehouse management levels

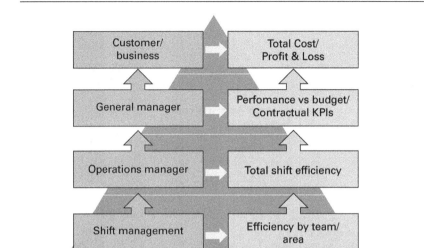

The model is therefore made up of four perspectives; namely financial, customer satisfaction, internal processes and learning and development. The former two perspectives are relevant to the here and now (customers and shareholders), and the latter are relevant to the future (people and processes), thus forming a balanced approach.

Many writers have looked to enhance the model by including other aspects within the business which require the attention of staff at all levels throughout the organization.

The following figure shows an adaptation of the Balanced Scorecard model produced by Performetrix, a software producer. Environmental issues have been added to the people quadrant.

The Balanced Scorecard has evolved from its early use as a simple performance measurement framework to a full strategic planning and management system.

The premise is to begin with a vision, determine a strategy or strategies to achieve this vision, and then break these down into activities which have their own measurements. The ideal scenario sees departments within the company all working towards the same vision with relevant and related KPIs.

Figure 7.5   Adaptation of the Balanced Scorecard

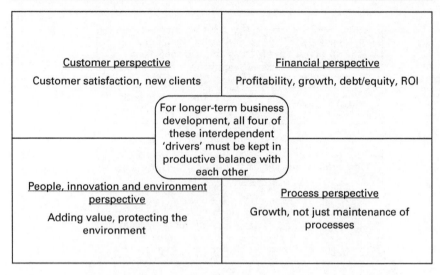

SOURCE reproduced by kind permission of Performetrix

As discussed, you need to set out the company's vision and the strategies to achieve this. A SWOT analysis – detailing strengths, weaknesses, opportunities and threats – is a good tool in this respect. Strengths and weaknesses tend to be internally-focused while opportunities and threats are externally-focused.

The perspectives mentioned above need to be clear and understandable to all, both within and outside the business.

The top-level scorecard needs to be translated into more detailed plans and tasks, and each department given measures and goals which will play a part in achieving the overall vision of the company.

The following steps need to be taken.

- As with the majority of new initiatives, you need to gain board commitment.

- Find a suitable project owner.

- Confirm, review or revise your company vision.

- Define your four business perspectives and ensure clarity and understanding.

- Formulate the overall strategic aims.

- Identify the critical success factors and create your initial KPIs with unambiguous definitions. Ensure they are SMART.

- Create the metrics for your KPIs. Each measure has objectives and targets which are measured against actual performance.

- Analyse the measures and ensure they provide 'balance'.

- Establish a comprehensive top-level scorecard and filter through the organization.

- Translate the vision into a strategy and the strategy into day-to-day tasks.

- Produce both long-term and short-term goals.

- Develop an action plan to achieve these goals.

- Continuously review and be prepared to change.

Note that this exercise can take up to two months to complete.

Figure 7.6 is an example of how a warehouse operation can assist in the success of the company's vision by providing performance which leads to the achievement of business goals.

The use of a Balanced Scorecard in this example should result in:

- improved staff safety;

- improved processes;

- motivated/educated employees;

- enhanced information systems;

- greater customer satisfaction;

- improved environmental credentials;

- increased profit.

Benchmarking

This section will look at benchmarking and how it can assist companies in their operation.

Benchmarking has been around since the early 19th century; however, it came to the fore in the 1980s when it was championed by Xerox Corporation.

It is a process of comparing performance with operations of other companies, or operations within the same company, identifying high-performance or best-in-class operations and learning what it is they do that allows them to achieve that high level of performance.

Figure 7.6 Example Balanced Scorecard with KPIs

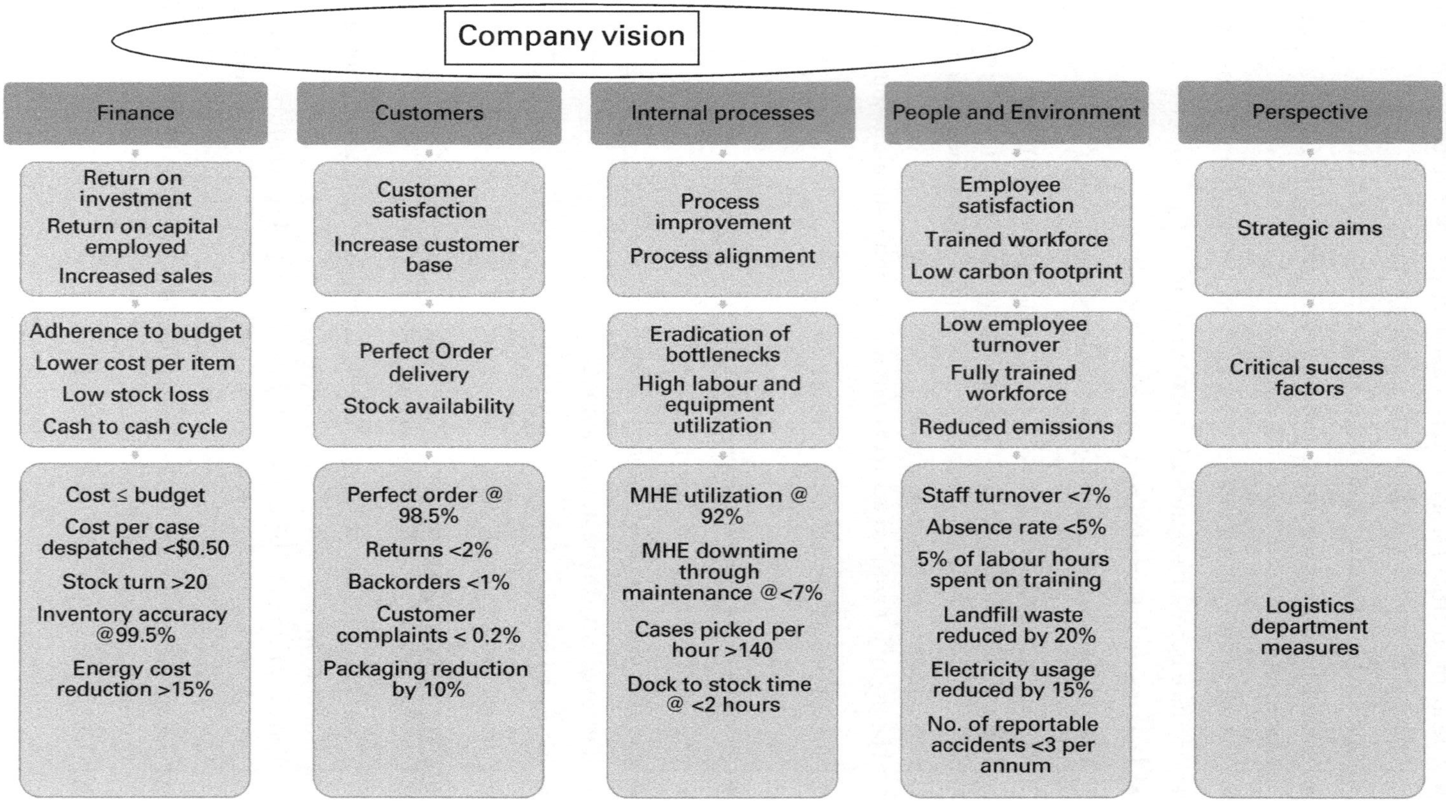

Company vision				
Finance	**Customers**	**Internal processes**	**People and Environment**	**Perspective**
Return on investment Return on capital employed Increased sales	Customer satisfaction Increase customer base	Process improvement Process alignment	Employee satisfaction Trained workforce Low carbon footprint	Strategic aims
Adherence to budget Lower cost per item Low stock loss Cash to cash cycle	Perfect Order delivery Stock availability	Eradication of bottlenecks High labour and equipment utilization	Low employee turnover Fully trained workforce Reduced emissions	Critical success factors
Cost ≤ budget Cost per case despatched <$0.50 Stock turn >20 Inventory accuracy @99.5% Energy cost reduction >15%	Perfect order @ 98.5% Returns <2% Backorders <1% Customer complaints < 0.2% Packaging reduction by 10%	MHE utilization @ 92% MHE downtime through maintenance @ <7% Cases picked per hour >140 Dock to stock time @ <2 hours	Staff turnover <7% Absence rate <5% 5% of labour hours spent on training Landfill waste reduced by 20% Electricity usage reduced by 15% No. of reportable accidents <3 per annum	Logistics department measures

Why should we benchmark?

Benchmarking enables us to:

- understand performance;
- identify any shortcomings;
- introduce training programmes;
- discover what others are doing better;
- identify performance targets that can be demonstrated to be achievable;
- accelerate and manage change;
- improve processes;
- understand best practice.

A word of caution. Benchmarking may point to best current practice, but not to best possible practice. 'As good as' is not 'better than'. It is not a substitute for creativity and innovation.

Benchmarking can be undertaken both internally and externally. There are a number of supply chain and logistics related benchmarking clubs, including the Chartered Institute of Logistics and Transport's Logmark, the Establish Davis Logistics Cost and Service Database, Benchmarking Success, and the United States' WERC.

In terms of external benchmarking, companies need to choose their partners carefully.

As in performance measurement, there are pitfalls to avoid. Benchmarking should not be considered until companies have an intimate knowledge of their own processes and results. Secondly, companies should not select processes to benchmark which don't have sufficient potential for improvement.

The principles of benchmarking are as follows:

- collaboration;
- confidentiality;
- value;
- flexibility;
- honesty;
- openness;
- reputation.

There is always likely to be a reluctance to share information with competitors. However, in order to produce meaningful results, honesty and openness are paramount.

One potential method of ensuring confidentiality and anonymity is to utilize a third party such as a benchmarking group, a consultancy or a university.

Companies who outsource part of their logistics operations and retain the remainder in-house are able to compare their own in-house operation with that of their third-party suppliers. However, the operations do need to be very similar to provide meaningful results.

An example is Sainsbury's in the UK who operate more than 20 DCs for their retail operations – some are operated internally, whilst others have been outsourced to LSPs. This provides an ideal scenario for benchmarking.

The example in the case study at the end of this chapter is from Mondelēz, who benchmark each of their distribution centres Europe-wide. All the centres work towards the same targets to enable a comparison across sites and ensure that best practice is achieved.

An interesting comment from the recent DC Measures survey (WERC, 2019) report is that 'performance management thrives on consistency'. However, each year sees a change in the top 12 metrics, and also in performance levels.

For companies striving for continuous improvement, and for LSPs looking to retain their clients, maintaining or improving performance is vital.

Monitoring supplier performance

According to the Chartered Institute of Procurement and Supply (CIPS), it is basic good practice to know that you are getting what you pay for. In terms of logistics, on-time-in-full (OTIF) delivery is an expectation from shippers and this needs to be monitored regularly.

The number of shipments undertaken by courier companies can be a significant number, and weekly invoices can total thousands of pounds for an e-commerce retailer. A 2 per cent failure rate on a thousand shipments per week can cost the company over £5,000 per annum.

There needs to be a process in place to ensure that all deliveries have been carried out within the contract terms, otherwise the shipper will be paying for a service which hasn't happened.

In the above example, if both parties agree joint goals (and jointly measure performance against these goals), the supplier can monitor its own performance provided a suitable process of validation is in place. Late or non-deliveries can be highlighted within the system and can provide a basis for discussion.

Companies can become complacent and allow slipping standards to go unnoticed. Problems need to be addressed when they are still minor issues and therefore easier to resolve. This why there is a need for measurement and monitoring of performance against the SLA included in the contract.

CIPS believes that it is important to hold regular review meetings where both parties seek to understand how they can make the contract perform better. Both parties need to learn from each other's feedback in order to improve their individual performance.

There are three aspects to the monitoring of supplier performance, post-contract:

1 compiling factual and therefore objective data on performance;

2 ascertaining customer experiences through interviews or surveys;

3 ensuring the supplier has the opportunity to discuss potential obstacles to the service such as increasingly late order cut-off times, customer hours of operation and poor delivery data, for example.

Figure 7.7 Assessment of supplier performance

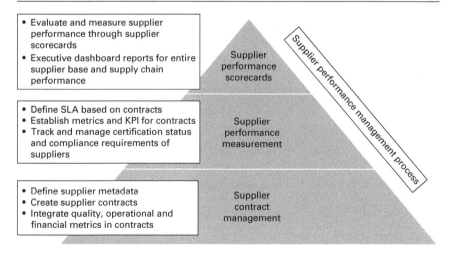

SOURCE MetricStream, n. d.

In the event that a supplier consistently fails to meet the shipper's requirements (and does not respond to feedback or suggestions), then the remedies set out in the contract must be brought into play.

In terms of who carries out the monitoring, this can be undertaken either by the procurement department or by the logistics department. Either way, they need sufficient authority and training in order to carry out their role effectively. This includes training in relationship management.

If financial penalties or rewards are part of the contract, CIPS suggests that the procurement and supplier management department are involved as they understand the commercial nuances, whilst the operational teams can discuss performance levels.

Not only should performance be monitored, but also the LSP's company growth, market share and financial standing. There have been a number of examples recently where LSPs have gone into administration, leaving their clients high and dry.

The level and frequency of performance monitoring is dependent on the value and criticality of the contract to the shipper.

Understanding SLAs

An SLA is normally included alongside a contract for the supply of services. In certain situations where the service is not significant, an SLA might be sufficient to provide the basis of the agreement provided it is coupled with the relevant Association terms and conditions. These can include RHA, UKWA and BIFA terms and conditions.

In such a fast-moving and changing market sector, an SLA formalizes the service 'sold' to the shipper and provides a level of comfort that service requirements are being met and guidelines followed.

The SLA needs to define which services are to be delivered, by whom and by when, and the levels of performance expected.

For an SLA to work, both parties must agree and commit to a set of common goals. The document might include, but not be limited to the following areas which may be further split into service and management elements:

- a description of the service being provided;
- the standards of the service expected;
- a timetable for delivery of the service(s);
- performance tracking and reporting;

- the responsibilities of both the supplier and the customer;
- a provision for legal and regulatory compliance;
- mechanisms for monitoring and reporting of the service;
- payment terms for the service supplier;
- how disputes will be resolved;
- issues of security – people, data, facilities, and so on;
- intellectual property rights;
- provisions for confidentiality and non-disclosure;
- conditions for termination;
- the supplier's price list or summary of expected charges;
- any dependencies that exist in delivering the service;
- a method for customization or variation of the services;
- cost and service trade-offs;
- protections and remedies to be implemented upon repeated failures.

The drafting of an SLA

The SLA should be drafted and ideally agreed between both parties prior to contract sign-off. This puts pressure on the customer to have a clear upfront definition of the operations being outsourced and existing delivery service levels.

Both these areas can be defined prior to starting the external phase of outsourcing insofar as talking with potential suppliers. In this way, the in-coming supplier has a clear indication from the customer of the operation being outsourced and the service level required.

This approach should lead to a more productive and longer-term alliance between both parties, as SLAs drive positive behaviours.

SLA issues

Many SLAs are industry-standard templates that have been drafted into a contract with less thought than was appropriate at the time. This begs the question as to which of the contracting parties produces the SLA. Experience suggests that the LSP produces a draft SLA, but works closely with the ship-per to populate the data and agree the main criteria. The LSP is more likely to have compiled numerous logistics-related SLAs in the past.

SLAs by their nature also emphasize the 'hard' and measurable aspects of performance rather than the softer aspects which might be more important such as the quality of people deployed to run the operation, language skills, approach to health and safety, and so on.

Steps to producing an acceptable SLA

In order to produce a workable and acceptable SLA, the parties need to:

- understand fully the shipper's requirements;
- understand exactly which services are being outsourced – both the hard and softer aspects;
- rank in level of importance the different elements of the services required;
- understand the current total cost of the operation – fixed, semi-variable and variable elements;
- understand the current service levels;
- produce a base level in terms of cost and service;
- produce a first-draft SLA (note this could well change once the contract has operated for a few months);
- ensure that rewards and penalties are agreed and fully understood;
- agree a 'honeymoon period' where the targets are not strictly imposed (more on this later in the chapter);
- ensure that penalties reflect the magnitude of the long-term business impact of a shortfall in service.

A progressive SLA can lead to an enhanced and long relationship between supplier and LSP. Sufficient time needs to be spent therefore on ensuring that the SLA is fit for purpose and acceptable to both parties.

The shipper needs to be prepared to adjust the SLA if operational experience shows the targets and requirements to be unrealistic – this is particularly true of new outsourcing contracts or the provision of specialist services.

Warehouse performance measures within an SLA

Having agreed to move forward with a particular LSP, there is now a requirement to produce the data and targets to be included within the SLA. This agreement will lay out the requirements and expectations of the LSP.

As discussed previously, the types of measures will very much depend on what is important to the client and its ultimate customers.

It is also important to ensure that you do not have too many measures in place which can take up valuable time with little reward. Note the word 'key' here. We only need a few KPIs; however, it may be prudent to have a number of supporting PIs.

Warehouse KPIs

Table 7.1 shows the top 12 metrics that companies use in their warehouse and DC operations, according to an annual survey carried out by WERC in the USA (WERC, 2019). As we can see, there is a mix of operational, employee and service metrics. The figures show the past four years' results.

The above metrics show 50 per cent of the metrics are specifically customer focused, whilst the other 50 per cent concentrate internally on capacity and employees and externally on supplier performance.

Capacity improvements and employee metrics are all operational and signify a concentration on cost reduction. As one of the most significant performance measures, cost reduction is important, but so is customer satisfaction. This is where there can be an issue in terms of expectation.

The choice of KPI will very much depend on who owns and operates the warehouse and whether it is a dedicated or shared-user facility. An LSP operating a shared-user warehouse is much more likely to concentrate on warehouse capacity.

The KPIs in Table 7.2 can be considered when entering an outsourced warehousing contract. The median and best-in-class figures are taken from the WERC 2019 report. Note that the respondents to the report come from a diverse group of companies in terms of size, longevity and capability. There is also a mix of own-account operators (shippers) and logistics service providers.

In addition to the above, the authors also suggest including lost time accident (LTA) ratios and inventory shrinkage. These measurements do not currently feature in the WERC top 36 metrics.

The best-in-class results relate to the top performing 20 per cent of respondents. Readers need to be careful not to take these figures and assume they are all achievable or required in their own industries. Some sectors will have higher failure rates, and companies will be at different stages in their development.

Table 7.1　WERC DC Measures report 2019 top 12 metrics

Metrics in order of popularity	2019	2018	2017	2016
Order picking accuracy (per cent by order) – customer	1	2	2	3
Average warehouse capacity used – capacity	2	1	1	2
Peak warehouse capacity used – capacity	3	3	4	7
On-time shipments – customer	4	5	3	1
Inventory count accuracy by location – customer	5	10	10	19
Percentage of supplier orders received damage free – supplier	6	11	11	6
Order fill rate – customer	7	14	12	10
Percentage of supplier orders received with correct documents – supplier	8	13	-	-
Dock to stock cycle time in hours – customer	9	16	-	4
On-time ready to ship – customer	10	12	8	12
Part-time workforce to total workforce – employee	11	7	5	46
Cross-trained percentage – employee	12	8	12	49

SOURCE WERC, 2019

According to Leonard (2019), Walmart in the US has tightened its OTIF policies to require suppliers to deliver full truckloads within a two-day window, 87 per cent of the time. This is up from a previous requirement of 85 per cent. Suppliers will be fined 3 per cent of the cost of goods sold if they fail to meet the requirements.

Table 7.3 shows that the Perfect Order index is made up of four specific measures which includes OTIF. In order to calculate the Perfect Order percentage, you need to multiply all four figures together. If we take the median figures from the WERC study, we note that the Perfect Order index is 93.3 per cent.

Companies will decide which are the most relevant KPIs for them, based on their ultimate customer requirements and their internal expectations.

Table 7.2   Suggested warehouse KPIs

KPI	Median	Best in class
Perfect Order index	93.3%	98.6%
Logistics cost as a % of cost of sales	4.8%	<1.76%
Total order cycle time	18 hours	<3.2 hours
Dock to stock time	7.5 hours	<2 hours
Inventory accuracy	98.4%	99.9%
Staff turnover	14%	<3%

Table 7.3   The Perfect Order index

KPI	Median	Best in class
Delivery on time	97%	>99.3%
Delivery in full	98.1%	99.7%
Delivery damage-free	99%	99.7%
Paperwork accuracy	99%	99.9%

A table to be included in an SLA could look like Table 7.4.

Note that each KPI is described in full so that there is no ambiguity when it comes to understanding its full meaning.

In Table 7.4, 'critical' is a situation whereby unless improvement is introduced quickly the business will fail. A 'failing' score denotes a requirement for immediate action to be taken to prevent the operation reaching a critical stage where loss of business is inevitable. 'Standard' is the level of performance which must be achieved for the warehouse, team or individual to be seen as being satisfactory – that is, the minimum level of acceptable performance.

Finally, 'target' is a level of performance above the standard performance level as set out in the SLA. A target-level performance is desirable to achieve in order for the LSP to impress the shipper and stretch the warehouse, team or individual. It is likely to be best-in-class in the industry.

Performance results need to be communicated both internally and externally. This can be achieved through regular operational meetings – weekly, monthly and or quarterly. Results can be posted on noticeboards for all staff to see.

Table 7.4 Performance indicators for customer service

KPI	Precise definition	Critical	Failing	Standard	Above standard	Target	How verified
On-time delivery	The number of orders delivered on or before the agreed-upon time, against the total number of orders received, expressed as a percentage.	<90	<95	97.5	98.5	99.5	System check/manual records
Orders in full first time	The number of orders which shipped completely, as per the initial order, against the total number of orders received, expressed as a percentage.	<90	<95.5	98	99	99.5	System check/manual records
Correct documentation	The number of orders for which the customers received an accurate invoice and other required documents, against the total number of orders despatched, expressed as a percentage.	<96	<98	99.3	99.7	100	System check/manual records
Damage claims	The number of customer orders received in good and usable condition, expressed as a percentage of total orders dispatched.	97.5	98.5	99.5	99.8	99.9	System check/manual records
Perfect Order	The result of multiplying the above four metrics together.	75.8	87.6	94.4	97	98.9	System check/manual records
Total order cycle time	The time taken in hours from placement of order to receipt of order by the customer.	>72	48–72	40	33	30	System check/manual records
Customer complaints	The time taken in hours to fully answer a customer query or complaint.	48	24	6	4	2	System check/manual records
Back orders	Back orders as a percentage. of total orders received.	>8	>4.5	2	0.6	0.2	System check/manual records

SOURCE reproduced by kind permission of Performetrix

Measuring freight transportation

A number of transport performance indicators are deemed to be important when managing a fleet of vehicles. Table 7.5 shows the KPIs which matter to the LSP, whilst Table 7.6 shows those which are relevant to the customer.

Unfortunately, there are no examples of actual freight transport related KPI scores, as with the WERC DC Measures (WERC, 2019).

As can be seen in these two tables, there is an overlap between the KPIs measured by LSPs and those of importance to the shipper. However, as mentioned in Figure 7.1, the LSP's metrics tend to be more operationally-focused.

Table 7.5 Example freight transport KPIs of importance to the LSP

Key performance indicator	Description
Kilometres per litre of fuel	Fuel consumption per vehicle.
Vehicle fill	The amount of full/part/empty running recorded.
Labour productivity	Productive vs unproductive hours per driver.
Maintenance costs	The total cost of maintaining the fleet of vehicles.
Profitability	The profit percentage per customer.
CO_2 produced per km	The average CO_2 produced (kg) per mile/km travelled by your fleet.
Loading/unloading delays	Time spent waiting to be loaded and unloaded over and above the agreed time.
Annual workforce turnover	The rate at which permanent employees are replaced (excludes casual or seasonal labour).
Accident record	Time lost through incidents, as a percentage of total working days.
Accident record	The number of days/miles/kms since the last reportable incident.

Measuring supply chains

Some LSPs and fourth-party logistics providers (4PLs) may well be managing a client's total supply chain. Table 7.7, which partially follows the Supply

Table 7.6   Example freight transport KPIs of importance to the client

Key performance indicator	Description
Average cost per unit delivered (£)	The average cost of delivering a specified unit (eg a pallet or tonne of goods).
Percentage of late deliveries	Late deliveries, as a percentage of total deliveries.
Percentage of in full deliveries	Complete deliveries, as a percentage of total deliveries.
Percentage of damaged items	Damaged items, as a percentage of all items delivered.
Number of insurance claims	The number of claims received, as a percentage of total deliveries.
Correct paperwork	The number of delivery notes, invoices etc completed correctly, as a percentage of total deliveries.
CO_2 produced per delivery	The amount of emissions per delivery undertaken.
On-time collection	The number of times the vehicle arrives at the designated time to collect the goods, as a percentage of total collections.
Freight transport costs as a percentage of cost of goods sold	The total cost of transport/total cost of goods sold.

Chain Operations Reference (SCOR®) model, suggests overall supply chain metrics, together with the expected performance level.

The column 'Disadvantage' shows company performance, which is suboptimal. 'Parity' is the norm, whilst 'Advantage' is close to best practice.

The SCOR® model is a product of the Supply Chain Council (SCC). It is a framework that links business process, metrics, best practices and technology features together into a unified structure to support communication between supply chain partners. It assists companies in improving the effectiveness of their supply chain management and related supply chain improvement activities.

SCOR® identifies five core supply chain performance attributes: Reliability, Responsiveness, Agility, Costs and Asset Management. Consideration of these attributes makes it possible to compare an organization that strategically chooses to be the low-cost provider against an organization that chooses to compete on reliability and performance.

Table 7.7 SCOR® level 1 metrics

KPI	Performance		
Delivery in full by line	95%–97%	97–99%	>99%
Delivery on time	95%–97%	97%–99%	>99%
Delivery OTIF	>90%	94%–98%	>98%
Total supply chain management cost	17%–10%	9%–7%	<7%
Cash-to-cash cycle time	>60 days	50–30 days	<20 days
Supplier deliveries OTIF	>89%	90%–95%	>97%
	Disadvantage	**Parity**	**Advantage**

(Best practice — spanning Advantage column)

SOURCE Logistics Bureau

Membership of the SCC is open to all companies and organizations interested in applying and advancing state-of-the-art supply chain management systems and practices. Member companies pay an annual fee to become involved.

The SCOR® process reference model contains:

- **Performance metrics**: standard metrics to measure process performance. There is a suite of KPIs, but first-line metrics include:
  - the Perfect Order – OTIF, damage free and complete document accuracy;
  - order fulfilment cycle time;
  - supply chain flexibility;
  - supply chain management cost;
  - cash-to-cash cycle time.
- **Processes**: standard descriptions of management processes and a framework of process relationships.
- **Practices**: management practices that produce best-in-class performance.
- **People**: training and skills requirements aligned with processes, best practices, and metrics.

According to BenchmarkingSuccess.com, organizations with best-in-class supply chains as measured by service level performance are able to operate at about half the cost of their peers who achieve average service levels. This is somewhat counterintuitive, as we normally associate higher service levels with increased costs.

Survey findings by Honeywell (2016) reported that the average global cost of one picking error is $59, resulting in distribution centres losing on average more than $400,000 annually on mis-picks. However, when operating at a high level of accuracy even a 0.5 per cent error rate can cost a significant amount, and therefore each error will need to be investigated and rectified.

Other supply chain metrics can include:

- inventory days on hand – raw materials and finished goods;
- lost sales due to stockout;
- back orders as a percentage of total lines;
- Perfect Order receipt from the supplier;
- average days of sales outstanding.

Actual KPI examples

During a recent ITT project for an e-commerce operation, the following KPIs and their targets were provided by three of the LSP participants to underline their commitment to service. When putting an RFP together, it is always suggested that LSPs should be asked to provide their main KPI, and the targets they currently work towards. Note the similarities between the indicators.

Example LSP 1

- Despatch on time – target 98.5 per cent.
- Delivered OTIF – target 98.5 per cent.
- Stock Accuracy – target 98.5 per cent.
- Pick accuracy – 99.97 per cent.

Example LSP 2

- Goods in completed within 24 hours – target: 99.8 per cent; minimum acceptable rate: 97.8 per cent.
- Order despatch – target: 100 per cent same day; minimum acceptable rate: 98 per cent.

- Returns completed – target: 100 per cent within 24 hours; minimum acceptable rate: 100 per cent.
- Stock accuracy – target: 99.9 per cent; minimum acceptable rate: 97.9 per cent.
- Pick accuracy – target: 99.9 per cent; minimum acceptable rate: 97.9 per cent.

Example LSP 3

- On-time receiving and availability – target: 98 per cent.
- On-time despatch – target: 99 per cent.
- On-time delivery for trackable deliveries via contracted carriers – target: 97 per cent.
- Accuracy of picking – target: 99 per cent.
- Inventory accuracy (annual absolute discrepancy) – target: 99 per cent.

Rewards and penalties

There is no point in having KPIs if they are not monitored and acted upon. If an LSP exceeds expectations, then there is no reason why they can't be rewarded. Achieving the standard is expected; however, exceeding the targets is likely to benefit the customer, and therefore the LSP should share in these benefits. They are more likely to look for further efficiencies if this is the case.

Conversely, if the LSP fails to achieve the minimum expected level then there is no reason why they shouldn't have a reduction in fees – although there has to be a degree of latitude when the LSP is not directly responsible for the shortfall in performance. An example could be bad weather causing highways to grind to a halt.

Following are three examples of a service credit in a recent SLA.

Example 1: Pick accuracy failure

Failure to hit minimum contractual levels will incur credits for the total monthly invoice exclusive of carriage and all rework charges, as detailed in the table.

Service credits for pick accuracy failure

Pick accuracy		Month number		
From	To	1	2	3
99.5%	100%	–	–	–
98%	99.5%	–	0.5%	1%
97%	97.99%	1%	1.5%	2%
96%	96.99%	1.5%	2%	2.5%

Example 2: On-time despatch

All non-palletized orders received by 5.30pm will be despatched on the day of order receipt. All orders received after this time to be shipped by the end of the following business day.

Failure to hit minimum contractual levels will incur credits for the total monthly invoice exclusive of carriage and all rework charges, as detailed in the table.

Service credits for on-time despatch

On-time despatch		Month number		
From	To	1	2	3
99%	100%	–	–	–
98%	98.99%	–	0.5%	1%
97%	97.99%	1%	1.5%	2%
95%	96.99%	1.5%	2%	2.5%

Example 3: On-time delivery

Failure to hit minimum contractual levels will incur credits for the total monthly invoice for carriage only, as detailed in the table.

Service credits for on-time delivery

On-time delivery		Month number		
From	To	1	2	3
99%	100%	–	–	–
97%	98.99%	–	0.5%	1%
95%	96.99%	1%	1.5%	2%
93%	94.99%	1.5%	2%	2.5%

CASE STUDY   Mondelēz (formerly Cadbury) – an example of Vested® Outsourcing

In September of 2008, Phil Wood took over the role of Head of Distribution for Cadbury in Britain and Ireland. He took on a network that was experiencing frequent issues in the UK, and consequently was regularly failing during periods of high seasonal volume.

It was a network that consisted of three dedicated primary DCs, each holding between 40,000 and 80,000 pallets. The largest was an in-house operation that had taken over from a previously outsourced LSP contract; the others were outsourced to two different LSPs on an open-book basis. To add to this complexity, the three DCs were served by three separate transport contracts with different LSPs, operating on a closed-book basis.

His initial perspective to fix the issues was to cut through the complexity and operate with one LSP nationally, and also consider potentially outsourcing the in-house operation to the same provider.

However, it quickly became apparent to him that the issues the network had experienced were less to do with structural complexity and far more to do with basic warehousing operations. Interestingly, he saw that there were examples of best practice especially in the LSPs that he wanted to share across the whole network.

Three factors came together that allowed him to do this effectively:

1 contractual arrangements;

2 LSP rivalry;

3 leadership approach.

1. Contractual arrangements

The logistics procurement lead had already informed him that they had built into the warehousing contract a clause that allowed for 'bonus-malus' KPIs. These needed to be agreed between Cadbury and the LSPs.

Bonus-malus is an incentive programme designed to give a negative bonus for poor performance. It is offset by a bonus scheme which rewards increased performance.

They agreed on six major KPIs in four categories:

- Health and safety:
  - **Reportable LTAs**. As these were dedicated operations Cadbury did not want their reputation to be tarnished by health and safety issues. Small sum gain for the LSP for no LTAs in a year; nil for one; small sum loss for two LTAs or more.
- Service:
  - **DC OTIF**: designed to get the DC LSPs working with their respective transport LSP. Small sum gain for the LSP for less than 0.5 per cent transport and warehousing OTIF loss in a year; nil for 0.5–0.55 per cent; small sum loss for more than 0.55 per cent.
  - **DC accountable**: Small sum gain for the LSP for less than 0.15 per cent service loss directly accountable to DC operations (pick accuracy, material handling equipment availability and so on) in a year; nil for 0.15–0.2 per cent; small sum loss for more than 0.2 per cent.
- Cost:
  - **Gain/loss share**: to a maximum 5 per cent of the agreed annual contract or budget which was volume/activity adjusted.
  - **Waste**: stock losses including damages. Small sum gain for the LSP for beating the budget agreed for the year by less than 5 per cent; nil for 5 per cent; small sum loss for exceeding the budget by more than 5 per cent.
- Audit compliance
  - **Audit findings**. Small sum gain for the LSP for no major and fewer than two minor audit findings; nil for no major and fewer than four minor audit findings; small sum loss for any major audit finding and/or five or more minor audit findings.

The small sum values were typically between £15–£20K, and the LSPs achieved most of the targets, but occasionally had to pay out against them. The LSPs exceeded the targets set, resulting in savings of between £100,000 and £150,000 at each site, of which the LSPs received 50 per cent of these savings.

The remaining 50 per cent enabled Cadbury to fund the small sum KPI, and thus remain within their original activity-based budget.

Other KPIs monitored and managed across the network are shown in Table 7.8.

There are 34 individual measures divided into eight major areas. Utilizing this benchmarking tool, the Cadbury team were able to compare its own in-house operations with those of their third-party logistics providers.

2. LSP rivalry

There was little doubt in Phil Wood's mind that the competition between the LSPs and the potential inducement for the best performing LSP to take over the transport contracts and the in-house operation, was a massive incentive for them to perform well.

Table 7.8 Cadbury benchmarking model

Category			Units
Warehouse	*Operational metrics*	Cases despatched (total)	Number
		Pallets despatched (total)	Number
		Case pick pallets despatched	Percentage
		Total warehouse cost including overheads	£
	KPIs	Full pallet pick	Percentage
		Cost per case despatched	£
		Cost per pallet despatched	£
Service	*KPIs*	Case fill (responsibility of Logistics Operations Department)	Percentage
		OTIF (responsibility of Logistics Operations Department)	Percentage

(continued)

Table 7.8   (Continued)

Category			Units
Transport Inbound	*Operational metrics*	Number of cases received	Number
		Number of pallets received	Number
		Number of loads received	Number
	KPIs	Vehicle utilization	Percentage
Transport Outbound	*Operational metrics*	Number of cases despatched	Number
		Number of pallets despatched	Number
		Number of loads despatched	Number
	KPIs	Vehicle utilization	Percentage
Inventory	*Operational metrics*	Total inventory value	€
		Total warehouse pallet capacity	Number
		Number of pallets in stock (month-end)	Number
		Value of inventory written off (responsibility of Logistics Operations Department)	€
	KPIs	Warehouse utilization	Percentage
Safety	*KPIs*	Lost time injury frequency rates (global definition)	Number
		Total number of accidents	Number
		Number of lost time accidents	Number
Quality	*Operational metrics*	Number of pallets on hold or in quarantine	Number
	KPIs	Cases damaged in transit	Number
		Cases damaged in warehouse	Number
		Transport security incidents reported	Number

(continued)

Table 7.8 (Continued)

Category			Units
Environment	*Operational metrics*	Electricity consumption	KWh
		Gas consumption	Litres^3
		Transport CO_2 emissions	Tonnes
	KPIs	Outbound CO_2 per pallet shipped	Tonnes
		Electricity consumption per pallet shipped	KWh

As a result, the people that he was dealing with at the LSPs were some of the best that he had encountered from the industry.

3. The leadership approach

Having established the contractual framework for the LSPs, Phil set about creating a forum for mutual co-operation, continuous improvement and best practice sharing.

It is important to note that the IT infrastructure was identical across all three DCs – that is, they all operated the same warehouse management system (WMS), equipment and interfaces to the Cadbury Systems Applications and Products in the Data Processing system. This aspect was fully funded and supported by Cadbury.

There were three forums:

- Health and Safety;
- Stock and Systems;
- Warehouse Operations.

Each was chaired by one of the DC general managers, with appropriate senior representation from the full network. They reported on their activities to the Distribution Leadership Team, which Phil chaired. This meeting had each of the DC leads, the UK transport manager, the Republic of Ireland logistics lead and associated support business partners from finance, HR and IT present their performance for the previous period.

All projects were reviewed and sanctioned by this meeting, including ideas for productivity generation at any of the sites. Where Cadbury was investing fully in a project such as WMS enhancement, the benefits were taken 100 per cent by Cadbury, as these were built into the open-book budget.

The business also required Phil's team to carry out internal compliance audits, such as for Sarbanes-Oxley and internal/external audit compliance. These audits were carried out on rotation between all the DCs, and interestingly the LSPs audited each other. The thoroughness of these audits were amazing, especially as each LSP knew that if they found issues it would impact their competitor financially!

Outcome

Besides gaining financially from the bonus-malus KPIs, the LSPs were rewarded by winning the transport contracts for the areas their DCs supported, and one of them was awarded the export warehouse contract which had been outsourced during the same period. Cadbury particularly benefited through best-practice sharing, increasing service levels and reducing costs during a period of growth, and also reaped the full rewards in its in-house DC operation.

Performance improvement highlights were as follows:

- Service levels moved from OTIF 97 per cent to 98.7 per cent (case fill) in 18 months. (Cadbury's customer service improvements were recognized when they were awarded the 2009 IGD Boxwood Business Transformation Award.)
- Overall costs were reduced from £60 million to £55 million.
- The network was able to deliver increasing sales volumes, so that costs as a percentage of Net Sales Value reduced from 5.2 per cent to 3.7 per cent between 2008 and 2011.
- Energy costs and CO_2 emissions were reduced by 33 per cent.
- LTAs were reduced by 50 per cent year-on-year.
- There were no compliance issues at any of the DCs.

Case study courtesy of Phil Wood, Associate Director of Order to Cash – Northern Europe, at Mondelēz International

Conclusion

The measurement of performance is key in any outsourced relationship. If expectations are to be realized, an agreement has to be made regarding the measures to be recorded.

There shouldn't be too many measures – only those that are relevant to the contract and are instrumental in driving the business forward should be chosen.

Not only should performance be measured, but the findings need to be acted upon to ensure that the business continues to move forward. Performance management is key in this respect.

Once a baseline has been recorded, companies are able to not only compare results historically, but can also compare results with their peers through benchmarking.

The risks associated with outsourcing

08

BY RICHARD GIBSON AND VICTORIA GIBSON

Introduction

Outsourcing can be a risky business, and when logistics services go wrong the consequences can impact on customers and business reputation very quickly. There are a number of high-profile cases of disruption related to the major transfer of business from one facility or supplier to another; a recent example of this is described in this chapter. There are many other examples where supplier insolvency or industrial relations disputes related to outsourcing have caused major disruption for the shippers involved.

The highest risk to a business may not be short-term disruption from a transfer or event, but years of lost opportunity and reputational damage from choosing the wrong supplier or failing to outsource properly. Even when there is no headline-catching disaster, the wrong logistics partner can delay or impede a wide range of supply chain initiatives and be very expensive to remove and replace.

This chapter will examine why managing risk is so important, what the likely risks are and how to mitigate these risks.

It will include a case study of a high-profile outsourcing contract which unfortunately was not a success; however, it does highlight the fact that managing all potential risks can be problematic. It will go on to discuss the aftermath, and how an initial disastrous handover became a lesson in good crisis management.

Why bother managing outsourcing risk?

If you contact any group of managers and ask them to discuss risk in the supply chain and their logistics operations, they will have widely varying views on what constitutes risk and what falls within the scope of supply chain and logistics. Logistics, particularly when outsourced, is frequently less visible within a business than its sales and manufacturing operations... until things go wrong!

So why is managing risk important? We automatically assess risk in our everyday lives, whether crossing a road, driving a car or using a sharp knife. Gibson and Savage (2013) argue that a similar set of decision-making processes should also influence the management of the supply chain, whether we are conscious of it or not.

A common definition of risk is 'exposure to the chance of injury or loss; a hazard or dangerous chance'. For logistics services, potential losses cover a spectrum from catastrophic loss of stock and facilities and a major interruption in supply to the more common losses of late deliveries, wrong product despatched and damage to customer service.

There are also risks associated with accidents, with consequences for staff or the general public and damage to the shipper's and LSP's reputations. Other risks associated with product safety, LSP solvency and potential loss of licences must also be considered.

Recognizing the assessment and mitigation of risk is a discipline. Resilience and robustness are often interchanged, but in supply chain terms they can acquire different connotations, as Christopher and Peck (2004) observe. Robustness relies on inbuilt strength or sturdiness during execution and covers more than the typical workplace risk assessments for, say, working at height or the once-in-a-lifetime disruptive event. They suggest that supply chain resilience may be defined as the ability of a system to return to its original state or move to a new, more desirable state after being disturbed.

Understanding robustness, resilience and our capacity for risk-taking is critical for organizational and supply chain success.

What is the risk problem?

The interdependencies between organizations and their supply chain and logistics operations mean that a supply chain can be at risk from a business (such as an LSP), just as a business can be at risk from its supply chain. Risks may further be categorized as:

- Risks internal to the organization – such as their process and degree of control. Examples here might include the risk to product contamination in the shipper's factory.

- Risks external to the organization but internal to the supply chain network in the areas of demand and supply – this is where logistics outsourcing and the majority of LSP delivery sits.

- Risks entirely external to the network – such as the wider environment (Christopher and Peck, 2004). Examples of this include Brexit, strikes at ports and road congestion.

Based on the work by Simchi-Levi (2013), Figure 8.1 describes supply chain risks in terms of whether they can be known, predicted, quantified or controlled.

When you consider the list above, no logistics operation is ever going to eliminate all of these risks, nor is it appropriate for each variant of the uncontrollable, unknown risks to be considered in depth. Instead, broad strategies, such as reducing single points of failure and having appropriate insurance, will be used for these categories, while more detailed action plans to improve resilience and robustness can be drawn up for controllable and known risks.

As ever with risk identification, it is easier to draw up plans for known risks than to identify unknown risks, and groups of logistics managers can

Figure 8.1   Sources of supply chain risks

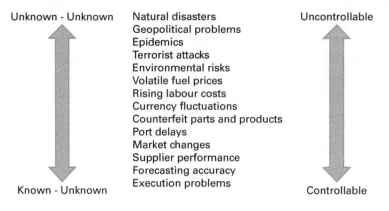

Unknown - Unknown	Natural disasters	Uncontrollable
	Geopolitical problems	
	Epidemics	
	Terrorist attacks	
	Environmental risks	
	Volatile fuel prices	
	Rising labour costs	
	Currency fluctuations	
	Counterfeit parts and products	
	Port delays	
	Market changes	
	Supplier performance	
	Forecasting accuracy	
Known - Unknown	Execution problems	Controllable

SOURCE Simchi-Levi, 2013

be subject to groupthink and not consider risks outside their experience. It is therefore helpful to broaden the participation for risk identification exercises and certainly to include procurement in the process.

Some risks may develop over several outsourcing cycles: a poorly run, biased process in one cycle is likely to reduce competition in subsequent phases.

Successive Transfer of Undertakings, Protection of Employment transfers of staff can also lead to poor morale or even industrial disputes, as in the 2011 fuel tanker drivers' dispute in the UK, which, according to the union, Unite, was 'triggered by an erosion of working conditions as major supermarkets and oil companies contracted out to haulage firms'.

Risk appetite and tolerance

The tanker drivers' dispute in 2011 had the potential to affect up to 90 per cent of petrol forecourts. Fresh in the mind of the government and the public were the fuel blockades and chaos of 2000; therefore the government's appetite for risking a repeat of this scenario was very low, and they suggested that the public fill up their cars just in case.

A standard definition for risk appetite is 'the amount and type of risk that an organization is prepared to seek, accept or tolerate' (ISO 31000:2018). Defining an organization's risk appetite can help in several ways. Within the outsourcing contract it helps to:

- ensure the organization is only taking a level and type of risk with which it is comfortable;

- ensure the risks you are exposed to are commensurate to the opportunity or reward to be gained;

- provide a framework within which to consider the acceptable risk level;

- enable staff to make dynamic judgements about risk acceptability where necessary;

- ensure any response to risks is proportionate – neither reckless nor prohibitive;

- ensure the risk limit is escalated and reports are made when your risk appetite is reached.

There is no perfect answer to what your risk appetite should be. No organization can make a sustainable profit without taking risks and the control culture of the organization is linked with its propensity to take risk. An organization's appetite for risk may be what it wants to do and how it goes about it, incorporating quantitative and qualitative measures such as financial targets and reputational impact.

Risk tolerance is about bearing risk, and can be expressed in absolutes – for example, the organization may refuse to deal with certain customers, market segments or even certain LSPs.

Which approach should we adopt?

Existing supply chain risk management literature is concerned with risk identification, risk assessment and risk mitigation, with responsiveness described in terms of operational or catastrophic risks.

When we have a disaster, each event will impact the supply chain in a unique way, and our mitigation strategies should be flexible enough to minimize the financial impact and the time taken to recover. These events allow us to manage and mitigate our risk appetite and tolerance for the benefit of the supply chain and organization.

Any approach to assessing and managing supply chain and logistics risk should recognize that the greater the complexity, the greater the opportunity for being ineffective. Simple is best, and some straightforward questions can initiate this process:

- What could go wrong?
- Can it be detected or predicted?
- What could be the effect of failure?
- What could be the cause of failure?
- What could trigger the failure?

This basic approach can be summarized with the acronym 'SOD' – that is, Severity of effect, the likelihood of Occurrence, and the likelihood of Detection (see Figure 8.2).

As an example, applying the approach to supply disruption of a single source product could give a high level of severity as operational service levels cease (S=5). However, the probability of this occurring may only be once in many years (O=1). The detectability could be high for a factory destroyed by fire (D=5), or low for an activity such as a change in technology (D=1).

Figure 8.2   SOD model for risk assessment

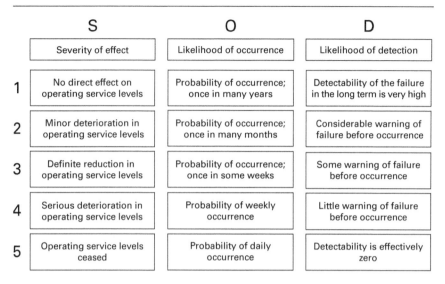

	S	O	D
	Severity of effect	Likelihood of occurrence	Likelihood of detection
1	No direct effect on operating service levels	Probability of occurrence; once in many years	Detectability of the failure in the long term is very high
2	Minor deterioration in operating service levels	Probability of occurrence; once in many months	Considerable warning of failure before occurrence
3	Definite reduction in operating service levels	Probability of occurrence; once in some weeks	Some warning of failure before occurrence
4	Serious deterioration in operating service levels	Probability of weekly occurrence	Little warning of failure before occurrence
5	Operating service levels ceased	Probability of daily occurrence	Detectability is effectively zero

SOURCE Slater, 2005

The overall score for this event would be S x O x D, giving a value of 25 for service levels stopping due to a factory fire. Each company will have a different level of tolerable risk for different elements of the supply chain.

For outsourced logistics, the shipper and LSP should undergo a joint SOD exercise at least once a year to identify and assess risks. Both parties should also identify risks in their own organizations or supply chains that are outside the scope of their service contract. For the shipper, an example of this could be the lack of an alternative supplier for this service; for the LSP, it could be the loss of a contract that might impact on the viability of the business.

Once this is done, both sides need to look at risk mitigation.

Some practical risk management applications

Outsourcing can give a sense of security, in terms of risk transfer, service delivery and customer satisfaction. In the 2018 Chartered Institute of Logistics and Transport Outsourcing Attitudes survey (CILT, 2018), public sector and charity sector shippers identified the transfer of risk to the LSP as a major benefit of outsourcing. However, can this sense of security some-times be misplaced?

The 'five Ts' of risk management are as follows:

1 Treat – take actions to reduce or remove the risk.

2 Tolerate – accept the current risk level.

3 Terminate – cease doing the activity from which the risk arises.

4 Take the opportunity – use the risk as a positive, to make gains.

5 Transfer – place all or part of the risk ownership elsewhere.

Examples of these strategies for the logistics sector are shown in Table 8.1.

The most common example of Transfer is insurance, where a company pays a premium to a third party to bear all or part of the cost of a risk. Outsourcing an activity is also commonly perceived as a form of risk trans-fer, in which at least some elements of the risk, for example financial or op-erational, are passed to the provider.

However, it is important to be aware of the implications of something going wrong and the impact it could have on your business. There have been complex legal cases in recent years involving local authorities' outsourcing activities – for example Woodland v Essex (Tench, 2013) which have shown that risk is not necessarily transferred by a contractual agreement.

When entering into any outsourcing arrangement, therefore, we should continually consider risk ownership. Which elements of the risk will we re-tain? Can we afford it if the risk materialized? Is the third party fully aware and in agreement? Is it (can it be?) fully documented?

Reputational damage is an aspect which is often overlooked when out-sourcing, but should remain high in contract management practices. Just because a service is being delivered by an LSP, the end-user almost certainly will not associate poor service with that third party and will expect the ship-per to rectify any defects (as demonstrated by the case study below). Many organizations have little awareness of their reputation as a business asset; it can be an intangible asset and therefore difficult to quantify, but if custom-ers start going elsewhere, its value will soon become apparent.

Let us consider the contract management process. Are all contracts for-mally documented? Does that documentation include partnerships, shared activities, memorandums of understanding and so on? A larger, more com-plex organization is likely to have robust contract and project management procedures in place, but may not have oversight of all the risk elements.

Table 8.1 The five Ts of risk management

Strategy	Risk example	Action examples
Treat	For shipper: LSP insolvency.	Check financial reports regularly. Maintain contact with unsuccessful bidders. Split the contract between two LSPs. Check on dependency on other contracts, and review regularly. Simplify requirements (if possible) to increase LSP alternatives.
	For the LSP: reduction in stock levels threatens recovery of fixed cost.	Agree minimum stock levels in charging mechanism. Negotiate the ability to sublet space.
Tolerate	Snow poses threat to deliveries as DC has exit with an incline.	Tolerate (in UK where snow is rare – this strategy would not be acceptable in Chicago!).
Terminate	Brexit causes major delay on route from Ireland to France via the UK, and fresh goods perish.	Many companies in Ireland are looking at direct sea routes to mainland Europe as an alternative.
Take the opportunity	Implementation of a new warehouse management system forces change to pick process.	Use as a way to change fixed behaviours; design for optimum routing.
Transfer	For the shipper: sales forecast inaccuracy leads to poor vehicle fill.	Outsource to an LSP with multiple clients.

A smaller company is likely to trust in previous good relationships. 'They've been doing our xxx for years' should be enough to ring a small warning bell.

Warning signals can be as simple as noticing unusual behaviours: staff and/or management leaving in numbers; not returning phone calls or emails; project slippage; unexpected costs, etc. Staying close to key suppliers is not only good practice, it's sound risk management. Having good governance of contracts will help to ensure that warning signs are spotted early on.

So, how do we know if we're doing it right? Remember, absence of failure is not necessarily the same as success, but there are some assurances that can be given:

- Do the key suppliers have business continuity plans in place?
- Where does the shipper factor in their plans? For example, if there's severe weather, or a fuel shortage, whose contract will be a priority for them – do they have service agreements with other businesses which may take precedence?
- Has the shipper made its risk appetite levels clear to the suppliers?
- Are there clear exit strategies in place?

Knowing the strategic importance of all the contracts is vital in terms of how the company engages, communicates and manages the risk. Who are the key players? Is there regular communication with them? Would the company know if anything was going wrong?

So, to use the clichéd question 'What keeps you awake at night?', it may be the scary zombie film you finished watching at 1am, or it may be that you don't know the strategic significance of your contracts and the impact on the business if something goes wrong. The message is 'it's all about proportionate risk management'. So:

- know the risks and manage them appropriately;
- understand the company's risk appetite and communicate this to suppliers;
- engage and communicate continually;
- identify the key players and manage them accordingly;
- monitor performance and look out for those alarm bells.

CASE STUDY   KFC and DHL

This case study is an extreme example of how an outsourcing contract can fail during a transfer between suppliers and a major network change.

Companies naturally do not like publicizing their failings, but the documented casualties of poor supply chain and outsourcing risk management are numerous, and include the 2018 debacle involving the KFC fast food retail outlets in the UK.

A new contract will 'revolutionize the UK food service distribution market' (Henderson, 2017) was the first indication to the wider UK logistics services market that something was about to happen between the restaurant chain KFC, their incumbent logistics partner and a new provider. It transpired that a joint venture formed between DHL and QSL (Quick Service Logistics) was awarded a contract by KFC in the UK in October 2017 to manage their supply chain operations. QSL had worked successfully with KFC in Germany for seven years.

KFC's Supply Chain Director said that they had specifically chosen DHL and QSL for their reputation for innovation in logistics across other industries. DHL would look after the physical logistics, while QSL would handle demand planning and stock management, operational purchasing and accounting using dedicated IT systems.

Move forward five months, and the theatre of this change in their supply chain had been played out, the KFC brand was re-asserted in the British psyche and the outsourcing incident was generating good copy for industry observers and logistics management schools.

At its peak, the failing transition between the KFC logistics service providers led to the closure of 604 KFC stores (69 per cent) (Priday, 2018), the waste of lorryloads of fresh chicken, and the launching of a hastily prepared marketing plan, which industry observers suggest was a great success, not withstanding the immediate shortages, for the brand in the medium term (Brownsell, 2018). What happened with KFC is a great example of failing to assess the risks in the outsourcing process.

To learn the lessons, we can look to the column inches written in the aftermath. Firstly, there was no single cause for the KFC distribution network collapsing. Commentators refer to a shortage of staff at the new facility in Rugby, operational chaos during start-up, system issues (O'Marah, 2018) and traffic chaos; not one causal effect. If you were involved in this incident, your viewpoint would differ dependent upon your position in the operational structure. As with all disasters, there were the 'told you so' commentators who predicted failure as the network was reduced from six sites to one site, KFC executives who claimed to know three weeks beforehand that it would not work, and union leaders who had expected failure (Sit, 2018).

As someone who has survived several start-ups, Richard Gibson suspects the reality lies amongst all these different viewpoints. Start-ups will always have their phases of chaos. There are always recruitment challenges, and system integration rarely works first time. Migrating to one site from six would have delivered a hefty cost benefit to the KFC risk takers, and a single warehouse model is common throughout the industry and throughout the world.

On 14 Feb 2018, completely out of the control of the LSP, the closure of Junctions 2 and 3 of the local M6 motorway led to gridlock of the local road network, and the BBC reported that truckloads of chickens were missing their intake times at this fast-moving food operation. Combined with people, system and start-up challenges, these delayed vehicles would have absorbed any contingency plans in terms of additional time and labour allocated, and the day-to-day chaos will have turned to operational seizure.

As the roads around the area became free-flowing, outbound and scheduled inbound trucks would have started to conflict, by which time the stock awaiting goods receipt would have been out of phase with the despatch schedule. In hindsight, at this point the best thing to do would have been to stop everything, clear the warehouse floor and start the next cycle on schedule, a nightmare scenario for any general manager and probably grounds for contract termination, but realistic under the circumstances. Instead, the operation became more congested and eventually ground to a halt.

The scene that the logistics operators were now dealing with was the result of a process that had taken many months of deliberation amongst some of the industry's finest and most experienced logistics specialists. Could they have seen the disaster coming? Possibly. If one of the causal effects had gone in their favour on the day, could they have got away with it? Probably. Only the operators at the heart of the incident know the answers to these questions.

Questions must be asked about the implementation of the contract and how the transition between Bidvest (now Best Food Logistics) and DHL/QSL was managed. How thorough was the risk assessment? Could the contract have been phased or was a 'big bang' approach the most effective? How thorough was the contingency plan? Was there a plan in place for supply issues such as those witnessed here?

You cannot have a contingency plan for every single, possible occurrence – however, a significant supply problem should have been planned for, be it a logistics issue, an inventory planning issue or a major supplier issue. According to Professor Richard Wilding of Cranfield School of Management, from evidence gathered, 10 per cent of supply chains are severely disrupted each year and therefore a risk management assessment is key.

Taking a step back, what are the lessons which can help to avoid this happening in other supply chains?

Drawing from Green (2018), the KFC crisis highlights the need for at least the following five activities to take place in an effort to de-risk these outsourcing scenarios:

1 Do due diligence. Not just financial robustness, but also commercial viability: understanding what other contracts and relationships the LSP has had. Might this have uncovered a failed Burger King contract years previously under very similar events? Also, the other aspect to consider being operational: can they really deliver this change?

2 Have a trial period. Outsource small chunks; in this instance slowly collapse the network into one hub. It might delay the savings, and in theory cost a bit more, but there is no need to do it at speed.

3 Weigh up the risks. Calculate the potential cost of lost sales versus the logistics cost saving of the intended change.

4 Contingency planning. Insist on the rigorous management of the preparation and operations set up, as well as the communication plan between both parties.

5 Get the contract right. In the KFC instance, the contract might specify the relationship between distribution failure, impact upon operations and an agreed remedy for each day that this occurs.

Cunliffe (n. d.) writes about the incident from a lawyer's perspective, identifying four areas to address as elements of a boilerplate approach (a standardized method or procedure):

- ensure robust contracts are in place to protect the business;
- define the terms of the supply agreement;
- check that insurance policies cover all known eventualities;
- create a disaster recovery plan.

Move forward to the present day, and what has been the lasting impact upon the organizations involved? The original LSP has regained the distribution business, and the KFC brand has been re-established within the British psyche.

The messages that KFC shared with the public during and after the crisis reached a combined audience of more than a billion people, and the marketing campaign has been recognized as 'rewriting the manual for crisis management' (Brownsell, 2018).

The loser was DHL who sold their vision, oversaw the crisis and were a higher-profile media target than their partner QSL. Other DHL customers were also impacted by the internal autopsy process that put an immediate stop on capital supply for developments, and slowed other customer activities as the LSP sought answers to 'what just happened?'.

Conclusion

This chapter has described how understanding robustness, resilience and the capacity for risk-taking is critical for organizational and supply chain success when outsourcing. The chapter has reviewed the interdependencies between organizations and their supply chains, summarizing these as sources of known and unknown risk. It has considered appetite and tolerance of risk.

The chapter included some practical management techniques and the message that getting this right is all about proportionate risk management.

The KFC example illustrates how a shipper chasing cost savings got it wrong, but turned it into a positive with clever marketing. The experience for both service providers in the short term was negative and, arguably, had KFC not reacted in the public way they did, the ramification in terms of profit and market share would be very different. The fact that the relationship between KFC and Bidvest had not soured as a result of the contract loss allowed both parties to work together again.

Managing
relationships

09

Introduction

Relationship management in the context of procurement and supply is often interpreted as building relationships between people in the entities concerned. Relationships between customer and supplier, however, are framed by the interdependency between their organizations and the impact each has on the other's performance. The relationship stretches beyond individual relationships, but is underpinned and supported by these.

In the early days of logistics outsourcing, logistics service providers (LSPs) were generally local and often developed their services alongside their customers. Relationships were close on both a personal level and on the business interdependency side. From local, daily interaction, LSPs had a good understanding and knowledge of their customer's priorities and business direction.

As economies of scale and industry consolidation on both sides have created national and global businesses, and procurement has become increasingly professionalized, many supplier/customer relationships have become more remote: senior managers on both sides are travelling and relationship knowledge is split across many different personnel, departments and sites. To solve this, two related disciplines have been developed: supplier relationship management (SRM) – an approach used primarily by procurement professionals, and customer relationship management (CRM) – the sister methodology and toolset on the supplier side. This chapter will focus on SRM and relationship management generally, although most of the principles apply equally to CRM.

The purpose of relationship management for a logistics service is to develop value through improving the long-term performance of that service. The performance management of logistics services is covered in Chapter 7. This chapter focuses on one component to achieve enhanced performance and therefore value. How that value is developed will depend on the needs of the customer organization. Its success will need the engagement of the LSP, and benefits will also need to accrue to the LSP from deeper engagement, as this takes time and effort.

Procurement Leaders (n. d.) define SRM as:

> '[F]irst and foremost an approach used for engaging with suppliers on a level that reflects the priorities of the customer organization and how best these needs can be achieved. It is a differentiation process that recognizes that not all suppliers are the same and therefore not all customer-supplier relationships should be dealt with through a single strategy.'

Relationship building in any walk of life is an investment, and resources are limited. This chapter will build on the theories explored in Chapter 4, and will look at appropriate relationship management for different categories of service, as well as the enablers for relationship development.

Why is relationship management important?

Two entities engaged in the buying and supplying of logistics services will naturally build up many relationships between their companies and between their personnel. These relationships are:

- between operational teams, related to the movement of goods across the supply chain;
- between finance teams, related to the raising and payment of invoices or the performance of goods receipt functions by the LSP;
- between quality management teams and operational personnel;
- between the LSP's delivery staff and/or distribution/fulfilment centre personnel and the shippers' end customers;
- between IT departments;
- between the shipper's customer services team and the LSP's operational team;
- between procurement and sales or account management teams.

While these relationships may be enough for day-to-day business, without conscious effort they are likely to be fragmented and insufficient to either drive step changes in performance or provide resilience against external events. In the 2018 Chartered Institute of Logistics and Transport Outsourcing Attitudes survey (CILT, 2018), 35 per cent of shippers that had terminated a logistics contract in the last five years, cited relationship issues or a lack of responsiveness by the LSP to issues or queries as a reason.

Without aspects of SRM such as joint plans and engagement, adverse events can lead to both continuous fire-fighting and the apportionment of blame. To achieve better outcomes, LSPs need to be deeply engaged with a customer's needs, and senior influencers must meet often enough to develop a good working relationship and understanding of each other's businesses.

> A good example here can be found in the Tate and Lyle case study in Chapter 5, where the LSP changed their strategy with significant consequences to Tate and Lyle's ongoing operations. A closer relationship at senior level could well have alerted Tate and Lyle sooner of the impending non-renewal of the lease.

To take advantage of all the potential opportunities related to a particular logistics service, change will usually be needed at the shipper's organization, or with their supply base, as well as at the LSP. To identify and get commitment for such changes, both sides will need to have built the right relationships across the lifetime of the contract including mutual respect, honesty and a track record of delivering against promises on both sides.

Performance management modes

The UK's Chartered Institute of Procurement and Supply (CIPS) identifies three levels of performance management for a supplier:

1 Contract management – this covers the development and management of the contract including performance management to the standards agreed.
2 Supplier management – this covers the areas of contract management but has more engagement to drive the performance of the supplier.
3 SRM – this includes contract management and supplier management, but looks to develop the relationship sufficiently to be able to predict and rely on the other party's response to an unforeseen event and to develop enhanced value from the contract.

For low-risk, relatively low-value services, contract management will be sufficient, and the short contract lengths of some of these services may preclude any other approach. If a supplier is not performing, then a new supplier can be found with relatively little impact on the business. A professional and good working relationship is still necessary, but not to the depth required for more significant contracts.

Suppliers providing a significant number of services where the change of supplier is more disruptive, or Bottleneck services, where there is little choice, will require the more involved approach of supplier management. Here the buying and operational teams may have supplier action plans, and will hold regular meetings with the supplier to develop performance including improving service or delivering cost savings.

State of Flux, a UK based procurement consultancy, recommends supplier relationship management for the most strategic suppliers used by an organization, and distinguishes this from other approaches in order 'to capture innovation, jointly develop new products and services, improve the efficiency of your operations and speed up your time to market requires a much broader and more relationship-based approach' (John, n. d.).

Characteristics of this approach are senior- and director-level engagement and time investment on both sides, a willingness from the customer to understand how they must change (rather than just how the supplier needs to change), and far broader discussions than performance management against contractual commitment allows. Again, it is worth re-iterating that this is an investment, and is only worthwhile where the potential benefits are significant and where contract duration supports such engagement.

Table 9.1 shows the features of contract management versus SRM.

Table 9.1   Contract management vs SRM

Contract management	SRM
Performance metrics	Relationship metrics
Contractual levers	Stakeholder engagement
Managing risk	Account management
Conflict	Relationship dynamics
Contingency planning	Supplier classification
Variation and change	Continuous improvement

SOURCE CIPS, n. d.b

Figure 9.1   The spectrum of supplier relationships

LOW	Quality of information exchange	HIGH
LOW	Trust	HIGH
LOW	Openness	HIGH
LOW	Commitment	HIGH
SHORT	Duration	LONG
INDIVIDUAL	Risk assessment and resilience	DONE TOGETHER
INDIVIDUAL	Risk management	INTEGRATED

COMPETITIVE ———————————————→ COLLABORATIVE

SOURCE CIPS, n. d.b

In practice, most organizations do not define their relationships neatly into the three performance management levels listed on page 235, but instead have a spectrum of different modes of engagement across the goods and services they buy or supply. Many, however, never actively review this and therefore invest too much time with non-strategic partners and fail to invest properly in relationships with the most potential. Without all participants understanding the engagement strategy, it is unlikely that such potential will be realized.

Figure 9.1 shows this spectrum well. To achieve fruitful SRM, all the attributes on the right side of this diagram need to be in place.

How to achieve success

As stated above, all contracts for services require some form of good professional working relationship. Without this, suppliers will find contracts less attractive, and may not compete for the business. Not surprisingly, the enablers and skills required for supplier relationship management are far greater than for contract management.

Enabler 1 – be the customer/supplier of choice

There is no point trying to develop a deep collaborative relationship if the basics are not in place. Buying organizations should:

- pay on time;
- specify requirements clearly;

- have fair contracts;
- acknowledge and react to changes to volume/specification;
- value good service;
- have staff who behave professionally at all levels;
- have clear decision-making processes;
- follow up on actions and commitments.

If there are issues which prevent these being delivered (such as a dramatic fall in volumes), this should be addressed in the SRM programme rather than being ignored.

Enabler 2 – alignment of purpose

For lower-level engagement and relationships, alignment on the long-term direction of the shipper is less important: an LSP may be happy enough to carry out a significant number of transport routes on a backhaul or tactical basis, even if this is not its long-term strategy.

True SRM will not get off the ground unless both parties are aligned to the strategic purpose of the relationship. If a shipper tries to engage deeply with an LSP that does not see this service as core to its business long-term, or considers the customer unattractive, success is likely to be elusive.

Enabler 3 – have a contract in place

Some organizations celebrate the fact that they do not have a written contract with key suppliers or customers. They are ignoring the fact that a contract is in place, be it verbal or assumed, but they do not know what it entails!

Better to have the expected service and contractual terms agreed and defined in a written contract, as a foundation for further strengthening the relationship and opportunities. If neither side refers to the contract regularly, this will demonstrate that the relationship is working.

Enabler 4 – contract length

Contract length will very much depend on the complexity of the work and the investment required. Contracts can range from months to five years, for example. To achieve value from strategic warehousing and fulfilment contracts and deeper engagement from an LSP, a significantly longer contract length will be necessary to allow investment in SRM, as well as assets such as automation and sophisticated technology.

In his interview later in this chapter, David Lowther talks about an initial fixed period contract followed by a rolling annual contract. This takes the focus away from contract renewal dates.

Enabler 5 – attitude

To build a long-term, mutually beneficial relationship, the attitude of personnel on both sides needs to be right: openness, honesty, mutual respect and reliability are key.

Enabler 6 – skills

Having the right attitude can be enough for contract management, but to really deliver SRM both supplier and customer must have personnel with the right skills. These can be divided into:

- personal skills: communication and negotiation;
- intellectual skills: reason, perspective and intellect;
- technical skills: sector experience, process understanding, technological, IT and legal.

The 21st-century fulfilment centre is often a blend of automated and semi-automated equipment, sophisticated IT and highly skilled human resources. Increasingly robotics and other technology are transforming operations; such facilities are closer to a modern factory rather than a traditional warehouse.

The skills needed to manage and develop such operations and contribute to the optimization of shippers' supply chains requires a high-level understanding of technology and process optimization by senior managers at the LSP. This may reside in the design and business development departments at the LSP, rather than at contract level. If this capability is not accessible at the contract level, it will limit the ability of the LSP to deliver improvements and to achieve a long-term role in the development of a customer's strategy and performance roadmap.

Interview with Dave Lowther, former Supply Chain, Customer Services and IT Director, Kingfisher Group

Note these views are those of Mr Lowther, and may not represent those of the Kingfisher Group of Companies.

During his working career, Dave Lowther has worked for a number of LSPs and supply chain operations. He has years of experience in outsourced logistics. Many of the contracts he was involved in included dedicated freight transport and warehouse management.

He emphasizes the key need to build relationships between parties, providing a number of recommendations to ensure a successful outsourcing relationship:

1 Concentrate on your own core competencies.

2 Concentrate on customer service, not price – 'do it better, not cheaper'.

3 Good service is always more cost-effective in the long run.

4 Pay a fair rate for good service – ensure the service level is in the upper quartile for the industry, and get the LSPs working together.

5 Do not outsource a problem – deal with it first internally.

6 Never outsource on price.

7 Don't continually re-tender the contract – provide the LSP with some long-term certainty if performing well.

8 An initial three-year or five-year contract followed by a rolling annual contract if the LSP is performing well is preferable.

9 In review meetings, always look forwards, not backwards.

10 Employ only the best people on both sides – get involved in the recruitment process.

11 Introduce achievable incentive schemes and encourage innovation.

12 Don't try to micromanage the contract – for example, never insist on having a senior member of staff working alongside the LSP.

13 Be honest – share data; share everything.

14 Continually talk through and agree the service proposition improvements.

15 Understand that any material change always brings risk.

According to Dave, good reasons for outsourcing include:

- LSPs tend to have greater expertise;
- they tend to have greater access to back up if anything goes wrong;
- they are continually developing systems, people and processes in logistics.

In terms of dedicated contracts, his advice to shippers is to own/lease the assets (IT, vehicles and warehouses), and operate an open-book contract and agree a management fee. This should preferably be an actual figure, not a percentage, plus an incentive/penalty package.

Examples

In a courier contract, Dave agreed a three-year deal with a single parcel carrier. (This ultimately became a 10-year deal, which is still ongoing.) An on-time percentage rate was agreed for next-day delivery, which was challenging, but fair. The earnings potential was also increased by up to 15 per cent if the targets were exceeded continually.

The courier company was also encouraged to be proactive – for example, the introduction of self-billing reduced the headcount by 16 people (a simple saving based on trust). Additionally, during periods of bad weather, the targets were suspended – another example of understanding the value and realities of the relationship.

Another example of LSPs being proactive saw vehicles belonging to a retailer being used for other retailers during counter-seasonal periods – a simple win–win situation.

These simple things are achievable if people can create relationships and are prepared to do something different. An LSP should always be better at the basics, but you do need to give them some freedom to be creative. Several small wins that improve the cost profile whilst improving service is what you are after.

It is, however, a long journey, and a sport for the truly patient.

SRM through the outsourcing lifecycle

Chapter 5 discussed the logistics outsourcing lifecycle, and the considerations at each stage. Relationship management should be part of the overall review and action plan that forms this lifecycle.

Step 1 – strategic review

Many companies start an outsourcing process or renew a contract without considering the relationship with their existing staff or with their current or potential LSP(s) and how they wish to develop these relationships. For strategic services, a consideration and recognition of the need for SRM should be part of the process at this stage, as it will be critical to both the process and partner selection.

Step 2 – planning

The process for selecting a strategic LSP where SRM is fundamental will be much longer than for other contracts. Where relationships are key, more time must be allowed for site visits and meetings with key personnel throughout the process.

Step 3 – market research

Market research will not only identify potential companies, but also the value that may be developed through the life of a contract or is already being developed by competitors and their LSPs. This in turn will influence the selection criteria for the service. Market research also provides a checkpoint for LSP credibility and honesty.

Step 4 – specifying requirements

For all contracts, specifying the service required and the volume of business and attributes of the service is key. For contracts with significant potential to transform the business, this specification needs to be broader and allow for the development of greater value through the life of the contract.

The expectations for innovation, and for the skill set of the LSP's personnel, should be explicit in the specification.

Step 5 – the tender process

As discussed in Chapter 5 and earlier in this chapter, when buying complex and strategic services, enough time is needed in the tender process to explore solutions, and to get to know the LSP's team and assess their capability. The process must match the type of service being bought, and be value-based rather than price-based.

Step 6 – evaluation, negotiation and selection

Where relationship management is key, it is vital that the purchasing organization satisfies itself that the long-term LSP team on the contract has the skills and attributes to support SRM. Sometimes, great rapport is built up with the sales and business development team who then withdraw once the contract starts.

It may be appropriate to have some safeguards to give the customer a role in the selection process, or in producing criteria for key roles on the LSP's team where these are critical to business success.

In the negotiation and contract stages of the process, it is important to remember that behaviour now will set the scene for years to come. An adversarial or short-term approach now will be remembered and impact on attitudes in the future.

Step 7 – contract

The contract needs to set out expectations for the value development of the service, as well as the roles and governance process for the contract. Where significant innovation or LSP provision of embedded personnel or project resource is required, this needs to be described and the reward for this (versus outputs or cost contribution) defined. Again, the spirit and terms of the contract negotiations will determine the relationship in the future.

Step 8 – managing performance

This is the critical, ongoing step for all forms of relationship and performance management. Regular contact at operational level and also senior level for SRM is critical. There must be a focus on joint objectives and joint achievements against these objectives. Clear and regularly reviewed agreements on how value progression is measured must be a function at this stage of the cycle.

Step 9 – renewal or exit

Few strategic relationships last forever and there will come a time when either the contract ends, is renewed in a similar form, or is renewed but with less strategic focus. Exiting should be done in the same spirit as the original negotiations and management phases, with professionalism and integrity on both sides.

Those contracts with extensive SRM will take longer to exit, and the risk of failure is greater, but the foundation of good relationships can be used to manage this change.

Both the KFC example in Chapter 8 and the Tate and Lyle example in Chapter 5 show the importance of maintaining relationships with previous suppliers and unsuccessful tenderers.

How to balance relationship management and competition

For those contracts where SRM is employed effectively, does this reduce the need for re-tendering the business periodically?

Firstly, as discussed elsewhere in this chapter, SRM is an investment, and time is needed to achieve a return on that investment. Full SRM will be employed on strategically important and longer-term contracts, where there is likely to be enough value opportunity and time for implementation to justify the investment on both sides.

The purpose of SRM is to achieve a higher level of performance in the long term, and there should be an assessment of the success of this approach both during the lifetime of the contract and before a decision to conduct a competitive tender is taken. There should be a clear rationale for going back to the market if value development is being achieved within the existing relationship.

However, the strength of the relationship and the personal relationships of the two teams should not remove the need for an unclouded assessment of the success of the contract and the alternatives that might be on offer. This is where the procurement department and Chief Procurement Officer can provide some independence and challenge to the logistics and supply chain departments. LSPs can change their focus, lose a technical edge or become less relevant to a business.

As a company can only support a relatively small number of strategic relationships, it is important for both sides that these are assessed and refreshed. Market research by the procurement department can identify how the market has developed since the last tender and where, if anywhere, the value challenges lie. Knowing that your customer has assessed the market and remains convinced that you remain the best value LSP, can strengthen a relationship rather than weaken it, if done honestly and professionally.

If the strategic importance of the contract to both sides remains and demonstrable value is being delivered, blanket procurement rules on re-tendering should be treated with caution. There may not be an alternative LSP capable of delivering the same value, and putting your existing LSP through an inappropriate process may halt progress and damage the relationship. However, renewal should never be a roll-over of the same objectives and incentives: it is important that both sides take stock and set new targets and processes for the next phase of their engagement.

Moving beyond – embedding LSPs and Vested®

As discussed earlier in this chapter, the broader scope of full SRM programmes is that both sides need to have a deep understanding of each other's businesses to identify and deliver opportunities for improvement. For supplier personnel to be able to do this, one option is to have embedded personnel at the customer's premises, attending strategy meetings and being dedicated to the customer's projects.

Kane is Able Inc, an LSP in the US, advocate such an approach and suggest that the cost of this resource should be paid for by the LSP, but that the rewards from the value opportunities achieved should be shared such that there is a return for the LSP on this investment.

Kane is Able describe SRM and embedding LSPs as the relationship management strand of Vested® Outsourcing; this is described next. Certainly, this kind of openness, joint working and shared risks and benefits are key to making Vested® a reality.

Vested® Outsourcing – an alternative approach

Used with permission. Vested®. www.vestedway.com. Vested® Outsourcing, Inc

Over the course of a four-year study, funded by the United States Air Force and led by Kate Vitasek, the University of Tennessee team examined companies with the very best outsourcing relationships and agreements, and identified '10 inherent ailments in today's flawed and old-school outsourcing agreements.' They looked at the challenge of aligning objectives in outsourcing relationships, and developed a new approach that they termed Vested®.

Vested® is a methodology that encourages companies and service providers to work collaboratively and become 'vested' in one another's success. It is applicable to a wide variety of outsourced relationships, including those in the field of logistics.

The aim of Vested® Outsourcing is to use collaborative economics or game theory, as well as incentive, to create a methodology for outsourcing that really binds the economics in that collaborative relationship to change the game. Kate Vitasek, who led the research, describes this as a 'what's in it for we?' relationship. Many negotiations come from a 'what's in it for me' perspective (although companies such as Mars Inc have long recognized that long-term relationships need to have a mutual benefit, and this is enshrined in one of Mars' Five Principles, 'Mutuality').

Vested® Outsourcing requires companies to sit on the same side of the table with their partners and work towards common goals.

The five rules of Vested® Outsourcing

One of the key premises of Vested® is its focus on buying results, as opposed to tasks or activities. A conventional outsourcing relationship, as described in Chapter 6, is activity- or transaction-based. Companies pay every time a product is touched, every time a pallet is stored and every time a call is answered. In other words, every transaction generates a fee from the outsourcing provider. As companies become more efficient and begin to eliminate transactions, they are literally creating a perverse incentive that penalizes outsource providers by reducing the number of transaction-based fees.

The idea behind Vested® is to change the way the shipper pays for services; instead of paying for activities, they pay for results.

The University of Tennessee research project identified five rules that should be applied any time you're structuring an outsourcing deal:

Rule 1: Replace the transaction-based business model with an outcome-based business model. The idea is to pay for the desired outcomes, not the individual activities. Begin by looking at the big picture. Ask yourself what you are trying to achieve. Are you trying to lower supply chain costs as a percentage of sales, cut overall transportation costs, or reduce inventory? Whatever your goals are, contract for the work based on outcomes. As David Lowther said earlier in this chapter – think about the service, not the cost.

Rule 2: Focus on the 'what', not the 'how'. Many conventional outsourcing agreements begin with a very long statement of work, dictating what the service provider will do. Vested® Outsourcing 'flips the concept on its head,' and asks the question, why would you outsource to experts and then tell them how to perform the work? Remember to allow your service providers to be innovative in defining how service is delivered.

Rule 3: Clearly define measurable, desired outcomes. Because payments will be released based on outcomes, it is essential to define what you're trying to achieve and how those achievements, or outcomes, will be measured.

Rule 4: Develop a pricing model with incentives that are optimized for service trade-offs. The idea is to create positive incentives that drive your outsource providers to solve a defined and measurable set of problems.

Rule 5: Develop a governance structure that focuses on insight, not oversight. Many companies have layers of people who are micromanaging their service providers. Move away from overseeing or micromanaging service providers, and move towards a more positive environment where you have insight that is used in a positive way to achieve your desired outcome.

The investment in senior management engagement to design a Vested® deal means that it is most suited to Strategic or perhaps Bottleneck relationships. Awareness of the concept of Vested® Outsourcing, however, is useful in setting a more positive relationship across a range of outsourced services.

CASE STUDY   Vested® case study – Intel and DHL Supply Chain

In 2012, Intel exited from its desktop motherboard business to focus on artificial intelligence, cloud computing, and other transformative technologies. While a great strategy for Intel, the exit of the business would mean a more than 50 per cent reduction in customer spend for DHL Supply Chain (DHLSC), Intel's supplier of choice for their reverse logistics operations in Europe, Middle East, and Africa. The decline in demand posed a severe challenge to the viability and sustainability of its reverse logistics operations managed out of the Netherlands.

John Hayes and Ruud de Groot were the leaders within Intel and DHLSC, respectively, who were tasked to come up with a new solution. Both wished to take their already good relationship to a higher level that would deliver innovation and transformative results to tackle the tough challenges in front of them. To accomplish this, they needed to do things differently.

Hayes and de Groot looked to a pilot project in Costa Rica that had transformative results using the University of Tennessee's sourcing business model, Vested®.

Global Reverse Logistics (GRL) is a department within Intel (Ireland), whose role is to provide warranty services to Intel's direct and indirect customers within Europe, the Middle East and Africa. The returned products are recovered where possible, and failure data provided to Intel to support product improvements.

GRL utilizes DHLSC as its service provider, to manage an integrated reverse logistics network comprising a central depot, four satellite depots, technical screening and multiple freight networks supporting inbound/outbound freight to customer, repair, and international replenishment shipments to Asia and the United States. GRL's inventory is characterized by a high number of stocking units, a diverse product range and a mix of fast-moving and slow-moving goods.

As a result of the change in the business, DHLSC developed a proposal outlining a tiered approach to invoicing – an increased price per unit if demand was reduced and a decreased price per unit if demand increased. Increasing demand would mean Intel benefiting from a lower cost per unit, yet in case of decreasing demand DHLSC would be protected against erosion of their fixed cost. The proposal was rejected by Intel for several reasons:

- The pricing model would be inconsistent from month to month or year to year, because Intel cannot control returns by the customer, making financial management more difficult.

- As returns decline, Intel wanted to see a proportionate reduction in costs.

- The tiered approach was complex to implement due to a diverse service mix.

Both companies then decided after long deliberation to go down the route of a Vested® approach.

The parties started by developing a baseline for their existing relationship and business. For Intel and DHLSC, baselining allowed a holistic view of the business in an objective manner. This also allowed the parties to openly discuss the presence and magnitude of the '10 ailments of outsourcing.' In summary, the workshops helped to:

- determine the main service, financial and operational drivers;

- understand the current level of performance;

- understand who the stakeholders are and their expectations;

- understand the partners' relationship within the context of the 10 ailments of outsourcing;

- determine the strong/weak points of the relationship;

- confirm the level of relationship maturity.

Table 9.2 Intel's and DHLSC's primary concerns

Intel's primary concerns	DHLSC primary concerns
1. Ensure no impacts to service delivery as a result of the transition from desktop board business.	5. Protect DHLSC's bottom line as Intel spend decreases.
2. Ensure spend tracks and preferably undercuts the decline in volume – eg if volume declines 20 per cent, then spend should decline 20 per cent.	6. Ensure the business is sustainable over time and has Intel's commitment.
3. Implement changes to processes to better meet the new business environment.	7. Revise the pricing model to meet local requirements.
4. Ensure there is a holistic view of the supply chain.	

SOURCE Vitasek *et al*, 2018

The parties ultimately agreed on five mutually Desired Outcomes as part of the initial workshop. These are listed in Table 9.3.

Results

- Intel's primary concern of zero impact on customers has been met with a 100 per cent satisfaction score, with 100 per cent of changes implemented on time.

- The Customer Excellence Score went from 93 per cent to 99 per cent, with on-time delivery at 99 per cent.

- The supplier performance score went from 87 per cent to 98 per cent.

- Even though the DHL supply chain experienced a 45 per cent cut in revenue associated from the drop in volume, the contract produced savings of $806,000 over a four-year period.

- Innovation increased and innovative solutions flowed consistently, resulting in the parties moving toward more transformational objectives.

Indeed, what began as an experimental pilot has evolved into best practice.

According to Dale Dean from Intel: 'The mechanics of change are not hard; they just take an open honest approach to working together. What is hard is changing the culture. If you put a supplier in a box for a lot of years

Table 9.3   Intel's and DHLSC's Desired Outcomes and incentives

Desired outcome	Incentive
A quality management structure to ensure outcomes are delivered to SLAs	Automatic renewal of contract once goals are met.
Delivery of operational excellence across the supply chain.	Automatic renewal of contract once goals are met.
Delivery of supply chain cost savings.	Gainsharing on decreases to planned spend, excluding demand-driven. Margin matching to support sustainability. Increased revenue from value-add activities.
Overall quality supplier performance.	Automatic renewal of contract once goals are met.
Change management – specific programme implementation within agreed timeframe and cost targets.	Automatic renewal of contract once goals are met.

SOURCE Vitasek *et al*, 2018

and tell them what to do, cost becomes the main driver. There is no value in it for them to do anything else. Vested® shares risk and reward and cultivates new ideas.'

Both companies found the non-adversarial nature of Vested® refreshing, helping them move away from the zero-sum nature of conventional buyer-supplier relationships. Hayes reflects, 'The old contract promoted an us vs them culture that could have led to perverse incentives and opportunism. With Vested®, our interests are truly aligned through mutually defined Desired Outcomes and economics that reward DHLSC for achieving the Desired Outcomes. Vested® helped us move from trying to shift risk to one where we win together. A win for DHLSC is a win for Intel.'

Andrew Allan, General Manager for DHLSC at the time, said 'Vested® is so collaborative. The master/slave relationship is gone. You feel like an equal partner.'

Courtesy of Kate Vitasek, Vested®

Conclusion

Relationship management is a critical component of all logistics outsourcing contracts. Even short-duration, low-risk contracts need good working relationships between the parties, with open, honest, professional behaviour on all sides. For strategic outsourcing, companies should proactively review their LSP relationship management, in addition to the performance management targets discussed in Chapter 7.

Full SRM requires investment in time and resource on both sides, and there needs to be an evaluation of the value opportunity before this is undertaken: starting a programme without the commitment of senior management will be doomed to failure. As discussed so often in this book, reviewing, prioritizing and planning are key to success.

IT in logistics outsourcing

10

BY LYNN PARNELL OF LOGISTICS PARTNERS CONSULTANCY LTD

Introduction

Traditionally, outsourcing tender processes for logistics services have focused on cost and physical service levels, with IT playing a small part in the decision-making process. However, outsourcing is not just about physical warehouses and trucks. IT and the related issues of data and data security are vital factors in today's world.

IT can deliver business-critical benefits in reducing lead times, improving operational efficiency, productivity and accuracy. Data generated from software running logistics services, reported properly, can support decision making and transform visibility. Therefore, all logistics outsourcing processes should carefully consider and plan for IT and technology in the decision-making process.

This chapter will discuss topics of importance both to the customer (the manufacturer, retailer or shipper) and the logistics service provider (LSP) with regard to IT, including which company should provide the IT solutions, the challenges to achieving effective IT solutions in an outsourced environment, and considerations for IT during the outsourcing lifecycle. IT in this context includes software such as warehouse management systems (WMSs), enterprise resource planning systems (ERPs), telematics and transport management systems, and technology such as radio frequency (RF) terminals, voice and vision picking, automation and electronic proof of delivery systems.

The importance of IT in outsourcing

The choice of technology deployed can have a significant effect on the efficiency, service levels and cost of a logistics operation. Increasingly, end customer experience is based on IT as expectations for lead times, pick accuracy and order fulfilment visibility are driven by leading edge technology companies such as Amazon, ASOS and Uber. The experience supply chain managers and customers have as consumers themselves in the B2C market is also driving B2B expectations. These expectations cannot be met without effective IT, and the pace of change is increasing, as discussed in Chapter 11.

IT is used by leading LSPs and in-house logistics operations to drive productivity in areas such as automation, warehouse picking, vehicle loading, vehicle routing and scheduling, load allocation and labour management. Software solutions can drive process conformation to raise service levels or to enforce compliance to safety or legal requirements. Real-time feedback and alerting can be built into workflow management. Data generated from logistics IT enables timely performance management, long-term business planning and reporting to authorities and customers.

WMSs and delivery management software ensures that the correct goods are despatched on time, to store or to the end customer and are critical to maintaining and enhancing a company's reputation. The IT solution bought as part of an outsourced logistics service can provide a direct link with end customers and consumers, giving real-time stock status and delivery tracking capability. It needs to be at the heart of any logistics outsourcing process.

There have been some very high-profile cases where IT has caused significant issues in an outsourced contract – the most recent UK example being when KFC changed to a new logistics provider with a new warehouse and operating new software (see Chapter 8). With newspaper stories of fresh food rotting on lorries and restaurants closing due to the lack of their main ingredient, the important role of software within the supply chain came to the fore.

If software doesn't work as intended, it can disrupt deliveries to the end customer, result in stock not being ordered and therefore not available for end customers, or cause issues with inbound deliveries resulting in trucks queuing on the highway. All of these will not only affect a company financially, but can also bring huge reputational damage.

When a company decides to outsource their logistics operations, there are some critical decisions to be made, including:

- which IT solutions are required;
- who will select, own and operate these solutions;
- whether the LSPs under consideration have the skills and resources to manage the IT aspect of the services;
- how the risks associated with systems implementations can be managed to ensure the benefits of outsourcing are realized.

Which IT solutions need to be considered?

The part of the supply chain being outsourced will dictate the type of software or technology needed to be considered as part of the tender process. These are not just the systems that will be operated by the outsourced provider, but also systems that will need to interface with those systems – a crucial area. These systems and technology include:

- WMSs, including labour management;
- ERP systems;
- Warehouse Control Systems (WCSs), automation and robotics;
- delivery and yard management solutions;
- Transport Management Solutions (TMSs) including vehicle and route optimization;
- vehicle telematics;
- digital tachograph management solutions;
- forecasting and procurement solutions;
- last-mile delivery and electronic Proof of Delivery (ePOD);
- job management solutions;
- executive reporting.

This list suggests that these systems and technologies are separate solutions; however, one of the key marketplace trends is for software providers to increase the scope of their solutions. Thus, ePOD solutions are likely to have job allocation and telematics capability; WMS solutions may include labour and yard management functionality.

Where discrete solutions are used, interfacing between them may be required. Even when there is a single solution at the LSP, interfacing with customer systems needs to be considered.

IT is increasingly an area of differentiation between LSPs. The 2019 Third-Party Logistics Study (Langley *et al*, 2019) included the following list of IT capabilities that LSPs should have, as reported by shippers and third-party logistics providers (3PLs)/LSPs:

Table 10.1 IT-based capabilities needed from 3PLs

IT-based capabilities	% reported by shippers	% reported by providers
Transport management (planning)	71%	79%
Warehouse/distribution centre management	67%	66%
Visibility (order, shipment, inventory, etc)	63%	75%
EDI data exchange – orders, advanced shipment notices, updates, invoicing	54%	73%
Transport management (scheduling)	54%	75%
Transportation sourcing	46%	56%
Global trade management tools (eg customs processing and document management)	42%	37%
Network modelling and optimization	39%	58%
Bar coding	39%	50%
Supply chain planning	39%	56%
Web portals for booking, order tracking, inventory management and billing	33%	56%
Customer order management	32%	50%
Cloud-based systems	30%	47%
Customer relationship management	29%	62%
Advanced analytics and data mining tools	27%	47%
Radio-frequency identification (RFID)	24%	23%
Distributed order management	23%	32%
Yard management	20%	26%
Blockchain	8%	15%

SOURCE Langley *et al*, 2019

Who should own the IT for an outsourced contract?

Once a company has identified what IT needs to be considered, then the next decision is whether the IT required for the contract should be provided by the LSP or by the customer. The answer will depend on the type of services to be outsourced and the length of contract.

Table 10.2   Who should provide the software?

Benefits of the LSP providing the IT solution	Benefits of the customer providing the IT solution
• The LSPs often already use standard software and technology that provides a high level of functionality.	• It allows the customer to contract parts of their supply chain to more than one LSP, but retain consistent systems across their network.
• The LSP takes full ownership of the IT, and is therefore able to innovate during the contract without involving the customer's IT team.	• The customer owns and has easy access to all the data collected by the operation.
• LSPs select their IT based on logistics functionality, whereas customers are often using software designed for purposes other than to control logistics – eg enterprise resource planning solutions such as SAP, Oracle and Microsoft Dynamics.	• There are fewer IT issues with interfacing data between companies and systems. • It allows continuity of systems at the end of the contract, reducing risk to the business during a transfer.
• It enables the LSP to operate facilities shared between several customers, thereby reducing costs to each customer.	• The customer will have contracts with all suppliers or end customers that need to interface with these solutions, and therefore will have greater ability to ensure integration takes place.
• The LSP may have less familiarity with a customer's IT, so may not be able to optimize the use of the system.	• The customer has full control of the security of data.
• The customer will not have to employ expensive IT management and development teams.	

Some complex outsourced logistics services may cover several different systems, some of which are provided by the customer and some by the LSP. Clarity on each of these is required. For all decisions on the ownership of systems, consideration should be given to the long-term development of the solution as well as the immediate requirements and the resources that will be needed for this.

If the customer owns the system, they need to ensure the LSP has appropriate training and an effective channel for future developments.

IT challenges in an outsourced environment

There are many challenges to getting the most appropriate IT when logistics services are outsourced. Common pitfalls include the following.

Focusing on cost rather than value

IT and innovation in IT can be expensive, but can bring great benefits in terms of service and efficiency. Customers do not always understand the benefits of specialist logistics software and technology such as warehouse management and labour systems, transport management systems, or voice and scanning technology.

LSPs may also be reluctant to propose these technology solutions because of the perceived development and hardware costs, in what is an overly cost-driven and sometimes short-term process. Any cost-benefit analysis of an outsourcing choice must include IT costs and benefits.

Lack of customer understanding of their IT requirements

If customers skimp on market research, fail to review their existing processes and systems and overlook future requirements, they will embark on the tender process without a proper understanding or definition of their software and technology needs. LSPs cannot propose innovative solutions during the tender if customer requirements are not clear.

Lack of involvement by customer IT teams

Many procurement and logistics teams embark on the outsourcing process without engaging sufficiently with their internal IT teams. This can mean vital elements of data security, interfacing and other IT aspects are missing from or inaccurate within the specification of requirements. It also means that timescales may be set unrealistically, and bidders are not properly evaluated. Good communication between the IT and operational teams on both sides is vital.

Lack of detail from the LSP

Unless specifically requested to do so through the RFP process, LSPs may not always include appropriate detail on the IT they will use to perform the contract. This may be because the tender timescale does not give the LSPs adequate time to get a full proposal from their IT teams, the LSP IT team is overstretched, or the LSP is reducing their risk (or cost of tendering) by not specifying their solution in detail.

No environment in which to discuss IT options

Although many service specifications neglect IT and system requirements, it is difficult to strike the balance between telling the LSP the service the company requires and ensuring that innovation within the contract proposal is not stifled.

In addition, a structured procurement process with several potential providers can preclude an individual LSP from having a detailed discussion with the customer about their requirements, and then having the opportunity to provide alternative solutions to meeting those requirements.

Interfaces

Interfaces between ERP systems and specialist logistics systems can be complex, and time needs to be allowed to ensure these are developed correctly. Interfaces often require resource from software providers and/or customer IT teams as well as the LSP. This may be an issue when it comes to implementation timescales and cost. This topic is discussed in more detail next.

Three key IT areas to consider

The importance of interfaces

In a modern supply chain, it is rare that data is created, used and reviewed within a single system. When looking at the systems that need to be considered in an outsourcing contract, companies cannot just focus on the systems that will be used to operate the contract being outsourced: data from those systems will also be required by various interested parties throughout the supply chain.

Examples of this include up-to-date stock balances in a WMS system being required in the customer's order processing system, and ePOD data from the transport LSP being required in customer service departments and accounts.

Integration can be a costly and time-intensive part of a project. All interfaces need to be designed, developed and tested. As integration requires the participation and co-operation of companies not directly involved in the outsourcing agreement (for example, software providers for multiple solutions), this can incur considerable costs for the LSP and their customers. On the customer's side, there may also be challenges accessing internal IT resource to agree the changes and manage or implement the interface.

The cost and time of integration can be reduced if the solutions bring integrated standard APIs (Application Programming Interfaces). This will mean there is a defined communication protocol and data structure for the interfaces into each solution, but these protocols and structure will not necessarily match across the solutions. Therefore, some integration work will still be required.

These challenges need to be recognized early in the procurement process: contracts may need to be awarded earlier to allow for development and testing, and internal and external resource identified and secured. Integration is also rarely static: companies in an end-to-end supply chain will be upgrading or changing systems or requiring enhancements to their data exchange throughout the life of a contract.

For an outsourced logistics contract that requires significant interfacing, such as warehousing or fulfilment contracts, it is highly recommended that the initial cost and time for developing an integration layer, or using a middleware solution, is managed, owned and paid for by the customer. This may be a service offering from the current ERP provider, or a company may develop an in-house system or use a specialized integration solution.

The use of such a layer means that bespoke interfaces are not required within the disparate solutions used throughout the supply chain. If a solution is changed, then only the interfaces from and to the changed solution need to be developed.

Data security

Within logistics, companies are constantly using and transferring data; data that is likely to be either personal data or company confidential data. Whichever it is, it is important that all data, whether held by the customer or the LSP is held securely and complies with all legislation.

In May 2018, the EU General Data Protection Regulation (GDPR) came into effect. In the UK this was also enshrined into UK law under the UK Data Protection Act (DPA 2018); this means that the legislation will remain post-Brexit. This law relates to all data that can personally identify an individual. Within the B2C logistics sector, personal data such as email addresses, postal addresses and telephone numbers are held throughout the supply chain.

If the data is collected by the customer, for example via an e-commerce website, then the customer has the responsibility to ensure that all data is held within the requirements of the law, and therefore the customer is defined as the 'controller' of the data. If this data is passed to a third party, such as an LSP, then the customer must ensure contractually that the LSP will also be complying with the law.

LSPs are likely to be considered 'processors' within the legislation. Processors also have some direct legal obligations: not only does a company risk a fine of up to €20 million or 4 per cent of global turnover, whichever is the greatest, for breaching GDPR or DPA 2018, but there is also great reputational risk from any data breach. The EU, UK and US press report on data breaches regularly, particularly when affecting household brands.

As a minimum, any company outsourcing logistics should undertake the following regardless of who owns the IT systems:

- ensure that they understand what personal data they will pass to the LSP;
- check that they have explicit permission from any data subjects that data can be shared with a third party;
- ensure that they are aware of where their customers' data will be stored and how it will be processed;
- be clear if any personal data is being passed to other systems via APIs, and ensure those systems are compliant;
- ask for evidence that all LSP employees, with access to personal data, have received GDPR/DPA training;
- ensure that they are aware of how the LSP intends to protect any data passed to them from a data breach;
- create a procedure to be able to provide all information relating to a data subject and the ability to delete that data;
- ensure their contract with the LSP requires the LSP to be compliant with GDPR and DPA 2018;
- regularly audit the LSP to ensure they are compliant with the legislation.

Ownership of data

In outsourced logistics contracts, ownership of assets such as vehicles and warehouses are often very detailed. This is not always the case for IT hardware assets or software, and rarely is the data generated during the life of the contract mentioned. But this data is crucial for the following reasons:

- Detailed historical order, stock and delivery data will be vital for any future tender document to allow prospective suppliers to understand and cost the operation.

- Data will be vital for decision making, not only within the customer's logistics team but potentially across the wider business also.

- Direct access to data enables customers to monitor the efficiency of their LSPs and ensure they are reaching the service levels agreed in the contract.

- Data can assist customers to model the effects of changes to their physical logistics operation; the customer may want to do this without involving the LSP.

- Data allows for comparison or benchmarking between contracts.

- Data allows for estimation of the profile of another part of the logistics operation, potentially provided by a different LSP.

IT and the logistics outsourcing lifecycle

In Chapter 5, typical steps in the outsourcing lifecycle were explored, with recommendations and actions that need to be carried out at each stage. The IT aspects of any outsourcing relationship need to be carefully considered, and may present the area of highest risk to the success of the process and eventual solution.

This section will review the outsourcing process from the viewpoint of IT hardware and software, to give guidance on how supplier solutions can be evaluated and how risk can be managed.

Prior to the tender

For all services that require some form of IT, data collection and exchange, customers need to take the following steps before embarking on a tender process:

- Document what IT they and/or their current LSP are using, to provide the current services. Ideally such documentation should be kept up to date throughout, so that no additional work is required when the services are (re-) tendered. Often this is not the case so this needs to take place before a tender is created for these services. If this is not done at an early stage the customer cannot be sure exactly what systems need to be provided in the contract.

- Review how the processes and/or IT solution for the services might need to change by the start of, or over the lifetime of, the contract.

- Ensure that the LSP can respond with suitable solutions, and that the estimated costs are accurate. It is vital that this stage takes place during the tender process, rather than after the contract has been awarded. After the award, the incumbent, if they have lost the contract, is likely to have reduced goodwill and would be very wary of passing on any intellectual property (IP) to a rival company.

- Be clear on ownership of current systems and the data held within those systems.

Tender specification and requirements

To have a successful outcome, and to ensure the IT related parts of the bid and solution are accurate and realistic, customers should:

- Define what customer owned IT the LSP will be expected to operate or interface with.

- Define what systems or solutions the LSP will need to supply as part of the contract.

- Give clear guidelines on the level of data security required (this is covered in more detail later in this chapter).

- Define what transactional data will need to be transferred between the parties as part of the contract.

- Define what management data will need to be shared during the contract, including the mechanism and format for data sharing. This should include monthly report data.

- Describe the processes that are required for the operation of the service. These should be provided in the form of an operations manual and/or process flowcharts (see Appendix V for an example flowchart).

As part of the tender response, the LSPs should be required to:

- Give a clear description of what IT will be used to fulfil the contract requirements. This should include whether the IT is already operated by the LSP on another contract, and also whether this is a standard package or customized solution.

- Provide full disaster recovery plans and explain how these will be regularly tested.

- Provide a statement of ownership and IP rights for all software and technology to be supplied as part of the contract.

- Provide a detailed systems implementation plan to ensure a smooth handover. This should include requirements gathering, modifications, training, testing and documentation. These plans should include details of the access the new provider will need from any incumbent provider, and how they plan to be able to gain this access within the Transfer of Undertakings, Protection of Employment (TUPE) legislation or equivalent framework.

Supplier assessment and selection

During the LSP selection process, the customer needs to perform due diligence of the IT solution proposed by each LSP and discuss the timeframe for any developments and integration mechanisms. The due diligence should be carried out by an IT professional with an understanding of the services, and should include:

- visiting the LSP to see the software solution(s) operating in a similar environment or receiving a demonstration of the actual solutions proposed;

- visiting the team that will be developing and supporting the software; this may be a team from within the LSP or a team from the IT solution provider.

Chapter 5 covered general selection criteria for different types of logistics services. In Table 10.3, specific criteria for the IT aspects of any proposal are listed. Some of these criteria will be less relevant for certain services (such as a simple full truck load transport contract), but data ownership, data security, interfaces, IT capability and business continuity will still need to be covered. Most warehousing and fulfilment contracts will need to cover all these criteria if the LSP is going to provide the software solutions or technology that will control the operation.

Some of the most important criteria are discussed in more detail below.

Table 10.3   IT selection criteria

Area	Criteria to be evaluated
Foundation software questions	Is the software operational at other LSP sites? Are the sites comparable to the existing operation? Has the customer seen the software in operation? Is the software bespoke or an off-the-shelf package?
Bespoke software	If it is an in-house development by the LSP, what is the size and make-up of the development team? How often is the solution upgraded? Which operating system is it using?
Packaged software	Are other companies in the sector operating this package/solution? If it is a package solution, has it been customized? Will it require changes to the customer's current processes? How might this affect the operation? If it is a cloud solution, what is the length of change contract, and what notice period does the software supplier need to give the LSP to withdraw access? If it is a cloud solution, where is the solution hosted? Is there evidence of due diligence from the software house?
Integration	Can the software easily integrate with upstream suppliers and downstream customers? What integration methods are available? If the warehouse is automated, does the solution have a track record of integrating with this automation?

(continued)

Table 10.3 (Continued)

Area	Criteria to be evaluated
Configuration, customization and future development	Does the software require customization for the initial go-live to achieve basic Day One functionality? If so, how long is this process likely to take? Who pays for future upgrades or changes to functionality? Who will drive innovation in IT and technology? How configurable is the solution to allow for future business change? Will the customer benefit from functionality changes developed for others?
Reporting and access	How will the company access the system to see live operational data? What reporting solution is available to both the LSP and the customer? Will there be additional charges for configuring reports to the customer's requirements?
Training and support	Does the LSP have existing training modules for this software? Does the LSP provide first-line support? If so, during which hours of the day, and how large is this team? Is there a requirement for the customer to train super-users?
Disaster recovery and data security	What disaster recovery procedure is in place for the hardware and processes? Is an ESCROW* agreement in place for the solution? Is the solution, including hosting and processes for data management and control, compliant with relevant legislation?

* ESCROW – a bond, deed, or other document kept in the custody of a third party and taking effect only when a specified condition has been fulfilled.

When reviewing the tender responses and meeting with the potential suppliers, the procuring team need to consider the following points.

New or bespoke solutions

Is the LSP proposing new solutions they do not currently operate, but will be purchasing or building for the first time for this contract? This could have extended development or implementation times, and may not be achievable in the timeframe before the new contract will start.

Ensure proposed development times and resources, and the LSP's track history of managing such developments, are scrutinized as part of the tender process.

Data access and ownership

What access will the customer have to data produced by systems operated by the LSP during the contract? What format will this data be in? Logistics data is key to data-driven decision making, so customers need full and flexible access, not just reports emailed once a month. Has the LSP made it clear how this will be achieved, and whether the customer will retain the data in the systems at the end of the contract?

Testing

Does the response include a clear plan on how new systems or technology will be tested before go-live? Who will be carrying out this testing – is there a separation between development and testing resource? Note: in-situ testing can be challenging if moving between LSPs at the same location.

Staff training

Does the response address how staff will be trained on any new systems prior to the contract start date, and what access will the new provider need to existing staff if they are transferring?

This can be particularly difficult if moving between competitive LSPs and a TUPE, or equivalent transfer is likely: how can LSPs retain their IP while training staff still employed by a rival LSP? If training only begins for some staff after the transfer, how can service be protected?

Stakeholder impact and engagement

What is the impact of proposed systems on external parties, ie end customers and suppliers? How will training and communication be rolled out in an affordable way for these stakeholders?

Is the solution reliant on a change of behaviour from one or more groups, such as different pallet and carton labelling by suppliers, or interface changes by couriers? If new interfacing is required, does the response include a plan of engagement and reasonable timescales?

Physical infrastructure and hardware

Is the tender response clear on what physical infrastructure will be required in the warehouse or transport depot for any new IT to operate, such as wireless access points and cabling? Is the amount of infrastructure technology suitable for the operation?

Is there a plan for installation that considers operational disruption, or that another LSP may currently be operating from the facility? If solutions are changed, will hardware currently operating the service also need changing, or can existing hardware such as screens, PCs, RF units or tablets be used? What is the ownership of this hardware, and has a transfer cost been allowed for?

Contract provisions for IT

Issues of data ownership and data security need to be addressed in any IT contract; however, for bespoke contracts for warehousing or other complex services, there are specific ways in which IT needs to be addressed in the final contract.

Include a provision that the operation, and therefore IT, may need to change during the contract, with a clear process for how this will be handled and who will fund any IT amendments or replacements. The customer should retain ownership of any bespoke solutions they have funded fully during the contract, or on a pro-rata basis if appropriate.

Ensure any software that is not owned by the customer is covered by an ESCROW agreement. In practice, for IT this means the source code can be deposited by the LSP or software house with a recognized independent body. This is normally an independent company that specializes in verifying and storing software code. There is then a legal agreement that the source code can only be retrieved by the customer in the event of the LSP or software house ceasing to trade.

This means that if an operation is reliant on software, and the LSP ceases trading, the customer could then continue using the software and have the ability to maintain or improve the software solution if needed.

The responsibility for providing the IT related to the services needs to be clearly defined in the contract, together with how licensing fees and service costs are funded. Any software used for the services must be licensed. The service levels required for software availability (that is, required uptime for the software) should be defined, with provision for remedy if service levels are in breach of the defined level.

Ensure that all data generated during the contract is owned by the customer, who has the right to access and use that data at any time. All data must also be stored and handled within GDPR and DPA 2018 requirements (see earlier in this chapter) – although note that these are EU and UK regulations, and other legislation will apply in different countries.

IT should be fully included in the end-of-contract provision, including:

- clear terms on who owns the IP for any software development paid for directly by the customer on systems owned and operated by the LSP;
- what historical data from the contract should be provided to the customer, and in what format;
- ownership of any IT hardware and infrastructure paid by and for the customer during the contract;
- clear direction on what should happen to data on laptops and desktops used during the contract;
- if possible, provision for the customer or another LSP to be able to run the services using the IT solution after the end of the contract for a defined period of time.

IT and implementation

Once a company has made the decision to outsource all or part of the logistics operation and has selected an LSP, a smooth implementation is key to the success of the ongoing operation. General implementation planning is discussed in Chapter 5; this section will look at the specific challenges related to the IT part of an implementation and how these challenges may be mitigated and managed.

One of the most common issues faced in this area is a lack of time: there is usually a contract termination-driven deadline for any implementation, and this may not be enough for an IT project that needs to involve a number of stakeholders and integrate with several systems. Procurement and logistics teams do not always consult IT colleagues in the early stages of tender planning, and therefore underestimate the time needed. Unless software providers have standard APIs that are appropriate for the implementation, the planning needs to include software provider integration implementation and testing and often customer ERP integration specialists, both of which may be resource-constrained.

Unless processes have been very carefully defined in the specification, and a full gap analysis carried out on the suppliers' systems, there may be insufficient understanding on both sides of the degree of software customization that is required to deliver the desired and promised, operational benefits.

New systems require in-depth testing by the LSP and by the customer, together with extensive training of operational personnel. If personnel are part of a TUPE transfer, getting access to them before the transfer may be difficult, and the new LSP will want to protect their IP from the incumbent. If personnel are new to an operation, they may not have sufficient experience to spot faults in the process design or software.

Potential mitigation for implementation challenges

There are several best practice steps a customer and LSP can take to mitigate the delays and risks associated with the IT part of an implementation. Most of these recommendations are also worth considering for significant developments during the life of a contract, as well as during an initial implementation.

Table 10.4 Mitigation for implementation challenges related to IT

Area	Mitigation
Implementation project management	• Customers must ensure they have full visibility of the LSP's project plans, and are updated regularly on progress. • The customer and LSP should agree key milestone delivery dates within the implementation phase. • The customer should have a contingency plan that can be triggered if these key milestones are missed. • Both sides must ensure there is appropriate contingency in the project timescales. • The customer and LSP should both have strong executive sponsors for the project – these should have the appropriate authority to be able to 'make things happen' and secure sufficient resource for the project, and the ability and authority to make decisions when needed. • Where there are prolonged development programmes, consider splitting the project into phases.

(continued)

Table 10.4   (Continued)

Area	Mitigation

Contingency planning	• Create a clear plan of action if any unavoidable delays occur that mean the IT solution is not going to be ready and operational by contract start date. This could be:
	  ○ the ability to extend the contract with an existing LSP for a short period;
	  ○ the ability for a new LSP to take over the systems of the incumbent LSP;
	  ○ the ability to run the operation without IT – this is only possible in some limited circumstances, and usually means a large increase in the labour needed to operate the contract.
	• Have clear dates when any emergency plans of action need to be adopted to protect service levels.
	• Ensure that the executive sponsors are willing and able to make the decision to invoke any emergency plans of action agreed.

Resource	• Ensure the LSP is clear about the skills and experience of the resource required for the project, as well as whether they are dedicated to the project underway. • The customer should consider appointing an experienced IT consultant or internal resource, together with an experienced project manager to oversee the overall project. • Resource at software suppliers, where needed for the success of the project, must be clarified and committed.
Engagement	• Engage with any end customers and suppliers affected by the change throughout the project.

(continued)

Table 10.4 (Continued)

Area	Mitigation
Testing	• Where transfer is relevant, consider whether key members of the existing LSP team should transfer across early to assist with the procedures and testing of solutions. • If the final site cannot be accessed, is it possible to test the solution on another site? • If the operation is not 24/7, can testing take place in the live warehouse during out-of-hours periods? • The customer should ensure that User Acceptance Testing is properly resourced, to assure themselves that the specified processes can be supported by the software changes provided.
Training and learning curve provision	• Look to ensure that transferring staff are released from the existing contract for training days at another site. • Look to mitigate the risk of new LSP management and new systems on the same date by considering the following alternatives: ○ Can the new LSP take over existing systems temporarily to remove the risk? ○ Can new systems be implemented on the site while still operated by the exiting LSP? ○ Is it possible to parallel-run live operations on another dummy site? • If the contract involves a new warehouse or operation, can the contract be transferred in phases to give new staff, procedures and systems time to bed in with lower volumes? • Training/education sessions should take place for all end customers and suppliers.

Conclusion

IT is likely to be required for most, if not all, logistics outsourcing contracts. The first decision a customer should make is who should own the software or technology. If this is to be the LSP, then this should become a key part of the tender process. The tender process should include some important due diligence for any solutions proposed, as well as the LSP's ability to manage the implementation of any proposed solution.

Once an LSP is selected, IT should be provisioned fully in the contract, including what happens at the end of the contract. Timescales between tender award and go-live should consider any IT development, testing and training. If changing LSP, then access to the physical operation and staff, prior to go-live, will be key to a successful implementation.

Over the life of the contract, particularly for warehousing and fulfilment contracts of three to 10 years, there will be the need to continuously improve and develop the service. Many initiatives will involve changes to systems and technology, and buyers must satisfy themselves that the LSP will have the capability and resource to manage such developments once the implementation team has been disbanded.

IT can play a transformational role in an outsourced logistics operation. Both parties need to place it at the heart of their proposals, assessments and implementation planning to achieve its potential; failure to do so may result in lost opportunity and risks reputational damage and service interruption.

The future of logistics outsourcing

11

Introduction

This chapter will outline the main innovation trends and technology advancements in the logistics sector, and discuss how many of these new technologies are currently being embraced by LSPs or will be in the future. Videos demonstrate many of the innovations currently being introduced.

It will look at how innovation can provide shippers and LSPs with a competitive edge, and also examine the barriers to introducing these new concepts and why LSPs don't always leverage these innovations across their portfolio of customers.

It will also examine the developments in outsourcing processes such as the Uberization of freight transport, the use of crowdsourcing, online auctions as an alternative to the traditional request for proposals, and the potential for greater collaboration between competing parties.

Finally, this chapter will examine the current and future trends in logistics outsourcing in terms of market growth and satisfaction levels with LSPs, based on data from recent surveys.

Logistics innovations

According to Steve Jobs, 'Innovation distinguishes between a leader and a follower'.

The ability to innovate has always set companies apart from the competition. In today's fast-moving and growing economies, we are seeing a higher corporate priority for innovation in the supply chain. The growth in e-commerce is one of the main factors driving this.

In addition, long-standing challenges such as a shrinking labour market and the demands of rapidly changing retail business models such as omni-channel are driving companies who run logistics operations towards introducing more sophisticated technologies into their transport and warehouse operations.

With increasing environmental concern and government policies to reduce transport emissions, there is pressure on both shippers and LSPs in the logistics sector to find solutions to reduce carbon, improve efficiency and reduce congestion and pollutants in cities.

LSPs that want to achieve growth alongside profitability typically rely on taking market share away from competitors and strengthening existing relationships with customers. Innovation can have a substantial effect on both of those strategies. Without innovation, LSPs will see their service offerings become commodities, and will lose any hope of maintaining long-term, profitable relationships.

According to a recent eft report (2018), manufacturers and retailers are transforming their businesses with digitalization, which means the supply chain will be expected to run much faster, everything will become more intelligent and connected, more autonomous devices will be operationalized and much more data will be generated.

Startus Insights see digital transformation as a major component in driving the innovation process. They believe this will account for €1.42 trillion in investments to be allocated to logistics by 2025. They identify a number of innovation areas that will alter the logistics industry as we know it today (Startus Insights, n. d.).

These innovation areas are depicted in Figure 11.1, along with additional innovations which the authors believe will have a significant impact on logistics in the future.

Miller (2018) believes that companies will need to embrace innovation and encourage new ideas. He suggests that companies need to prepare for technologies in three 'waves':

1 exploit the opportunities provided by technologies that are past the tipping point, such as analytics, digital collaboration, the Internet of Things (IoT) and robotic process automation (RPA);

2 swiftly embrace emerging technologies such as blockchain, connected vehicles and drones, as these will disrupt the industry within the next five years;

3 prepare for technology disruption of deep learning, augmented or virtual reality and 3D printing.

Figure 11.1   Innovations in logistics

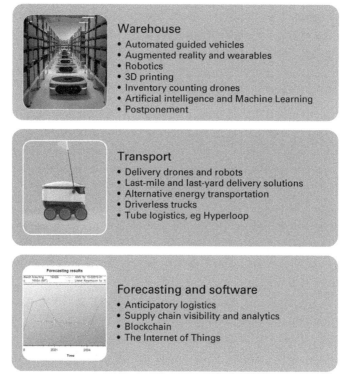

Warehouse
- Automated guided vehicles
- Augmented reality and wearables
- Robotics
- 3D printing
- Inventory counting drones
- Artificial intelligence and Machine Learning
- Postponement

Transport
- Delivery drones and robots
- Last-mile and last-yard delivery solutions
- Alternative energy transportation
- Driverless trucks
- Tube logistics, eg Hyperloop

Forecasting and software
- Anticipatory logistics
- Supply chain visibility and analytics
- Blockchain
- The Internet of Things

SOURCE adapted from Startus Insights, n. d.
Photographs courtesy of Eiratech, C4FF and Starship

The next section will examine each of the three areas of innovation, and provide examples of where LSPs and/or industry disruptors are introducing these technologies.

However, at this juncture we also need to point out that the logistics industry isn't quick to embrace technology.

A recent survey of 549 industry professionals by the Warehousing Education and Research Council found that 35 per cent of warehouses are not using a warehouse management system (WMS) as of 2018. A number of companies are still using Excel as their primary operating system (Kapadia, 2018).

Warehouse innovations

As discussed, the introduction of the following technologies coincides with an increasing shortage of warehouse labour in many markets. This is one of the main drivers of technology in the logistics industry, alongside more dynamic retailing models such as omni-channel and customer demands for quicker deliveries.

Within this section we have included videos of the innovations, so that the reader can see how these advances in technology work.

Automated guided vehicles (AGVs)

AGVs are increasingly being used in today's warehouses in a move from person-to-goods picking to goods-to-person picking strategies.

There are many different types of AGV operating within warehouses. The most newsworthy are those operated by Amazon in many of their fulfilment centres. These AGVs are utilized to bring the product to the person on moveable shelving. The technology was pioneered by Kiva Systems, which was then purchased by Amazon. Other automation companies have now introduced similar systems, including Grey Orange, Eiratech and Swisslog.

A video example of this technology can be found at http://bit.ly/2DZEE0B (DB Schenker, n. d.).

AGVs are also used for the horizontal movement of both cartons and pallets throughout the warehouse.

We are also seeing driverless forklift trucks replacing forklift operators, as these trucks have become more sophisticated and are able to transfer goods both horizontally and vertically. One of the main reasons for the change is that a fork-lift truck driver accounts for approximately 70 per cent of the operating cost of the truck. A video of this technology, introduced by Toyota, can be found at http://bit.ly/2YgQQSj (Toyota, n. d.).

DB Schenker has recently introduced the CarryPick solution by Swisslog into its e-commerce operation. This system can be seen in the Swisslog video previously mentioned. The company has also collaborated with IAM Robotics on the deployment of mobile manipulation solutions – the type of robots that can both pick up and transport goods.

John Stikes, DB Schenker's Director of Innovation and E-Commerce, says: 'Through automation, companies can achieve compelling economic advantages while alleviating their labour issues, and then redeploy that labour to more thought-involved processes and gain enhanced flexibility in their operations.'

Augmented reality and wearables

The use of vision technology in warehouses is growing apace. Companies are using vision technology, not only for outbound checking of orders but also for the pick operation itself. Here the operator wears a pair of glasses equipped with a camera, which guides the operator to each pick location, provides an image of the item to be picked, and once picked captures an image of the barcode in order to update the system in real-time.

> DHL is working with Ricoh on augmented reality and wearables, as can be seen in the video example at http://bit.ly/2Vc5ZT1 (DHL and Ricoh (n. d.). This first vision picking deployment at DHL completed with Ricoh demonstrates a 25 per cent performance increase when using smart glasses in logistics. Benefits come from the real-time connectivity of the devices to the WMS, the innovative user interface, and hands-free operation.

One point to note here is that recent studies are showing staff experiencing neck ache and headaches. However, this technology is very early in its development.

Robotics

Robotics and automation will become an integral part of future logistics operations, and in the last two years we have seen the first wave of collaborative robots entering the logistics workforce. More advances in technology and affordability will enable the eventual automation of many key logistics tasks, and create new roles in the logistics industry.

According to Deloitte's global outsourcing survey (2018), organizations are embracing disruptive solutions such as RPA. Rather than create bespoke software through an API (application programming interface), the operator is observed whilst undertaking the task and then those tasks are repeated, which is a much quicker process.

Robotics in the warehouse comes in many forms including robotic arms to transfer items from tote to tote – as can be seen in the following video: http://bit.ly/2LvSY7d (Knapp, n. d.) – and their use for de-layering cartons from pallets onto conveyor belts. A video showing the use of robots in a JD.com warehouse can be found at http://bit.ly/2H9ILsR (JD Logistics, n. d.).

Companies such as Boston Dynamics and Ocado, an online grocery retailer, are also working on humanoid robots which can pick up and transfer products. This technology is a few years away from perfection at the moment.

Ocado entered the outsourcing market through introducing innovative solutions into its own operations, and then extending the system out to other retailers including Morrisons, Groupe Casino and Kroger. Ocado's technology division comes up with the innovations and trials them at Ocado's own warehouses, and then deploys them to other clients.

Ocado Technology recently announced a major development in the pursuit of creating robotic grocery picking solutions for Ocado's highly-automated warehouses. The Ocado Technology robotics team has created a robotic arm capable of safely grasping a wide variety of products, including many from Ocado's current range which includes over 48,000 hypermarket items. This can be viewed at the following website: http://bit.ly/2HkIWTt (Tech Insider, n. d.).

They have also introduced a similar system to that operated by Asda Walmart in the UK (Autostore) and Yusen Logistics in Singapore – see http://bit.ly/2JH8cnl (Swisslog, n. d.).

3D printing

3D printing or additive manufacturing is a process of making three dimensional solid objects from a digital file.

The creation of a 3D printed object is achieved using additive processes. In an additive process, an object is created by laying down successive layers of material until the object is created. Each of these layers can be seen as a thinly sliced horizontal cross-section of the eventual object.

3D printing enables you to produce complex (functional) shapes using less material than traditional manufacturing methods.

A high take-up of 3D printing will drastically reduce stock levels in affected industries such as service logistics, automotive parts operations and many others. It will also reduce reliance on demand forecasting.

Warehouses will connect production with logistics, offering extended postponement services on behalf of customers. With 3D printing and other mobile automation technologies, logistics providers can take over final assembly and/or product customization. They can also use their global networks to customize stock and deliver closer to the point of demand.

> UPS has partnered with Fast Radius, which has located a 3D printing factory just minutes from the UPS global air hub in the United States, to speed shipping of 3D printed parts. UPS customers can have parts printed at the Fast Radius factory or at one of 60 UPS Stores equipped with 3D printers, and then shipped to them.
>
> The proximity to the air hub will allow orders to be manufactured up to the 1:00 a.m. pick-up time, and delivered anywhere in the US the next morning.

Inventory counting drones

The use of drones within the warehouse to count inventory is at its early stages. However, companies including Walmart in the US are currently trialling this technology.

Stock counting is very time-consuming and takes up significant labour and equipment time. These drones will be able to count full pallets within the warehouse and, if products are fitted with RFID tags, will also be able to capture quantities within a carton.

> GEODIS and DELTA DRONE have collaborated to produce an inventory counting drone. The system combines a ground-based robot equipped with a battery that provides the energy needed to navigate a warehouse, and a quadcopter drone equipped with four high-definition cameras. This set, equipped with indoor geolocation technology, operates autonomously during the hours the site is closed.
>
> From an IT point of view, the solution enables the counting and reporting of data in real time, the processing of data, and its restitution in the warehouse's information system. The tests conducted during this initial development phase show that the solution enables inventory to be managed reliably with rates close to 100 per cent.

Artificial intelligence (AI) and machine learning (ML)

Automation has always been paramount to achieving speed and efficiency, but in the future the industry will see AI add a new layer of sophistication to logistics processes.

This will lead to increasing connectivity within the warehouse environment. Integrated, cloud-based programmes will provide a real-time, bird's-eye view across all of the disparate elements of supply chain management.

These new technologies are becoming more mature, and as a result the LSPs are seeing potential in introducing them to improve efficiency and reduce costs over time – something their clients have been demanding for a long time. This video, a collaboration between SAP and Vuzix not only introduces augmented reality but also shows examples of AI, ML and the IoT: http://bit.ly/2vMcQrR (SAP, n. d.).

Postponement

Retailers and manufacturers are now providing an even greater variety of products, and these products are also being customized for clients. As a result, there is an increasing need for more value-adding services closer to the point of sale with a move away from finishing products at the manufacturing site. Products are only configured and finished at the final stage of the supply chain after receiving the order.

Panalpina has introduced Logistics Manufacturing Services (LMS) in response to a rapidly changing global manufacturing and supply chain landscape where speed to market, product customization and the influence of the end consumer are of paramount importance.

Large companies, especially but not exclusively in the technology sector, are rethinking their manufacturing strategies and redesigning their global supply chains as two major manufacturing trends are unfolding: production is moving closer to the end user again, and more and more products are being customized.

Panalpina's global network of dispersed facilities allow companies to push manufacturing operations down the supply chain and closer to the end user. In this new postponement model, rather than centralizing production in one location, manufacturing is broken down into various stages at several locations.

Transport innovation

Within freight transport and last-mile delivery operations, we are seeing the growth of technology companies. Some of these companies are working closely with traditional logistics service providers (LSPs) – however, others are providing services directly to the end user.

Last-mile and last-yard delivery solutions

Shippers recognize the need for capable, last-yard logistics services. Increasing customer demands, urban congestion, a green agenda and greater competition are driving companies to come up with greater choice for consumers in terms of last-mile delivery.

The 'last yard' refers to what happens to a shipment once it is delivered to a customer, and then how it is routed within the customer organization to the specific location where it may be needed or used. The concept extends to both B2B and B2C situations, as the principal question is how well incoming shipments or packages make their way to recipients who will actually use or benefit from receiving what has been delivered.

In the 2019 Third-Party Logistics Study (Langley *et al*, 2019), 77 per cent of shippers felt that last-yard logistics services will play a critical role in how LSPs differentiate themselves and add value for their customers. An even higher number, 87 per cent, of shippers felt that LSPs can create a source of competitive advantage by extending their reach and fulfilment services beyond the receiving dock.

Innovative last yard capabilities required by shippers include the following:

- real-time delivery change options whilst in transit;
- consolidation;
- stockroom replenishment management;
- reducing the quantity of unnecessary inventory;
- appliance/furniture delivery, installation and cleaning up;
- returns exchange service at the point of delivery;
- moving stock to point-of-use, such as an engineer's van;
- sequencing/production line feeding;
- separating product by department within a building;
- medical device/high-tech appliance demos from trained personnel;
- experiential marketing services at the doorstep.

LSPs will need to increase their service menu to accommodate these requirements if they are to remain competitive in this rapidly changing market.

Delivery drones   An offshoot of Google has become the first drone operator to receive government approval as an airline, an important step that gives it the legal authority to begin delivering products to actual customers in the State of Virginia.

Drone regulations still don't permit most flights over crowds and urban areas, limiting where the company can operate. But the approvals give the company the ability to charge for deliveries of clients' goods in Virginia and apply for permission to expand to other regions.

Both UPS and DHL amongst others are trialling drones for last-mile delivery, as shown in the video: http://bit.ly/2Q1la0c (UPS, 2019).

Delivery robots   We are now beginning to see robots travelling along our streets and university and work campuses making deliveries.

Starship robots are now delivering food, drinks, parcels and other items on corporate and academic campuses around the world. This new service allows staff the freedom to choose how and where to spend their time during the day. Starship's initiative is the first large-scale deployment of autonomous delivery services, supporting campuses by implementing robots to assist in work and school environments.

The robots offer on-demand delivery anywhere on participating campuses via an app, offering employees the flexibility and convenience of having food delivery when and where they want, eliminating unwanted errands and waiting in line, or transporting items to and from other locations on campus.

Each robot has a sensor suite to enable it to drive autonomously, avoid obstacles and cross roads safely. The robot is locked during a delivery and has tracking to the nearest inch, cameras and alarms: http://bit.ly/2LtsGlY (Starship, n. d.).

Hybrid   Many companies are utilizing a combination of delivery methods to undertake the last-mile delivery. To enable a fast and efficient response to orders, these companies rely heavily on their sophisticated IT systems. Companies such as Collect Plus, Parcelly, Doddle, myHermes and HubBox provide collection points close to the consumer, removing the need for home delivery when people are not available.

It's not only the large courier companies who are introducing these services. There are a number of start-up companies such as Go-Jek in Asia, Shutl in the UK and Go-Share in the US.

London-based start-up Quiqup is at the forefront of providing businesses with affordable on-demand logistics. Their solution – the Quiqees fleet – will shop, pick up and drop anything needed, offering transportation of a package by car, scooter or bicycle alongside providing real-time tracking for each delivery.

The Parcelly platform enables city dwellers including businesses to turn redundant storage space into parcel storage and pick-up points. Consumers can choose their preferred pick-up location from over 1,500 Parcelly points across the UK, enabling greater flexibility and convenience. Logistics companies benefit from augmenting their existing networks with additional service points to improve service to customers and increase coverage.

Parcelly has recently teamed up with the charity Barnardo's to utilize their shops as PUDO (pick up, drop off) locations.

Passel, based in Australia and Ireland, are using crowdsourcing to undertake deliveries from store to home. Once you have signed up to the scheme and downloaded the app, Passel will alert you when you are close to a store which requires a delivery to be made. You collect the item(s), and as long as you make the delivery within three hours you receive payment.

Alternative energy in transportation

Alternative energy is another potential differentiator as LSPs look to enhance their green credentials. The need to innovate in this area is as a result of pressure, not only from shippers but also by government legislation, public awareness of particulates and the realization that saving energy – and as a result lowering emissions – can reduce costs significantly for all parties.

FedEx has announced that it has placed a reservation for 20 Tesla semi trucks. The fully-electric trucks, which are scheduled to begin production in 2019, will be operated by FedEx Freight, its less-than-truckload unit (Post & Parcel, 2018).

'FedEx has a long history of innovation and incorporating sustainability efforts throughout its global network,' says FedEx Freight president and CEO Mike Ducker. 'Our investment in these trucks is part of our commitment to improving road safety while also reducing our environmental impact.'

The company suggests that the electric energy costs are half those of diesel.

DHL are currently working on lightweight solar panels for its delivery fleet. They were recent winners of the Chartered Institute of Logistics and Transport (CILT) Supply Chain Innovation Awards 2018. DHL are also producing their own electric delivery vehicle called StreetScooter. With more than 5,000 in deployment and plans to produce 20,000 annually, the electrification of logistics fleets will help to save significant amounts of CO_2 emissions.

DHL has also introduced the eco-friendly Cubicycle, which can carry 125-kg containers for inner-city deliveries across several European cities. This optimized container format replaces 60 per cent of inner-city vehicle journeys. Custom dimensions enable quick and easy transfer across different modes of transport (vehicles or cycles). The container can also be reloaded with new shipments, increasing sustainability and enabling circular economy concepts.

Driverless trucks

According to Freightflow (n. d.), the potential saving to the freight transportation industry of the introduction of driverless trucks is estimated at $168 billion annually, broken down into:

- reduced labour: $70 billion;
- increased fuel efficiency: $35 billion;
- increased productivity: $27 billion;
- reduction in accidents: $36 billion.

Truck drivers are limited by driving hours legislation, and therefore loads will arrive quicker thus increasing productivity. Drivers also require significant training and are in short supply in many markets. These driverless trucks solve these problems, and will be driven in the most efficient and economical mode and should reduce the number of accidents caused through human error. However, there remains a public concern regarding prioritization of passengers (if applicable) and third-party safety.

Tesla has produced a semi-autonomous, electric powered truck with a 500-mile range on a full charge. An enhanced autopilot feature provides an advanced driver-assistance system that includes adaptive cruise control, lane centring and self-parking, and enables the truck to be summoned from a parked position. Tesla has planned for fully autonomous driving capabilities once regulatory, technical, and legal hurdles have been overcome.

The biggest risk to third party logistics companies comes when a technology company, such as Uber, begins to make driverless trucks available to shippers just as they currently make Uber drivers available to people.

AI

According to Markets and Markets (2017), AI in the transportation market is projected to grow at a compound annual growth rate of 17.87 per cent between 2017 and 2030, and the market size is expected to grow from US$ 1.21 billion in 2017 to US$ 10.30 billion by 2030. The increasing government regulations for vehicle safety, growing adoption of advanced driver assistance systems and development of autonomous vehicles play a significant role in the growth of this market.

Deep learning technology is estimated to be the largest and fastest growing segment of the AI-in-transportation market. It is widely used in the development of autonomous vehicles, which need to see, think, drive and learn.

Truck platooning is projected to be the next emerging segment for AI – technologies such as sensor fusion, signal recognition, forward collision warning, and lane keep assist are its key drivers. Growing environmental concerns, increasing fuel efficiency, stringent government regulations for emissions and concerns over traffic congestion have accelerated the growth of the truck platooning market.

Tube logistics

Tube logistics is a visionary trend which has received increased media attention in recent years. This is mainly due to an announcement over plans to build a Hyperloop network between San Francisco and Los Angeles, in which passengers and freight would be transported in pods propelled at supersonic speeds. The 600km journey could take less than 30 minutes.

Motivated by growing congestion in megacities, there is renewed interest in the use of existing and new tube infrastructures for cargo transportation. Innovations such as the Hyperloop could one day provide rapid cargo transit within and between cities for express shipments, or even passenger traffic.

Despite recent scepticism from the UK's Department for Transport Science Advisory Council about the viability of Elon Musk's Hyperloop technology to transport passengers and freight in a high-speed pipe-based system, Mole Solutions has completed feasibility tests in Northampton, UK for its underground logistics system and the Chinese and United Arab Emirates transport authorities are actively considering supporting this UK innovation.

Mole Solutions' Underground Logistics System plans to transport a wide range of freight such as crates, pallets and shipping containers in simple capsules by magnetic forces on smart guideways in enclosed pipelines.

Forecasting and software innovations

We are seeing significant advances in the development of software systems for the logistics market. The following section looks at advances in this area.

Anticipatory logistics

Anticipatory logistics is one of the lesser-known innovation areas. It is implemented via software solutions that predict demand before it occurs. Empowering logistics companies to substantially improve efficiency through reduced delivery times and better utilization of their transport capacity and network, Big Data predictive algorithms contribute to precisely this.

Predictive logistics can be enhanced by AI to shift the logistics industry from operating reactively with planning forecasts to proactive operations with predictive intelligence. An example is predictive demand planning using data from online shops and forums to predict unexpected volume spikes for trending products.

Logistics providers and suppliers can then avoid costly overstocks or out-of-stock situations that result in lost sales for both the supplier and the consumer.

It is estimated that 24 per cent of the road freight km in Europe are driven by trucks which are completely empty. Bulgarian-based start-up Transmetrics is providing logistics companies with network optimization and demand forecasts using predictive analytics and Big Data.

Supply chain visibility and analytics

According to the 2019 Third-Party Logistics Study (Langley *et al*, 2019), 75 per cent of respondents are planning on investing in 'Control Towers' for greater visibility, and more than 50 per cent are planning on investing in predictive analytics and anticipatory logistics.

Bill Goodgion, President, Ascent Global Logistics, commenting in the eft Global Logistics Report 2019 (eft, 2019), says:

> 'When we are able to provide customers with improved business intelligence surrounding the work we do for them, it increases the level of trust and moves the conversation away from only focusing on costs and rates. We want to be more involved upstream with our customers and steer our discussions more about planning, forecasting and where their business is headed. We want to be more than just a transactional provider for our customers.'

Blockchain

Another finding from the 2019 Third-Party Logistics Study is that the need for greater visibility across the supply chain is increasing interest in block-chain technology. This technology breaks each movement down into 'blocks', and documents transactions every time a shipment changes hands.

The technology improves security because each transaction is validated and recorded by an independent third party. No one party can modify, delete or append any record without a validation of the edit from others in the network. The goal is to create one version of the truth, link information and create transparency.

By using blockchain, LSPs and shippers will be able to gain additional value from the supply chain. Data generated through blockchain technology will provide more opportunity to analyse information, which is becoming more important in today's data-driven supply chain. However, blockchain technology remains in its early stages.

In the 2019 Third-Party Logistics Study, 9 per cent of shippers said they're investing in blockchain technology, compared to 7 per cent of LSPs. In addition, 8 per cent of shippers said that LSPs must have blockchain capabilities to successfully serve them, compared to 15 per cent of third-party logistics providers (3PLs) that said it was necessary.

In the 2018 eft survey (eft, 2018), 52.79 per cent of LSP respondents suggested that blockchain is a game-changer for logistics right now, closely followed by AI, robotics and autonomous vehicles.

Conversely, only 5 per cent of companies in the survey have invested more than $1 million in the technology to date, with 50 per cent stating that they have yet to invest anything.

Shippers, logistics providers and carriers have come together to form the Blockchain in Transport Alliance (BiTA). BiTA provides a forum to promote and educate, while encouraging the development of blockchain application within the transportation industry.

Some of the key areas BiTA plans to address include smart contracts, freight payments, asset maintenance and ownership history, grey trailer pools, and transparency and chain of custody of freight.

The container shipping industry is an early adopter of this technology.

The IoT

Smart warehousing, real-time transport visibility, and predictive delivery are just some of the key areas for IoT innovation in logistics. Smart objects will be capable of taking part in event-driven processes, while internet protocols will facilitate communication between sensor data and applications.

IoT adds tremendous value across the entire supply chain, including warehousing, last-mile delivery and freight transportation.

DHL has been working with US tech specialist Cisco to bring IoT to three major warehouse operations across Europe. DHL Supply Chain is testing the technology at three pilot sites in Germany, the Netherlands and Poland.

The solution enables DHL to monitor operational activities in real-time through a responsive graphical visualization of operational data aggregated from sensors on scanners and material handling equipment and from DHL's WMS.

Visualizing operational data with heat maps has changed the way data is analysed and used at the pilot sites, and is expected to contribute to operational efficiencies and improved employee safety.

CargoSense is an IoT startup which has the capacity to easily track valuable assets via their platform. The software taps into data provided by internet-connected sensors, thereby guaranteeing logistics companies full transparency as to what happens to a package until reception by the customer.

Up until now, only a few IoT applications in logistics have experienced widespread adoption, due to the total cost of deployment, security concerns, and an absence of standards in what remains a fragmented logistics industry. However, vehicle tracking is now standard in most operations, and as battery life improves and costs come down, the widespread tracking of assets, equipment and stock will become the norm.

Big Data and advanced analytics

The increasing scope of enterprise solutions to manage and track supply chain activity has led to a step change in control and visibility in many organizations. However, it has also provided an opportunity for the system providers to harness the vast amounts of data generated in their systems to provide insights to customers and to market new services to these customers. This approach has been pioneered by companies such as Facebook and Google, but is just as relevant to the providers of supply chain and logistics management software.

These companies will increasingly be making use of supply chain data, not only to suggest improvements to management decisions (using journey times, job completion rates, transaction times, transaction costs and other historic data points across thousands or millions of transactions to predict outcomes), but to sell cross-company, industry datasets for marketing, benchmarking or even national planning purposes.

For shippers it will be important to access these industry datasets and the insights they will bring; this functionality, rather than the traditional core functionalities of scheduling, tracking or managing flows will be where competition moves over the next five years.

Other advancements

The innovation areas outlined above are just a few of the crucial advances in the logistics industry we see today. Others include logistics as a service, cloud logistics and digital identifiers.

As well as growth in companies providing freight and storage matching services for companies in the logistics sector, there is also increasing sophistication and digitalization of these services. Examples of companies offering such services include Timocom, Haulage Exchange, ReturnLoads, Flexe, LogistCompare, Stowga, Freightex, Transporeon and TGMatrix.

In its simplest form this service is similar to a dating agency, where loads and truck capacity are posted on freight boards or haulier exchanges and the service supports pairing them up. Both the pairing and the end-to-end transaction require human intervention. The transaction may not be digitized (captured in digital form), and little data is available for future analysis.

Some companies offer a degree of automation for the matching and/or the transaction, with a greater degree of digitization of the process and therefore better data management and the potential for enhanced analytics.

The ultimate form of this service is using full digitization of the process, combined with ML and historic data to predict and pre-empt shipper and carrier behaviour. By predicting which loads a shipper will need, or what capacity will be available when, the system can prompt and suggest actions – such as when to buy and when to monitor end-to-end progress of the transaction.

By working with a group of large shippers and drawing from a network of more than 4 million GPS/electronic logging devices, FourKites is able to identify capacity based on real-time conditions, including delays at stops, traffic congestion and weather events, and thereby help to match loads with empty trailers and reduce transportation costs. This is a form of anticipatory logistics for reducing empty running that again requires collaboration between the LSPs and technology firms.

A new service from UPS called Ware2Go matches available warehouse space and fulfilment services with merchants looking for secure storage and swift fulfilment. UPS Ware2Go recruits and certifies warehouses in strategic locations, establishing a network of vetted fulfilment partners. Merchants can then position products closer to their customers without the need for researching or vetting providers or making long-term volume and time commitments (Wilson, 2018).

Another trend is for software solution providers to create communities of their users to facilitate sub-contracting to companies with the same IT capabilities as themselves.

BigChange is a provider of cloud-based job management software for mobile workers, including transport drivers. They have created the BigChange Network which enables companies to sub-contract work to other BigChange users, whilst ensuring that their job workflows are followed. To the end-customer the service, real time visibility and branding are identical.

A related trend is the creation of service gateways, where solution providers enable their customers to access a wider variety of synergistic services from other providers via their portal. For the user, it means fewer services to find and fewer portals to log into; for the solution provider, it improves their value proposition.

The evolution of logistics outsourcing services

Logistics outsourcing began in earnest during the 1980s when retailers looked to LSPs to operate their distribution centres (DCs), and freight transport more efficiently and coincided with the growth in globalization.

During this time and up to the turn of the century, LSPs focused on scaling capacity by building and consolidating their networks and becoming more efficient and cost-effective in serving their markets. The emphasis was on reducing costs through operational improvements with very little concentration on innovation and new technology.

The LSPs built warehouses and cross-dock centres, introduced track and trace systems and provided some value-adding service capabilities. This was also a time of significant industry consolidation.

In 1997 Gwynne Richards wrote his Master's dissertation on 'Innovation in third-party logistics – or lack of it'. Back in those days LSPs were constantly being criticized for not being innovative or proactive. There were a few isolated examples of innovation, but it was universally acknowledged that LSP managers were having to spend a great deal of time micro-managing daily operations and thus weren't able to take a step back and look at the whole picture. Also, margins were not sufficient enough to plough back into the operation, contracts were still too short, and the majority of LSPs were risk-averse.

In Figure 11.2 we see this evolution from inward-looking companies to a more outward-looking approach. As we moved into the new millennium, we saw and continue to see a move towards greater digitization, automation and disruptive technologies.

Innovation drivers for LSPs

In today's market, margins remain low; however, there is an increasing realization that in order to survive and grow, LSPs need to innovate and harness new technologies in order to increase their own and their clients' margins.

Secondly shippers are increasingly aware that if they do not have the technological capabilities to accomplish their goals, they need to partner with those that do.

In the 2019 Third-Party Logistics Study (Langley *et al*, 2019), the majority of shippers – 93 per cent – agreed that IT capabilities are a necessary element of LSP expertise, but only 55 per cent stated that they are satisfied with LSP IT capabilities. Thus, LSPs need to enhance their IT capabilities in order to keep up with the emerging trends that are listed below.

According to LCP Consulting (2016), the following trends require innovative/extended services from LSPs:

- multi-channel/omni-channel integration;
- returns management and recycling;
- packaging, merchandising, postponement and more complicated value-added services;
- process integration from the order release point to final delivery;
- increase in shared user operations for economies of scale;
- cost transparency, benchmarking and collaboration;
- trade/inventory financing and responsibility;
- performance-related contracts;
- service-dominant logic (SDL).

Figure 11.2 From industrialization to digitization

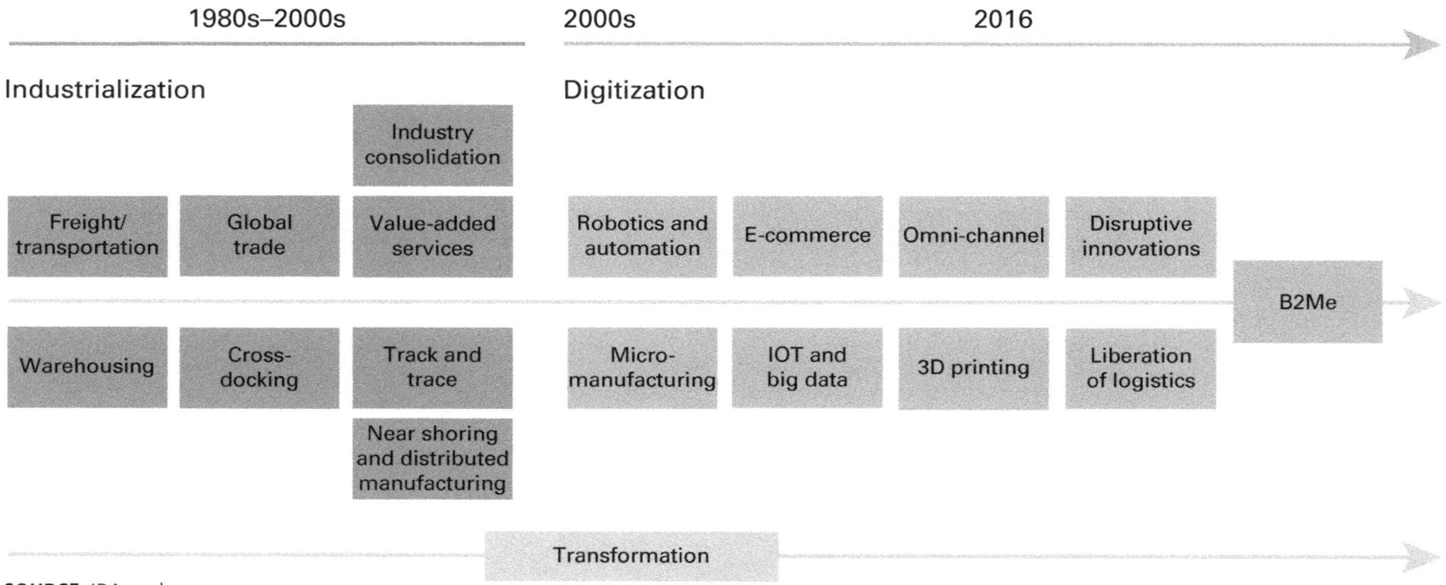

	1980s–2000s	2000s	2016
	Industrialization	Digitization	

Freight/transportation · Global trade · Industry consolidation

Value-added services

Robotics and automation · E-commerce · Omni-channel · Disruptive innovations

Warehousing · Cross-docking · Track and trace

Near shoring and distributed manufacturing

Micro-manufacturing · IOT and big data · 3D printing · Liberation of logistics

B2Me

Transformation

SOURCE JDA, n. d.

The rise in omni-channel in the B2C environment has now set new expectations in B2B markets. Buyers of logistics services want the same quality and level of service as provided by companies such as Amazon, Alibaba and JD.com.

Services such as real-time information on order status and location, next or even same-day delivery and on-demand delivery are today's e-commerce battleground. The expectation is that these services will also be free of charge in the near future.

LSPs are required to not only deliver products, but also provide additional value-adding services as outlined above. The economy is becoming more service-driven, where logistics is no longer a commodity but has been transformed into an all-encompassing service – hence the emergence of SDL.

Alongside the above, we also see that the global workforce is shrinking, with fewer millennials entering the industry than logistics personnel retiring. This shortage, together with a move away from traditional off-shore manufacturing, has seen a significant rise in labour rates.

In the 2017 Shippers and 3PL Benchmark study (Supply Chain Digest and JDA Software, 2017), shippers were asked 'When considering a new 3PL provider (LSP), do you evaluate their ability to innovate in some way?

The results were as shown in Figure 11.3.

The fact that shippers see innovation in 3PLs as a differentiator is certainly one of the main drivers for LSPs to become more proactive and innovative.

Figure 11.3   The value of an LSP's ability to innovate – responses

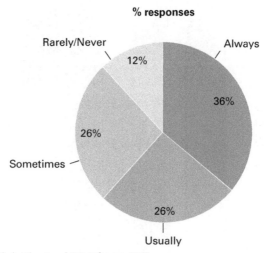

SOURCE Supply Chain Digest and JDA Software, 2017

Interestingly both studies showed that some shippers do not, or very rarely require their LSPs to be innovative. This might be because the operation is very standard and straightforward and is not critical to the shipper's business strategy, or the shipper prefers to undertake the innovation themselves. This is sometimes the case when companies are introducing automation into the operation and prefer to work with the automation equipment supplier as opposed to the LSP. We are, however, seeing all three parties working together on certain projects.

Comments from the study include: 'Innovation is important if it is needed. No need to make changes for change itself', and 'Innovation is important but operational excellence must be established first'.

This need for improvement is mirrored in the 2018 UK CILT Outsourcing Attitudes survey, with 18 per cent of shippers reporting that they had terminated a logistics contract in the last five years because of lack of innovation and improvement. The importance of improvement progress in the 2018 study is shown in Figure 11.4.

Recent research by the CILT's Outsourcing and Procurement Forum and Cranfield School of Management (Gibson, Saghiri and Godsmark, 2017) showed that many shippers are poor at defining and communicating what they mean by innovation in a contract. While the shippers and LSPs who were interviewed believed that LSPs should bring new technologies or new solutions to solve customers' problems, there was also a recognition that shippers need to tell LSPs what they need and what targets they want to achieve.

Figure 11.4   Importance of continuous innovation by LSPs – responses

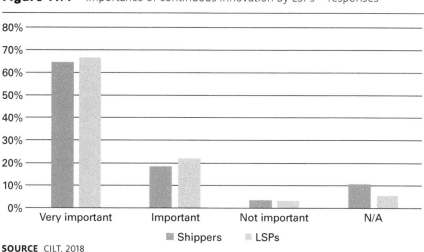

SOURCE CILT, 2018

How innovative are LSPs?

As seen in the examples earlier in this chapter, LSPs are introducing innovation into their contracts with their customers.

In the 2019 Third-Party Logistics Study (Langley *et al*, 2019), 73 per cent of shippers and 91 per cent of LSPs agreed that LSPs provided new and innovative ways to improve logistics effectiveness.

LSPs have been and increasingly are, working with Automated Materials Handling Systems (AMHSs) in their operations. This is unsurprising, bearing in mind the growing investment in AMHSs in many industrial sectors and markets around the world. Knapp, an automation systems supplier, now quite regularly find themselves working in concert with end users, their chosen 3PL provider and often a logistics consultant in the employ of the end user.

The advantages of such a collaboration are obvious. It is no surprise that where projects in which the overall supply chain, customer experience, AMHS design and operation have been considered holistically, these are, in Knapp's experience, more likely to be successful. This, in comparison to instances when either the 3PL or indeed the 'in-house' operator is not involved in the design and implementation phases of a project. In a collaborative example such as this, Knapp has always been contracted by the end user (the shipper).

This is not to say that LSPs are not investing in technology and automation. Some companies are introducing innovative services and products into their customer relationships either in partnership or autonomously.

Knapp are currently noticing a discernible increase in interest from LSPs for a variety of reasons, amongst them an awareness that several (end user) customers have taken an operation back 'in-house' because they felt the business case for an AMHS was compelling, but could not be supported by their LSP.

LSPs are also actively finding innovative ways to secure profitable business in this environment, and there are signs they are being assisted by financiers, equally prepared to be innovative in the pursuit of profitable business. Previously, they have been reluctant to invest.

So, what are LSPs doing to enable them to be more innovative?

In the eft 2018 survey, only 27 per cent of LSPs contacted said that they have a dedicated centre of excellence or innovation lab.

LSPs need to embrace these technologies in order to ensure that they, together with their clients, are the ones driving change in the industry.

Figure 11.5 Level of innovation capability within LSPs – responses

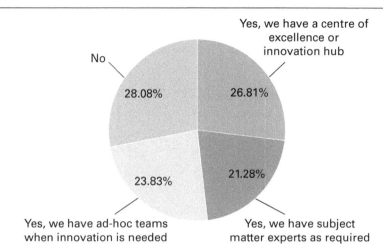

No 28.08%

Yes, we have a centre of excellence or innovation hub 26.81%

Yes, we have ad-hoc teams when innovation is needed 23.83%

Yes, we have subject matter experts as required 21.28%

SOURCE eft, 2018

In a similar survey by Supply Chain Digest and JDA Software (2017), both shippers and LSPs were asked the following question: 'Overall, how would you rate the LSP sector in terms of process innovation capabilities?' The results can be seen in Figure 11.6.

A further question was: 'Overall, how would you rate the LSP sector in terms of technology innovation capabilities? The results can be seen in Figure 11.7.

Interestingly, 80 per cent of LSPs in response to this question said that they had modest or high innovation technology capability. There is certainly a gap between what shippers expect and what LSPs think they can deliver.

In the most recent Eye For Transport survey, LSPs were asked: 'How much focus is there in your organization to identify technologies that will enable higher productivity or unlock efficiencies?' Fifty per cent said they had a dedicated team of people, and 42 per cent said they operated with ad-hoc teams, whilst 8 per cent were not focusing on this area.

Technologies can provide competitive edge, and companies which are seen to be leading the field, providing of course they can demonstrate cost-effective solutions, will gain more customers and utilize this scale to provide overall cost savings.

In response to this need for innovation, one of the leading LSPs, Kuehne + Nagel, has opened two innovation centres, one in the Netherlands and the other in Singapore.

Figure 11.6   LSPs' process innovation capabilities – responses

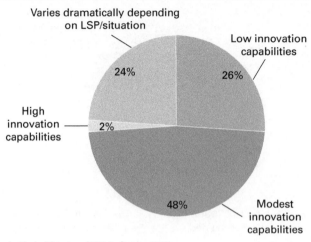

SOURCE Supply Chain Digest and JDA Software, 2017

Figure 11.7   LSPs' technological innovation capabilities – responses

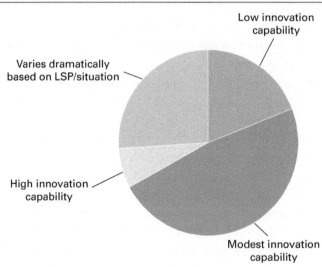

SOURCE Supply Chain Digest and JDA Software, 2017

Another 3PL to recognize the value of innovation is GEFCO. Their Innovation Factory is designed to nurture a culture of innovation, empowering every employee to invent and explore innovative ideas, with the potential of developing them into solutions to support business growth. The Group's aim is to boost the creative spirit of its employees by providing an internal incubator for their most promising new concepts.

The Group is actively monitoring innovative developments and adopting a 'test and learn' approach to new technologies, using for instance robots for warehouse management in France or drones for counting warehouse inventories in Spain.

Another LSP at the forefront of innovation is XPO, who have partnered with Nestlé to build a next-generation DC in the UK, due for completion in 2020. The centre will feature predictive analytics, robotics and other intelligent machines, and act as an incubator for innovations developed in their on-site technology lab.

DHL Supply Chain, the contract logistics arm of Deutsche Post DHL Group, reported in 2018 that they will spend $300 million to introduce emerging technologies in its North American facilities and transportation control towers in an effort to help its clients address e-commerce and omnichannel challenges. Technology platforms involved will include robotics, augmented reality, RPA, the IoT, and DHL's proprietary end-to-end visibility solution My Supply Chain (Ames, 2018).

DHL also keeps a close eye on innovations in logistics and produces a regular Logistics Trend Radar, updating readers on what is happening in the logistics industry across all modes and operations.

LSP alternatives

Customers can increasingly choose from a large variety of logistics services globally, thanks to the cloud-powered online marketplaces and start-ups that are unbundling traditional logistics integrators.

Companies not necessarily classed as LSPs but which provide a third-party service are at the forefront. These include Amazon, Ocado, JD.com and Alibaba. These companies began as retailers, but have become suppliers of logistics services based on the technologies they are developing.

According to David Jinks from ParcelHero, Amazon spent $61.7 bn on logistics in 2018 – 26.5 per cent of its net sales – because it knows deliveries are a marketing tool, rather than just a necessary evil (Post & Parcel, 2019).

Within 18 years, Alibaba has risen to become the world's largest and most valuable retailer, with operations in more than 200 countries. Beyond its e-commerce activities, Alibaba is continuously increasing its reach into the logistics realm by heavily investing (more than US$ 15 billion within the next five years) to build a global logistics network. The ambition is to build the most efficient logistics network around the world, heading towards a 'supergrid' approach.

Alibaba-owned Hema supermarkets in Beijing and Shanghai now offer a round-the-clock, 30-minute delivery service that has proven highly popular with nocturnal shoppers. This will further shake up the logistics sector.

We are also seeing a significant number of technology start-up companies entering the logistics market. Some of these companies will work closely with LSPs, whilst others will introduce their own network and utilize their own assets.

Why LSPs don't always leverage innovations

According to Wagner and Franklin (2008), LSPs often struggle to extend customized solutions created for specific customers to a broader customer base. The reasons for this are as follows.

Firstly, logistics service innovation often arises not because of formal plans or processes but as an ad-hoc response to a customer request. Because of the geographically dispersed nature of the logistics service business, innovative offerings tend to start out as unique solutions developed for a single customer in a single region. Furthermore, the solution development processes used by the LSP often vary depending on the background of the response team, the team members' familiarity with formal corporate guidelines and processes and the nature of the customer's request.

Secondly, customers impose strict schedules on the innovation project. Time pressures force the field team to make rapid decisions about the innovation's design in order to satisfy the customer's immediate need. As a result, the service may only satisfy the specific customer for which it was developed.

Thirdly, innovations are usually composed of existing tools and processes combined in a new way. Because these tools and processes were originally developed for other applications, the solution generally is not scalable or usable for other customers with similar problems.

Finally, because these innovations are co-produced with the customer, the tools, processes, and human factors used to create them may include components from the customer or third parties. These external components may not be available for other competing companies or require a payment to purchase the intellectual property (IP).

For all of these reasons, an LSP that wants to extend an innovation to a broader customer base typically must re-engineer the innovation to ensure that it can be supported by the firm and can be applied in a reliable manner to other customers.

Product-focused processes assume that innovation can be managed and controlled centrally, and they target broad market segments of customers rather than individual customers. Central control is difficult for many LSPs as they can be set up geographically or by product/service classification. They also tend to be individual profit centres, and in fact some LSPs become their own competition when adopting this silo approach.

Many innovations result when the customer draws from its internal knowledge of what is required and then leverages the LSP's core competency in logistics to arrive at novel services that provide competitive advantage.

The formation of innovation centres should not only produce new ideas, but also disseminate innovations created throughout the company so that they can be shared with other group companies.

Barriers to innovation

The 2018 eft survey produced the following obstacles to innovation, according to the LSPs surveyed.

As shown, it isn't the lack of talent that is holding companies back, but resistance to change and investment. We would also add contract length to this list.

Figure 11.8   The biggest obstacles to innovation – responses

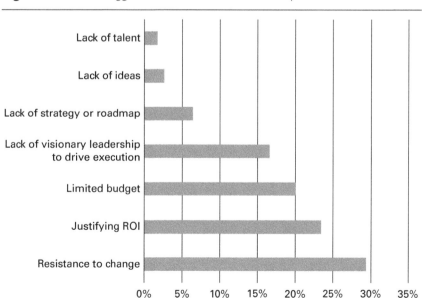

SOURCE eft, 2018

In the same survey they found the following average contract lengths:

- six months to four years – 77.11 per cent;
- five to 10 years – 14.44 per cent;
- more than 10 years – 8.45 per cent;

This is an improvement over 2013, where 90 per cent of respondents fell within the three years or less category. If the trend of longer contracts continues it will make it more conducive to collaboration and innovation.

As mentioned earlier in the book, margins remain quite low for LSPs, with the Motor Transport top 100 LSPs showing an average margin of 2.2 per cent. Such low margins restrict LSPs in terms of investing in outsourced relationships. As discussed, many innovations are held back as a result of the short-term nature of contracts and low margins.

In the 2017 Supply Chain Digest survey, respondents were asked 'What is your company's perspective on gainsharing?' The results are shown in Figure 11.9.

As can be seen, less than 10 per cent of companies use gainsharing as a mechanism to fund innovation. In the same survey, the following aspects were seen as potential barriers to innovation by LSPs:

- the culture of the two parties;
- the nature of the contract;
- the technological capabilities of both parties;
- the lack of a strategic relationship.

Figure 11.9 Use of gainsharing as a mechanism to fund innovation – responses

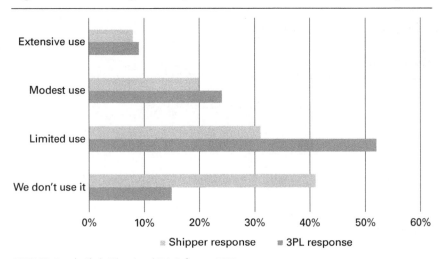

SOURCE Supply Chain Digest and JDA Software, 2017

The highest barrier identified in response to the question by both parties was that relationships were not strategic enough.

According to David James from automation systems provider Knapp, traditionally, LSPs have been infrequent and low investors in AMHSs, probably for conjoined reasons:

1 the typical length of their contracts;

2 asset ownership/capital spend and financing options.

If an LSP is awarded a contract for, say, two to five years, there will not be a business case to be made for investment in an AMHS. There are possibly exceptions to this – for example, where the investment is underwritten by the customer. This enables the customer to transfer contracts between the LSPs, but retain the equipment. This is subject to the building also being owned/leased by the customer.

Where an LSP has invested in an AMHS, it is usually in shared-user facilities/operations, where their risk analysis suggests a strong likelihood of renewed contracts and/or a ready supply of potential replacement contracts. Some of these exist in the grocery retail (e-commerce), pharmaceutical/healthcare and financial services sectors.

According to David, traditionally and currently, Knapp's order intake from 3PL providers represents a tiny proportion of their overall annual order intake – less than 5 per cent. There are, however, strong indications that this may be about to change going forward.

In a recent interview with HSS (2019), Andrew Hoyle, automation director at Wincanton, a leading UK LSP, said that there is a trend towards a more modular form of automation which is a lot more accessible to LSPs.

There is also increased competition among the automation suppliers and, as a result, return on investment is improving. He goes on to say that the 'often short length of logistics contracts can be perceived as a barrier to automated investment, but using robots could make it easier to move assets between sites as demand changes'.

In order to introduce innovation there needs to be collaboration between the parties. In the Supply Chain Digest and JDA Software survey, when asked about relationships in terms of innovation, the following results as shown in Figure 11.10 were seen.

We can see that shippers are still quite prescriptive in how they deal with their LSPs. This can be because they do not want to lose control of the business, because they don't believe the LSP capable, or because the shipper doesn't value innovation or foster strategic collaboration.

Figure 11.10 Relationships with regard to innovation – responses

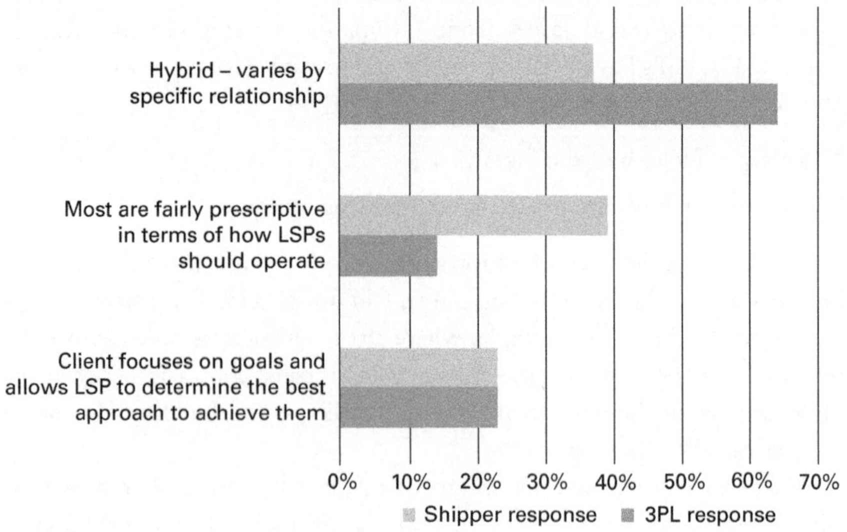

Hybrid – varies by specific relationship

Most are fairly prescriptive in terms of how LSPs should operate

Client focuses on goals and allows LSP to determine the best approach to achieve them

0% 10% 20% 30% 40% 50% 60% 70%

Shipper response   3PL response

SOURCE Supply Chain Digest and JDA Software, 2017

Future trends in logistics processes

Crowdsourcing

A T Kearney (Zimmerman, Sonthalia and Deshmukh, 2017) see the benefits of crowdsourcing in three specific areas:

- Crowdsourcing can potentially produce cost savings and productivity gains by exploiting the combined talents and insights of industry players who have a more comprehensive view of the logistics landscape than any individual shipper.
- Shippers and LSPs working together can design stronger logistics networks with the agility to meet rapidly changing customer needs and better resilience to withstand supply chain disruptions.
- Collaboration makes implementation quicker and easier, delivering benefits faster. It can also avoid roadblocks that can derail networks.

They have produced a short questionnaire to determine whether a crowd-sourced network optimization (CNO) is the right thing to do. If a company answers 'yes' to two of the following questions, then CNO is a possibility:

1 Was your last network optimization event held more than two years ago?

2 Does your organization spend more than $200 million per annum on distribution?

3 Have your distribution costs increased in two of the last three years, or are they about to?

4 Do your LSP contracts lack the provision for continuous improvement and profit sharing?

5 Has your network volume increased by more than 15 per cent in the past two years?

The following case study shows how crowdsourcing can have a significant effect on logistics costs.

CASE STUDY   Crowdsourcing delivers for chemical giant

A large global chemicals company knew it was time to rationalize the sprawling, complex logistics network it had assembled over years of acquisitions, divestitures and market expansions. The fragmented system encompassed 10 individual networks serving various regions and end markets. Some 800 warehouse locations and more than 100,000 shipping lanes spanned the Americas, Asia, Europe, the Middle East and Africa.

With more than 200 logistics providers, including several underutilized LSPs, the multi-layered network operated well below peak efficiency at a cost of more than $1 billion annually. Senior executives wanted to streamline without losing the capabilities to serve a diverse customer base with widely varying and sometimes incompatible shipping and handling requirements – the company ships everything from food ingredients to hazardous materials.

Adopting a crowdsourcing model, the company reached out to more than 1,000 industry participants for input on logistics options. Network planners analysed the responses to identify the local, regional and global capabilities of 800 LSPs. Using 'centre of gravity' modelling, they outlined more than 20 network consolidation scenarios with various configurations of warehouse locations, routes and transportation modes.

A market event staged to gauge costs for each scenario drew bids from more than 200 providers. Based on the bids, the company's logistics buyers and planners developed implementation strategies for each of the most promising scenarios.

Crowdsourcing yielded new options that helped the company score quick wins, lock in longer-term benefits and surpass its rationalization and cost reduction goals.

Conversations with providers revealed readily available warehouse capacity previously unknown to the company, and the collaborative process elicited stronger commitment from suppliers. Some providers expanded their offerings in return for lower operating costs, while others added capacity to serve the company's future network needs.

Securing capacity for short-term and future requirements ensured a smooth implementation and a faster transition to the future network.

Ultimately, crowdsourced network optimization eliminated one-third of the company's warehouses and culled 40 per cent of its logistics providers, enabling it to focus on strategic relationships with a core group of stronger LSPs.

The fit-for-purpose network design won quick buy-in at all levels, contributing to an accelerated implementation that had the new system up and running within 18 months. Customer service and inventory levels improved while annual logistics costs dropped by $100 million – a 10 per cent reduction. Strong cross-functional collaboration between procurement and supply chain from the get-go and enterprise-wide programme visibility and C-suite support were crucial factors for success.

Courtesy of A T Kearney

Through crowdsourcing, suppliers help unlock options across the whole network. The above company was able to access the combined insights of many industry experts, who have a broader view of the logistics landscape than any individual shipper.

Having the shippers and providers working closely together can also bring its rewards. The sharing of information and trusting in their relationships can result in stronger networks and allows companies to plan for the future, overcoming any possible disruption to the supply chain.

This is an interesting approach as it requires a great deal of time and effort to analyse each response and produce an effective network. If the company has sufficient resource in-house, then this approach can work.

We do, however, caution the reader when using consultants in this role, as the cost can escalate significantly. It may be more beneficial in certain circumstances to directly target potential LSPs having undertaken a significant amount of market research.

Collaboration

There are a number of different types of collaboration within logistics outsourcing, namely:

- shipper and LSP;
- LSP and technology supplier;
- LSP and LSP;
- shipper and shipper facilitated by a 3PL.

The increased complexity of supply chains and continually changing customer requirements and demands is forcing companies towards greater collaboration – both at a customer–provider level and at a provider–provider level.

Shipper and LSP

The 2019 Third-Party Logistics Study (Langley *et al*, 2019) shows that shippers and their LSPs are increasingly moving towards meaningful partnerships and working together to accomplish their supply chain goals.

We have seen examples of shipper–LSP collaboration in our section on Vested® in Chapter 9.

LSP and technology supplier

We are beginning to see collaboration between technology suppliers and LSPs. LSPs have the knowledge and experience of operating logistics whilst the technology companies are looking to introduce new tech into the industry. Examples include the relationship between D B Schenker and IAM Robotics.

IAM CEO Joel Reed says: 'This is the goal that the entire logistics industry is working toward, fully flexible distribution solutions and models – the kind of capability that allows organizations to be responsive to the accelerated pace of change.'

John Stikes, DB Schenker's Director of Innovation and E-Commerce, adds: 'To achieve this vision, we're having open dialogues about customers' needs, a roadmap for the future and where those two intersect. In the warehouse, fully-automated applications will be the key to sustainability and competitiveness in the new marketplace.'

LSP and LSP

This is probably still the most contentious type of collaboration, as trust between companies has always been an issue here. We do see LSPs working with couriers to effect deliveries on their behalf; however, this tends to be on a supplier/customer basis as opposed to a true partnership.

An interesting example of supplier collaboration is in the last-mile delivery within the Highlands and Islands of Scotland. Delivery to remote homesteads and businesses has always been a challenge to courier companies – low population density, low delivery volumes, difficult terrain and road congestion during the summer tourist season are all challenges – however, they are also strategically important in order to provide a truly national service.

As a result, Menzies Distribution, an LSP in its own right, has set up an operation in the Highlands and Islands which delivers to these homes. The company is seen as a neutral consolidator or carrier's carrier. Reducing costs is the key motivation – which can be four to five times higher if undertaken by individual carriers.

This model could be replicated in other remote areas, but also in densely populated areas where congestion, restricted access and parking are issues. For example, Gnewt, a carrier's carrier based four miles from the centre of London operates an all-electric fleet which overcomes the London congestion and low emission charges, and operates on behalf of a number of major courier companies. However, brand identity and fierce competition have been barriers to extending this further.

The likelihood of other global cities introducing low emission zones could, in future, force LSPs not only to invest in alternative energy vehicles, but also into greater collaboration.

Shipper and shipper

This is by far the most difficult collaboration to instigate. There are barriers such as trust, competitive advantage and marketing and sales issues, which are very similar to those in LSP/LSP collaboration. There are examples, such as Nestlé and United Biscuits sharing vehicles; however, these tend to be the exception rather than the rule.

Uberization of freight transport

Uber has revolutionized the way that the public hails a ride at any time of day or night, by utilizing sophisticated software and harnessing the power of mobile devices.

There is a movement towards the use of similar technology for load matching services. This isn't new – as discussed earlier in the chapter, freight matching websites have been around for a number of years. The difference today is that many more shippers and carriers can be reached through app-based technology.

Although termed 'Uberization', a number of companies are working on similar apps. According to Todd Dills of *Overdrive* (Dills, 2016) Amazon is also working on app-based systems that will make truck-stop recommendations and include pick-up and drop-off options for payment and order tracking.

According to Cerasis (n. d.), there are risks in the 'Uberization' of trucking that must be considered. Goods may be perishable, time-sensitive or very high-value, and therefore there is a significant need for authentication, vetting and verification. There may be a requirement for intermodal transport options, and the movement of goods is very different to the movement of people in terms of the types of vehicles required.

Compliance is always growing stricter in the logistics industry, and shippers are demanding more versatility in pick-up windows and back-house costs. Meanwhile, demand on the trucking industry is already high and charges are likely to be more volatile. Ensuring goods are insured to the correct value should things go wrong is also crucial.

In many countries up to 80 per cent of freight transport is already outsourced to LSPs, and therefore the most likely users of this service will be the top-tier LSPs themselves. The threat to the LSPs will be if shippers decide to deal directly with the hauliers and truckers through these apps. This reverts back to a commodity service, as opposed to the value-adding services discussed previously in this book.

E-auctions

Freight e-auctions are internet platforms for the procurement of transport. There are two types:

1 private networks for specific shippers and vetted LSPs;
2 open networks which are available to all shippers and LSPs through membership fees.

The advantages of utilizing a system such as this are as follows:

- ease of use;
- speed of use;
- easy transference of data;

- a wide range of potential carriers;
- global coverage;
- management resource savings;
- real-time discussions and transactions;
- shorter negotiation process;
- the ability to obtain competitive quotations across many lanes with many LSPs at once.

The correspondence below is a typical introductory note to potential LSPs who may be interested in quoting for a freight transport contract.

'ABC Ltd is a leading world manufacturer of beverage cans, with sites in the UK, Poland, Russia, Finland, Romania, India and Dubai.

We would like to announce that from 26 October to 15 November we will be holding our annual local and global freight e-tender. This e-tender is for both UK and European routes, and is open to all carriers wishing to participate.

In the UK alone, we have circa 12,000 to 14,000 full loads on mega trailers to UK destinations, plus around 7,000 export loads per annum.

If any carrier wishes to participate and register for this event, please visit https://www.transport.abc.eu and follow the instructions online for registering.

If you have any problems or require any further information, please contact info@abc.co.uk.

Don't miss out on this exciting opportunity to participate in this event.'

This type of procurement is only suitable for routine and leverage services where there are many suppliers and services that can be clearly specified and easily quoted. Charges for running such auctions, on the sophisticated platforms available, are relatively high, so this approach is only used in the main by high-volume shippers of palletized goods. In open auctions, the quality of the carriers needs to be established during the process; but open auctions allow new carriers to be identified.

There are certain disadvantages, especially when LSPs base their quotations on back-haul. This can have a significant effect on the quality of the service if the LSP loses its original contract. The quality of each carrier is also unknown unless a thorough vetting process has taken place.

What is the future of logistics outsourcing?

The outsourcing of logistics is likely to continue, despite some shippers taking their logistics operations back in-house. The difference now is that shippers are becoming more demanding and requiring their suppliers to be more proactive and innovative.

The 2019 Third-Party Logistics Study (Langley *et al*, 2019) shows that the majority of shippers – 91 per cent – report that the relationships they have with their LSPs generally have been successful. A higher number – 98 per cent – of LSPs agree that their customer relationships generally have been successful.

Among respondents, 89 per cent of shippers and 98 per cent of 3PL providers agree that the use of LSPs has contributed to improving services to the ultimate customers. The study shows that there is consistency in terms of the percentage of companies who increase their use of outsourcing and those who have insourced throughout the 23 years of the survey.

Overall, there is a positive growth in companies using LSP services. In 2019, only 28 per cent of the companies surveyed indicated that they are returning to insourcing services currently outsourced.

The survey did go on to state that 61 per cent of the companies surveyed report reducing or consolidating the number of LSPs they use.

Conclusion

The trend is that companies will continue to outsource; however, LSPs will need to up their game if they are to see further growth and stop companies from insourcing. Shippers will continue to ask more of their LSPs both in terms of services provided and innovation in order that they can remain competitive.

LSPs need to evolve to offer greater scope and more complex solutions. Providers increasingly need to choose between serving a large commodity segment and the more demanding, yet faster growing, high-process conformance segments.

According to IBM back in 2006, the future LSP industry would be:

'…more global, more concentrated, more segmented around customer types and universally better at execution. Business processes will be standardized and systems integrated. There will be better visibility of end-to-end supply chain information, and integration with partners and customers. Providers will develop a single view of their larger global customers.'

This holds true today.

Finally, according to the Supply Chain Digest and JDA Software innovation report:

> 'Becoming a thought leader and being able to show shippers the art of the possible requires an investment from the LSP community. When Henry Ford asked people what they wanted their answer was "faster horses". Innovators everywhere need to actively create a viable vision for the future, rather than just continuing to do what they do now but faster, better, cheaper.' (Supply Chain Digest and JDA Software, 2017)

LSPs need to fully understand this, and shippers need to trust in the capabilities of their suppliers.

APPENDIX I
LSP warehouse audit checklists

Warehouse audit – external

Carried out by:				Location:			
Date:							
Item	**No**	**Poor**	**Good**	**Excellent**	**N/a**	**Comments**	
Comprehensive signage for delivery drivers in multiple languages							
Comprehensive signage for visitors							
Separate routes for trucks and pedestrians							
Staff cars parked away from warehouse exits							
Disabled access into the building							
Perimeter fencing in good order							
Security gates/barriers in good working order							
External ground in good condition							
Exterior lighting sufficient and in good order							

(continued)

(Continued)

Item	No	Poor	Good	Excellent	N/a	Comments
Carried out by:			**Location:**			
Date:						
Access to the external storage area unobstructed						
External storage area clearly marked – gridlines						
Products protected from the elements – canopy, sheeting						
Safe stack heights adhered to and stacks stored safely						
Separation from pedestrian walkways						
Sufficient space and separation for stock counting						
Stacks labelled clearly						
Separate area for storage of waste packaging, away from the main building						
Broken pallets and defective equipment stored safely and away from the main building						
Vehicle speeds controlled						
Sufficient space for goods vehicle parking						
Sufficient turning space for all types of vehicles						

Warehouse audit – general operations

Carried out by:			Location:			
Date:						
Item	**No**	**Poor**	**Good**	**Excellent**	**N/a**	**Comments**
Personnel security checks on entry and exit						
All exits secure						
Visitors and attendance books available for inspection and accurate						
Visitors are given safety briefing/ instructions						
Visitors escorted at all times						
Disabled access into the warehouse						
Intruder alarm systems installed and inspected regularly						
Stock adequately protected from theft and pilferage						
Building, including the roof, wind- and watertight						
Floor surface in good condition (clean and dry)						
Floor capable of taking the weight of the storage medium and load in terms of point loading						

(continued)

(Continued)

Carried out by:			Location:			
Date:						
Item	**No**	**Poor**	**Good**	**Excellent**	**N/a**	**Comments**
Sufficient doors for volume of traffic entering and leaving the warehouse						
Warehouse is clean and tidy						
Documented cleaning schedule in place						
Adequate pest control in place						
Teams given responsibility for cleanliness of own areas						
Exits clearly lit, marked and obstruction free						
Adequate number of personnel exit doors						
Fire escapes, fire doors clearly marked						
Sufficient fire doors						
Fire doors obstruction-free						
Fire protection system in place, eg sprinklers						
Fire alarms tested weekly						
Fire alarm drills carried out periodically						

(continued)

(Continued)

Carried out by:			Location:			
Date:						
Item	**No**	**Poor**	**Good**	**Excellent**	**N/a**	**Comments**
Fire extinguishers and water hoses clearly marked						
Escape routes clearly marked and obstruction free						
Doors and windows fitted with safety glass						
Sufficient space between rack ends and external walls						
No Smoking signs clearly visible						
Safety equipment regularly inspected, checked and maintained						
First aid boxes provided and fully stocked						
Eye wash facilities available						
Named and suitably trained first aiders						
At least one first aider per 50 staff						
Lighting sufficient in each section						
Sufficient natural light available						
Eco lighting used						

(*continued*)

(Continued)

Carried out by:			Location:			
Date:						
Item	**No**	**Poor**	**Good**	**Excellent**	**N/a**	**Comments**
Lights switched off when area not in use						
Clerestory windows and roof lights cleaned regularly						
Sufficient emergency lighting provided in areas where staff are at risk						
Air quality acceptable						
Audible alarm to detect unsafe areas with poor ventilation						
Noise at an acceptable level						
Temperature conducive to working						
Sufficient, visible thermometers						
Battery-charging areas marked adequately and clear of obstruction						
Trucks recharged in a well-ventilated and risk-free area						
Suitable safety information signage at the battery-charge area						

(*continued*)

(Continued)

Carried out by:				Location:		
Date:						
Item	**No**	**Poor**	**Good**	**Excellent**	**N/a**	**Comments**
Tools and packing materials stored in their designated areas						
Racking condition checked regularly and reported						
Racking is independently inspected regularly						
No broken or collapsing pallets in the racking						
No overhanging pallets in the racks						
Weight capacity visible on the end of the racks						
Waste receptacles at the end of each aisle						
Racking legs protected						

Warehouse audit – systems and equipment

Carried out by:			Location:			
Date						
Item	**No**	**Poor**	**Good**	**Excellent**	**N/a**	**Comments**
Warehouse IT systems						
Warehouse management system in place						
System adequate for the current operation						
Data backups taken daily and stored off-site						
Display Equipment Regulations adhered to						
Mechanical handling equipment						
Staff have correct licence for type of truck operated						
Responsible staff trained to operate material handling equipment (MHE)						
Record of safety training kept up to date						
MHE appropriate for the tasks						
MHE serviced regularly						
Service chart visible for all MHE						
Service and repair records kept up to date						

(continued)

(Continued)

Carried out by:			Location:			
Date						
Item	**No**	**Poor**	**Good**	**Excellent**	**N/a**	**Comments**
Pre-operational daily, weekly and monthly checks carried out on the equipment and recorded						
Inspections carried out on lifting equipment every six months						
All defects reported to the employer immediately						
Safe working load limits clearly marked						
Audible signals used when trucks reversing and turning corners						
Forklifts travel at safe speeds						
Equipment parked in designated areas when not in use, keys removed and forks lowered						
Contingency planning						
Documented contingency plan in place for equipment downtime						
Documented contingency plan in place for system downtime						

(*continued*)

(Continued)

Carried out by:		Location:				
Date						
Item	**No**	**Poor**	**Good**	**Excellent**	**N/a**	**Comments**
Documented contingency plan in place for labour issues						
Documented contingency plan in place for supplier issues						
Documented contingency plan in place for other emergencies						
List of emergency contact numbers held and updated						

Warehouse audit – inbound operation

Carried out by:		Location:				
Date:						
Item	**No**	**Poor**	**Good**	**Excellent**	**N/a**	**Comments**
Inbound processes manual available						
Vehicle booking-in system utilized						
Scheduling of vehicle arrivals						
Pre-notification of goods to be received						
Vehicle immobilized during unloading						

(*continued*)

(Continued)

Carried out by:			Location:			
Date:						
Item	**No**	**Poor**	**Good**	**Excellent**	**N/a**	**Comments**
Delivery drivers given instructions on what to do whilst on site						
Drivers' instructions in multiple languages						
Instructions for inbound goods handling provided						
Dock area clear of stored materials and obstructions						
Sufficient stock of empty pallets available						
Sufficient space for empty pallet storage						
Sufficient space to lay out goods for checking						
Recording of number of pallets received						
Pallet exchange system in place						
Product quantity and condition check						
Log of supplier non-conformance kept, eg incorrect paperwork, quantities, products, condition of goods, condition of packaging, TiHi met, pallet overhang						

(continued)

(Continued)

Carried out by:			Location:			
Date:						
Item	**No**	**Poor**	**Good**	**Excellent**	**N/a**	**Comments**
Sufficient handling equipment provided						
Recording of unloading times (dock to stock time)						
Quarantine area for non-compliance						
Quality control area provided						
All non-conforming stock dealt with quickly						
Returned items dealt with immediately						

Warehouse audit – putaway and storage

Carried out by:			Location:			
Date:						
Item	**No**	**Poor**	**Good**	**Excellent**	**N/a**	**Comments**
System/ management directed put-away						
FIFO stock rotation is followed correctly						
Best-before-date stock is managed						
ABC analysis used for product location						
Location IDs marked clearly						

(*continued*)

(Continued)

Carried out by:			Location:			
Date:						
Item	**No**	**Poor**	**Good**	**Excellent**	**N/a**	**Comments**
Accurate recording of stock location						
Task-interleaving/ dual cycling undertaken – one pallet in, one pallet out						
Slotting used effectively						
Random location system used						
Stock transferred between locations based on ABC analysis						
Cube utilization of locations efficient						
Location utilization between 80% and 90%						
Space usage monitored and action taken to minimize wasted or excess space						
Part pallets consolidated where feasible						
Product tracking in place						
Damaged items promptly identified and dealt with appropriately						

(continued)

(Continued)

Carried out by:			Location:			
Date:						
Item	**No**	**Poor**	**Good**	**Excellent**	**N/a**	**Comments**
Items do not overhang pallets						
Stock control						
FIFO rotation is adhered to						
Items stored in the correct location						
High-value goods stored securely						
Hazardous items stored under the correct conditions						
Non-moving items regularly reviewed, eg FISH (first in still here)?						
Perpetual inventory counting takes place						
Stock counting accuracy measured						
Stock counts use the 'blind' count method (quantity not revealed to counter)						
Errors investigated thoroughly						

Warehouse audit – picking

Carried out by:			Location:			
Date:						
Item	**No**	**Poor**	**Good**	**Excellent**	**N/a**	**Comments**
Forward pick areas close to despatch						
Pick locations replenished efficiently						
Replenishment does not take place during picking						
Sufficient stock held in each location for each shift						
Items that sell together located next to each other						
Very similar items separated						
Fast-moving items in the most accessible locations						
Stock arranged with consideration to product size and weight						
Fast-moving items on middle shelves						
Pick list provides efficient pick path						
Heavier items picked first						
Pick instructions are clear and concise						

(*continued*)

(Continued)

Carried out by:			Location:			
Date:						
Item	**No**	**Poor**	**Good**	**Excellent**	**N/a**	**Comments**
Sufficient scanners/ voice units available for the team						
Pyramid picking evident						
Pick accuracy measured and monitored						
Despatch						
Departure times are planned						
Sufficient space given to lay out despatches						
Products packed securely and safely						
Load optimization apparent						
Products packed to minimize transport costs						
Outbound pallets recorded						

Warehouse audit – other areas

Item	No	Poor	Good	Excellent	N/a	Comments
Carried out by:			Location:			
Date:						
Staff and housekeeping						
Daily and weekly resource planning takes place						
Daily work tasks balanced and prioritized						
Tasks checked from an ergonomic point of view						
Resources maximized to avoid idle time						
Activities timed and compared against target						
Activities reviewed regularly						
Staff trained regularly						
Staff encouraged to suggest improvements						
Staff are uniformed and smart						
Staff issued with PPE						
PPE adequate for the tasks required						

(*continued*)

(Continued)

Carried out by:			Location:				
Date:							
Performance management							
Performance measured							
Suite of relevant performance measures exists							
Performance measures shared with staff and visible in the warehouse							
Staff productivity measured							
Productivity data shared with staff							

Warehouse audit – legislative/health and safety requirements

Carried out by:			Location:				
Date:							
Item	**No**	**Poor**	**Good**	**Excellent**	**N/a**	**Comments**	
Warehouse safety policy document available for inspection/displayed							
Risk assessments carried out							
Risk assessments available for inspection							
Near-miss record book kept							

(*continued*)

(Continued)

Item	No	Poor	Good	Excellent	N/a	Comments
Carried out by:			**Location:**			
Date:						
Accident book kept						
Accident book up to date						
Manual handling assessment available for inspection						
COSHH assessment carried out						
Equipment statutory inspection certificates available for inspection						
Waste disposal arrangements in place						
Notices displayed						
Employer's liability and public liability certificate						
Health and safety information for Employee Regulations 1999						
Health and safety policy						
COSHH information signage						
Electric shock signage						

(*continued*)

(Continued)

Item	No	Poor	Good	Excellent	N/a	Comments
Carried out by:			Location:			
Date:						
Staff awareness of following regulations						
Health and Safety Executive requirements (UK)						
Occupational Safety and Health Administration requirements (USA)						
Health and Safety (Signs & Signals) Regulations 1996						
Health & Safety (First Aid) Regulations 1981						
Provision and Use at Work Equipment Regulations 1998						
Lifting Operations and Lifting Equipment Regulations 1998						
Display Screen Equipment Regulations 1992						
Regulatory Reform (Fire Safety) Order 2005						
Pollution Prevention and Control Act 1999						
Environmental Protection Act 1990						

(continued)

(Continued)

Carried out by:			Location:			
Date:						
Item	**No**	**Poor**	**Good**	**Excellent**	**N/a**	**Comments**
Hazardous Waste Regulations						
Producer Responsibility Obligations (Packaging Waste) Regulations						
Waste Electrical & Electronic Equipment Regulations 2007						

* Note that different countries will have different requirements and legislation

Further information

This audit can be downloaded in Excel format from www.howtologistics. com for a small fee.

APPENDIX II
LSP transport audit checklists

This section provides audit checklists for a road freight transport operation. These lists are not exhaustive, and can be added to by the auditor to meet their own requirements.

Transport audit – transport yard

Carried out by:			Location:	
Date:				
Item	**No**	**Yes**	**N/a**	**Comments**
Sufficient space for goods vehicle parking				
Comprehensive signage for drivers in multiple languages				
Comprehensive signage for visitors				
Staff cars parked away from vehicles				
Perimeter fencing in good order				
Security gates/barriers in good working order				
External ground in good condition				
LPG gas and diesel kept in suitably safe and secure area				
Vehicle and trailer wash facilities available				

Transport audit – maintenance

Carried out by:			Location:	
Date:				
Item	**No**	**Yes**	**N/a**	**Comments**
Vehicle maintenance schedule visible in office				
All vehicles and trailers on the plan				
Future service dates shown				
Future MOT dates shown				
Plan updated weekly				
Tachograph calibration dates shown				
Road tax expiry date shown				
Other inspection dates shown, eg tail-lift				
Comprehensive file kept for every fleet vehicle				
Vehicle service/ inspection sheets filed in date order				
Maintenance sheet signed by the fitter and supervisor				
Sheet stamped by the repair garage (if external)				
Driver vehicle defect sheets filed in date order				

(*continued*)

(Continued)

Carried out by:			Location:	
Date:				
Item	**No**	**Yes**	**N/a**	**Comments**
Sample check of defects reported				
All reported defects checked, signed and actioned				
Defect report book kept				
Vehicle records kept for at least 18 months				
Safety inspections carried out (frequency)				
Automated vehicle scheduling system in place				
Whiteboard used for scheduling				
KPIs in place				
KPIs on view				
KPIs shared with staff				

Transport audit – administration

Carried out by:		Location:			
Date:					
Item	**No**	**Yes**	**N/a**	**Comments**	
CPC holder (nominated professionally competent person) on site					
All current vehicles recorded on licence					
Details of operator's licence (enter in comments): • issue date • valid until • number of vehicles • margin for additional vehicles					
Operator's licence sufficient for current fleet numbers and has spare capacity					
Rented vehicles over 28 days shown on operator's licence					
Log kept recording how long vehicles have been on rental					
Trigger mechanism for transferring long-term rental vehicles onto the operator's licence					
Rental agreements filed in date order					
Copies of drivers' licences held in office					

(*continued*)

(Continued)

Carried out by:			Location:	
Date:				
Item	**No**	**Yes**	**N/a**	**Comments**
Licences checked within the last six months				
Driving licence register kept				
Copy of vehicle VTG 6 plating certificate kept on file				
MOT certificate on file for each vehicle				
Valid vehicle insurance certificate on file				
Copy of each vehicle tachograph calibration on file				
Valid tail-lift inspection certificate in place (if applicable)				
Valid crane inspection certificate (if applicable)				
Notification log for infringements and medical conditions kept				
Copies of drivers' digital cards held on file				
Company digital card in office				
Log of drivers' hours kept				
Training log kept for Drivers' CPC*				

*A Driver CPC (Certificate of Professional Competence) was introduced across the EU to ensure high driving standards and improve road safety. All professional road freight drivers in the EU must hold a Driver CPC (with some exceptions).

A Driver CPC lasts for five years. To retain a CPC, drivers need to complete 35 hours of periodic training every five years to continue to drive professionally.

APPENDIX III
Sample non-disclosure agreement

CONFIDENTIALITY AGREEMENT
THIS AGREEMENT is made between the PARTIES

1 **Apprise Consulting Ltd** (Registration number:4987218) whose registered office is at: 22, Ensign Business Centre, Westwood Way, Westwood Business Park, Coventry CV4 8JA acting on behalf of **ABC Ltd**

and

2

Please enter the name of your company, registration number and registered office address

BACKGROUND
"Apprise Consulting Ltd" acting on behalf of (**ABC**) wish to disclose information to you relating to (**ABC**) businesses for the purpose of producing a proposal for the warehousing and distribution of ABC's products in the UK.

IT IS AGREED as follows:

1 In this Agreement:

   a. "Authorized Representative(s)" means those employees, officers and directors of the receiving party or any member of its group together with its professional advisers;

   b. "Confidential Information" means any information or data relating to the disclosing party, any member of the disclosing party's Group or to their respective businesses which is in written, electronic or other visual or machine readable form or which is communicated orally, including but not limited to, any kind of commercial or technical information, business, financial and marketing information, computer software and know-how which is made available to the receiving party in connection with the Purpose;

2 PROVIDED THAT Confidential Information does not include any information which the receiving party is able to demonstrate:

a. is already in the public domain or which becomes available to the public through no breach of this Agreement by the receiving party or its Authorized Representatives;

b. was in the possession of the receiving party prior to receipt from the disclosing party;

c. is independently developed by the receiving party without any use of Confidential Information;

d. is approved for release by the written agreement of the disclosing party; or

e. is required to be disclosed by law or the rules of any governmental or regulatory organization;

3 "Group" means the group of companies comprising the company in question together with its subsidiaries and affiliates as implied by the company registration number above.

4 The territory covered by this agreement is the UK.

5 For a period of five years following the date of this Agreement the receiving party shall procure that the members of its Group and its Authorized Representatives shall:

a. keep the confidential information confidential and shall not disclose it to anyone other than to its Authorized Representatives who need to know such information for the purposes of considering or advising in relation to the Purpose; and

b. use the Confidential Information exclusively for the Purpose and shall not permit the Confidential Information to go out of its possession or control; and

c. not make any announcement concerning, or otherwise publicize, the Purpose or any other arrangement with the receiving party in any way relating to the Purpose; and

d. procure that each Authorized Representative to whom disclosure of Confidential information is made, is made aware in advance of disclosure of the provisions of this Agreement and shall procure that each Authorized Representative adheres to these provisions as if such person were a party to this Agreement; and

e. immediately upon request by the disclosing party deliver to the disclosing party all Confidential Information (including all copies, analyses, memoranda or other notes made by the receiving party or its Authorized Representatives) and delete all electronically held Confidential Information or, with the consent of the disclosing party, destroy the same and provide the disclosing party with a certificate confirming that the provisions of this clause 5.e have been complied with.

6 No right or licence is granted to the receiving party in relation to the Confidential Information otherwise than as set out in the Agreement.

7 The receiving party acknowledges that damages would not be a sufficient remedy for any threatened or actual breach of this Agreement and that the disclosing party will be entitled to other remedies, including but not limited to, injunctive relief and specific performance.

8 The receiving party acknowledges that neither disclosing party nor any of its Authorized Representatives makes any express or implied warranty about, or accepts responsibility for, the accuracy or completeness of any of the information supplied under this Agreement.

9 Neither party shall assign this Agreement without prior written consent of the other party.

10 Notices under this Agreement shall be in writing and shall be deemed validly given if delivered by hand, e-mail, fax (supported by positive transmission report) or post (recorded delivery, with proof of posting) and shall be deemed served on the date of despatch.

11 This Agreement shall be governed by and construed in accordance with the laws of England and Wales.

SIGNED by
duly authorized for and on behalf of

....

Print name:
Date:

SIGNED by
duly authorized for and on behalf of
APPRISE CONSULTING LTD

Print name: Gwynne Richards
Date:

APPENDIX IV
LSP outsourcing contract – typical headings

Table of Contents

APPENDIX V
Sample receiving process flow

Sample receiving process flow

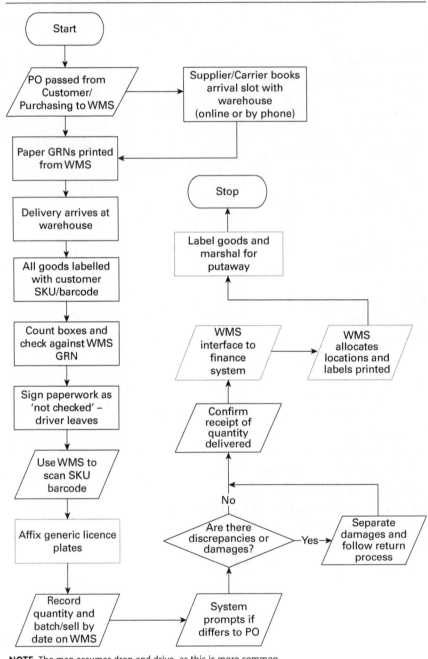

NOTE The map assumes drop and drive, as this is more common
SOURCE © Logistics Partners Consultancy Limited 2019

APPENDIX VI
Sample customer questionnaire

CUSTOMER: ....

CONTACT: ....

TEL NO: ....

DATE: ....

PRODUCT TYPES: ....

<u>Incoming</u>:

Please indicate
no per annum

MODES OF TRANSPORT: I) Road   (i) 20' container

(ii) 40'/45' container

(iii) 8.0m rigid vehicle

(iv) 13.6m trailer

(v) Parcel deliveries

<u>Product loading</u>

(i) Loose: No of items   Per   20' container   ....

Per   40'/45' container   ....

(ii) Palletized: No of pallets Per 20' Container/Trailer   ....

Per 40'/45' Container/Trailer   ....

(iii) Average number of pallets received on intake   ....

Size and type of pallet used:

1,000	x	1,200 mm		GKN Chep
1,000	x	1,000 mm		UK white
800	x	1,200 mm		Euro pallet
Other	(please state)			American pallet
	....			Other

Height of pallet: Min .... Average .... Max ....

Weight of pallet: Min .... Average .... Max ....

No of lines per incoming
shipment   Min .... Average .... Max ....

No of incoming pallets/   ....
items per wk

No of cartons per pallet   Min .... Average .... Max ....

Average carton sizes   (a) ....
                            (b) ....
                            (c) ....
                            (d) ....

Average carton weight

Warehousing

Temperature   N/A ☐   Min ☐   Max ☐
Is product hazardous? Yes ☐   No ☐
If yes: classes   ....

Storage requirement: No of pallets   ☐

                        No of shelf locations (0.2 m³)   ☐

                        Additional sq m for other activities   ☐

                        Bin locations   ☐

or   Total m² (dedicated)   ....

Potential expansion/reduction requirement   +
                                                   -      ....

Stock turnaround   _____   times per annum

Total no of product lines (SKU)   ....

Storage status: Excise bonded: ☐
                        Customs bonded: ☐
                        Free movement: ☐

Are pallets stackable?   Yes ☐   No ☐

If yes, how high? ☐ pallets inc base pallet

Value-added services required

		% of total items
Labelling	☐	....
Barcoding	☐	....
Packaging	☐	....
Stretch wrapping pallets	☐	....
Product configuration/assembly	☐	....
Product repair	☐	....
Other	☐	....

Please state details of other ....
....
....

Total percentage of returns .... %

Outgoing

No of orders per week   Min ....   Average ....   Max ....
No of lines per order   Min ....   Average ....   Max ....
No of units per order   Min ....   Average ....   Max ....

Average despatch order size   Cartons ....

No of pallets despatched per week   Pallets ....

No of units/outers per order line   ....
No of outers despatched per wk   ....

Method of order receipt   EDI ☐

Email ☐

Post ☐

Telephone ☐

Fax ☐

Warehouse management system

Current warehouse management system
used (if applicable):   ....

Inventory control procedure   ....
(eg FIFO, batch no, etc):
                                         ....

Required order processing time: .... days

Required delivery time: .... days

Volumes

Seasonal pattern	Incoming pallets	Incoming cartons	Av. no of pallets stored per week or space required	Outgoing orders	Average units per order
January					
February					
March					
April					
May					
June					
July					
August					
September					
October					
November					
December					

<u>Administration</u>

Office accommodation required?   Yes ☐   No ☐   Number of staff ☐

Services required:

Order processing ☐

Credit control ☐

Invoicing ☐

Stock updates   Daily ☐   Weekly ☐   Monthly ☐

Other services ☐

Please state   ....
....

Service objectives

1.   --------% of orders delivered in -------- days from receipt of order.

2.   Warehousing costs are a maximum of--------% of annual turnover.

3.   Distribution costs are a maximum of ---------% of annual turnover.

Any other requirements (please state)

....
....
....
....

Length of contract envisaged ....

APPENDIX VII
Useful websites

Useful websites

Company	Website	Type
Alibaba	www.alibaba.com	Retailer
Amazon Robotics	www.amazonrobotics.com	Technology company
Association for Supply Chain Management (ASCM)	www.ascm.org/	Professional body
Apprise Consulting Ltd	www.appriseconsulting.co.uk	Consultancy
Ascent Global Logistics	ascentgl.com/	LSP
Benchmarking Success	www.benchmarkingsuccess.com	Benchmarking company
BigChange	www.bigchangeapps.com	Technology company and consultancy
Blockchain in Transport Alliance (BITA)	www.bita.studio	Blockchain alliance
Boston Dynamics	www.bostondynamics.com	Technology company
British Association of Removers	bar.co.uk	Trade association
British International Freight Association	www.bifa.org	Trade association
C4FF	www.c4ff.co.uk	Technology company
Cargosense	www.cargosense.com	Technology company
Cerasis	cerasis.com	Technology company

(continued)

(Continued)

Company	Website	Type
Chartered Institute of Logistics and Transport (CILT)	ciltuk.org.uk/	Professional body
	ciltuk.org.uk/Knowledge	Knowledge library (member access only)
Chartered Institute of Procurement and Supply (CIPS)	www.cips.org	Professional body
Chartered Institution of Highways & Transportation (CIHT)	www.ciht.org.uk/	Professional body
Cisco	www.cisco.com	Technology company
Cold Chain Federation	www.coldchainfederation.org.uk/	Trade association
CollectPlus	www.collectplus.co.uk/	Last-mile delivery
Council of Supply Chain Management Professionals (CSCMP)	cscmp.org/	Professional body
Croner	croner.co.uk/	HR services including wage cost data
DC Velocity	www.dcvelocity.com/	Magazine/blog
Delta Drone	www.deltadrone.com/en/	Technology company
Department for Transport	www.gov.uk/government/organisations/department-for-transport	UK government department
DHL	www.dhl.com	LSP
eft	www.eft.com	Business intelligence
Eiratech	www.eiratech.com	Technology company
Excello Law	excellolaw.co.uk/	Law firm

(*continued*)

(Continued)

Company	Website	Type
Fast Radius	www.fastradius.com	3D printing
Fleet Operator Recognition Scheme	www.fors-online.org.uk/cms/	Government scheme for transport
FourKites	www.fourkites.com	Technology company
Freight Transport Association	fta.co.uk	Trade association
	fta.co.uk/services/affinity-services/fuel-price-information-service/services/fuel-price-information-service/	Fuel information
Gnewt	www.gnewt.co.uk	Last-mile delivery
Go-Jek	www.gojek.com	Last-mile delivery
GOV.UK statistics	www.gov.uk/search/research-and-statistics	Government statistics on inflation measures including RPI/CPI
Grey Orange	www.greyorange.com	Technology company
Health and Safety Executive	www.hse.gov.uk	UK government agency
HowtoLogistics	howtologistics.com/	Consultancy and technology
IAM Robotics	www.iamrobotics.com	Technology company
Inbound Logistics	www.inboundlogistics.com/cms/	Magazine/blog
Institute of Chartered Shipbrokers	www.ics.org.uk/	Professional body
Internet Retailing	internetretailing.net/magazine/magazine	Magazine/blog
JD.com	www.jd.com	Retailer
JDA Software	www.jda.com	Technology company
A T Kearney	www.atkearney.co.uk	Consultancy

(continued)

(Continued)

Company	Website	Type
Knapp	www.knapp.com	Automation supplier
LCP Consulting	www.bearingpoint.com	Consultancy
Lloyds Loading List	www.lloydsloadinglist.com	Freight community news
Logistics Bureau	www.logisticsbureau.com	Consultancy
Logistics Management	www.logisticsmgmt.com	Magazine/blog
Logistics Manager	www.logisticsmanager.com	Magazine/blog
Logistics Partners Consultancy Limited	www.logisticspartners.co.uk	Logistics IT consultancy
Logistics World	www.logisticsworld.com	Directory
Manufacturing and Logistics IT	www.logisticsit.com	Magazine/blog
Menzies	www.menziesdistribution.com	LSP
MetricStream	www.metricstream.com	Technology company
Modern Material Handling	www.mmh.com	Magazine/blog
Mole Solutions	www.molesolutions.co.uk	Technology company
Motor Transport	motortransport.co.uk/top-100/	Publication
National Industrial Transportation League	www.nitl.org	Professional body
Ocado Technology	www.ocadotechnology.com	Technology company
Occupational Safety and Health Administration	www.osha.gov	US government agency
Palletforce	www.palletforce.com	LSP
Panalpina	www.panalpina.com	LSP
Parcelly	parcelly.com	Last-mile delivery

(*continued*)

(Continued)

Company	Website	Type
PWC	www.pwc.co.uk	Consultancy
Quiqup	www.quiqup.com	Last-mile delivery
Road Haulage Association	rha.org.uk/	Trade association
Shutl	shutl.com/uk	Last-mile delivery
Starship Robots	www.starship.xyz	Last-mile delivery
Startus-Insights	www.startus-insights.com	Technology company
Statista	www.statista.com	Business intelligence
Storage Handling and Distribution	www.shdlogistics.com	Magazine/blog
Supply Chain Brain	www.supplychainbrain.com	Magazine/blog
Supply Chain Digest	www.scdigest.com	Magazine/blog
Supply Chain Dive	www.supplychaindive.com	Magazine/blog
Supply Chain Management Review	www.scmr.com	Magazine/blog
Supply Chain Movement	www.supplychainmovement.com	Magazine/blog
Swisslog	www.swisslog.com	Technology company
Tesla	www.tesla.com	Technology company
Timocom	www.timocom.co.uk	Technology company
Transmetrics	transmetrics.eu/	Technology company
Transport for London	tfl.gov.uk	UK local government body
Transport Intelligence	www.ti-insight.com	Business Intelligence
UK Chamber of Shipping	www.ukchamberofshipping.com	Trade association

(*continued*)

(Continued)

Company	Website	Type
United Kingdom Warehousing Association	www.ukwa.org.uk	Trade association
Vested®	www.vestedway.com	Consultancy
Vuzix	www.vuzix.com	Technology company
Warehouse and Logistics News	warehousenews.co.uk/	Magazine/blog
Warehousing Education and Research Council (WERC)	werc.org	Professional body

REFERENCES AND FURTHER READING

Accenture (n. d.) [accessed 7 August 2019] World-Class 4PL Capabilities, *Accenture* [Online] https://www.accenture.com/au-en/topic-fourth-party-logistics (archived at https://perma.cc/5BH3-7AWP)

Adams, K (2018) [accessed 7 August 2019] Culina enters baked goods space, *Flickread* [Online] http://flickread.com/edition/html/index.php?pdf=5abbf07f8f5b0#6 (archived at https://perma.cc/9TEB-KAFR)

Air Cargo News (2018) [accessed 27 July 2019] Top 25 Air Freight Carriers 2018, *Air Cargo News* [Online] https://www.aircargonews.net/data-hub/top-25-cargo-airlines-2017/ (archived at https://perma.cc/K6UZ-ZKY3)

Ames, B (2018) [accessed 39 July 2019] DHL to invest $300 million in emerging technologies, *DC Velocity* [Online] https://www.dcvelocity.com/articles/20181130-dhl-to-invest--300-million-in-emerging-technologies (archived at https://perma.cc/4VZM-RYU3)

Armstrong & Associates (2017b) [accessed 1 June 2019] 3PL Customers Report Identifies Service Trends, 3PL Market Segment Sizes and Growth Rates, *Armstrong & Associates* [Online] https://www.3plogistics.com/3pl-customers-report-identifies-service-trends-3pl-market-segment-sizes-growth-rates/ (archived at https://perma.cc/L8P2-LXW7)

Armstrong & Associates (2017c) [accessed 1 June 2019] LSP global market size estimates, *Armstrong & Associates* [Online] https://www.3plogistics.com/3pl-market-info-resources/3pl-market-information/global-3pl-market-size-estimates/ (archived at https://perma.cc/Q28X-EE8W)

Armstrong & Associates Inc (2017a) *Global and Regional Infrastructure, Logistics Costs, and Third-Party Logistics Market Trends and Analysis*, available at: https://www.3plogistics.com/product/global-regional-infrastructure-logistics-costs-third-party-logistics-market-trends-analysis/ (archived at https://perma.cc/R6P7-KE5U)

Armstrong, E (2019) [accessed 7 August 2019] 2018 Was a Year of Extraordinary Growth for 3PLs, *Transport Topics* [Online] https://www.ttnews.com/articles/2018-was-year-extraordinary-growth-3pls (archived at https://perma.cc/85YE-T6DD)

Armstrong, R (2014) [accessed 28 July 2019] Where the 3PL Action Is: A Scan of Logistics Providers & Services Worldwide, *Supply Chain Brain* [Online] https://www.supplychainbrain.com/articles/18817-where-the-3pl-action-is-a-scan-of-logistics-providers-services-worldwide (archived at https://perma.cc/U6V9-Q7L9)

AXSMarine (2019) [accessed 7 June 2019] Alphaliner Top 100, *AXSMarine* [Online] https://alphaliner.axsmarine.com/PublicTop100/ (archived at https://perma.cc/2LPK-AXMM)

Badasha, K (2012) [accessed 28 July 2019] 'Think small and focused' when writing an RFP, *CIPS* [Online] https://www.cips.org/en-GB/supply-management/news/2012/august/think-small-and-focused-when-writing-an-rfp/ (archived at https://perma.cc/WQ7F-VBAB)

Bailey, N (2018) [accessed 12 August 2019] Top read: Global freight forwarding market sees rapid growth in 2017 as large forwarders seek to transform themselves from within, *Transport Intelligence* [Online] https://www.ti-insight.com/top-read-global-freight-forwarding-market-sees-rapid-growth-in-2017-as-large-forwarders-seek-to-transform-themselves-from-within/ (archived at https://perma.cc/NJ2C-MUBM)

Barnes, D (2008) *Operations Management: An international perspective*, Thomson Learning, London

Boeing (n. d.a) [accessed 28 July 2019] World Air Cargo Forecast 2018–2037, *Boeing* [Online] https://www.boeing.com/commercial/market/cargo-forecast/ (archived at https://perma.cc/5MGZ-Z97V)

Boeing (n. d.b) [accessed 30 July 2019] Importance of freighters in the air cargo industry, *Boeing* [Online] https://www.boeing.com/commercial/market/cargo-forecast/importance-of-freighters/ (archived at https://perma.cc/VSJ2-8N2F)

Brightpearl (2018) *Returns Tsunami for Retail*, available at: https://info.brightpearl.com/returns-tsunami-for-retail (archived at https://perma.cc/TD62-PSRQ)

Brownsell, A (2018) [accessed 11 May 2019] KFC: A very fcking clever campaign, *Campaign* [Online] https://www.campaignlive.co.uk/article/kfc-fcking-clever-campaign/1498912 (archived at https://perma.cc/MYN9-LZH2)

Chartered Institute of Logistics and Transport (CILT) (2011) [accessed 12 August 2019] Vision 2035, *CILT* [Online] https://ciltuk.org.uk/Portals/0/Documents/About%20Us/Vision2035.pdf (archived at https://perma.cc/62XL-PFBM)

Chartered Institute of Logistics and Transport (2018) Outsourcing Attitudes survey, *CILT* [Online] https://ciltuk.org.uk/About-Us/Professional-Sectors-Forums/Forums/Outsourcing-Procurement/Surveys (archived at https://perma.cc/M4DG-4E79)

Chartered Institute of Procurement & Supply (CIPS) (n. d.a) [accessed 1 June 2019] P&SM: Monitoring the Performance of Suppliers, *CIPS* [Online] https://www.cips.org/Documents/Knowledge/Procurement-Topics-and-Skills/10-Developing-and-Managing-Contracts/Performance-Analysis-and-Management/POP-Monitoring_the_Performance_of_Suppliers.pdf (archived at https://perma.cc/YTE2-XN3R)

Chartered Institute of Procurement & Supply (n. d.b) [accessed 12 August 2019] Supplier Relationship Management (members-only content), *CIPS* [Online]

https://www.cips.org/knowledge/procurement-topics-and-skills/srm-and-sc-management/supplier-relationship--management/ (archived at https://perma.cc/9L5A-DGCX)

Christopher, M and Peck, H (2004) Building the Resilient Supply Chain, *International Journal of Logistics Management*, **15** (2), pp 1–14

Council of Supply Chain Management Professionals (2013) *CSCMP Glossary*, available at: https://cscmp.org/CSCMP/Academia/SCM_Definitions_and_Glossary_of_Terms/CSCMP/Educate/SCM_Definitions_and_Glossary_of_Terms.aspx?hkey=60879588-f65f-4ab5-8c4b-6878815ef921 (archived at https://perma.cc/VN3Y-DLPB)

Covey, S (1989) *The 7 Habits of Highly Effective People*, New York, Free Press

Cunliffe, R (n. d.) [accessed 27 July 2019] What can KFC teach us about supply chain management? *Hillyer-McKeown* [Online] https://www.hillyermckeown.co.uk/can-kfc-teach-us-supply-chain-management/ (archived at https://perma.cc/6P2Z-XR53)

Dani, S *et al* (2018) Investigating the influencers of commoditisation within logistics outsourcing, LRN conference paper (unpublished)

Davis, C (2011) A T Kearney CILT Outsourcing and Procurement Forum presentation

DB Schenker (n. d.) [accessed 7 August 2019] VIDEO 5.12 CarryPick system from Swisslog, *YouTube* [Online] https://www.youtube.com/watch?v=ga1GaYn-grI&t=14s (archived at https://perma.cc/79KR-7C2U)

Deloitte (2018) [accessed 7 June 2019] 2018 global outsourcing survey, *Deloitte* [Online] https://www2.deloitte.com/us/en/pages/operations/articles/global-outsourcing-survey.html (archived at https://perma.cc/L5WS-VT6B)

DHL and Ricoh (n. d.) [accessed 7 August 2019] DHL Vision Picking Final 1080p 1, *YouTube* [Online] https://www.youtube.com/watch?v=2NPJtJX1YU8&feature=youtu.be (archived at https://perma.cc/QKA6-BCB5)

Dills, T [accessed 29 July 2019] Trucking 'uberization' and the 'new 800-pound gorilla that everyone will have to be aware of', *Overdrive* [Online] https://www.overdriveonline.com/trucking-uberization-the-new-800-pound-gorilla-that-everyone-will-have-to-be-aware-of/ (archived at https://perma.cc/3X2V-FN76)

Dornier, P *et al* (1998) *Global Operations and Logistics: Text and cases*, New York, John Wiley

eft (2018) [accessed 7 June 2019] 2018 eft Global Logistics Report, *JDA Software* [Online] https://jda.com/knowledge-center/collateral/2018-eft-global-logistics-report (archived at https://perma.cc/5HQG-VZBX)

eft (2019) [accessed 29 July 2019] 2019 eft Global Logistics Report, *JDA Software* [Online] https://jda.com/knowledge-center/collateral/2019-eft-global-logistics-report (archived at https://perma.cc/9GZ6-VTUK)

European Conference of Minsters of Transport (2001) *Short Sea Shipping in Europe*, available at: https://www.oecd-ilibrary.org/transport/short-sea-shipping-in-europe_9789282113271-en (archived at https://perma.cc/QK3T-7ZFW)

Eurostat (2018) [accessed 6 June 2019] Road freight transport by journey characteristics, *Eurostat* [Online] https://ec.europa.eu/eurostat/statistics-explained/index.php?title=Road_freight_transport_by_journey_characteristics&oldid=429430 (archived at https://perma.cc/352Y-B5GD)

Forwarder Magazine (2018) [accessed 7 August 2019] Logistics sector facing a "perfect storm" says UKWA CEO, *Forwarder Magazine* [Online] https://forwardermagazine.com/logistics-sector-facing-a-perfect-storm-says-ukwa-ceo/ (archived at https://perma.cc/4VVQ-G6T3)

Freight Transport Association [accessed 30 July 2019] Tips for using rail freight, *Freight Transport Association* [Online] https://fta.co.uk/compliance-and-advice/rail/case-studies/tips-for-using-rail-freight (archived at https://perma.cc/M3KL-DBCY)

Freightflow (n. d.) [accessed 5 May 2019] What Self-Driving Trucks Mean for Your Third Party Logistics Company, *Freightflow* [Online] https://www.freightflow.co/posts/self-driving-trucks-mean-third-party-logistics-company/ (archived at https://perma.cc/VK7S-25XX)

Frost, F A and Kumar, M (2000) INTSERVQUAL: an internal adaptation of the GAP model in a large service organization, *Journal of Service Marketing*, **14** (5), pp 358–77

Gadde, L-E and Hulthén, K (2011) Logistics outsourcing and the role of logistics service providers from an industrial network perspective, *Industrial Marketing and Purchasing Group* [Online] https://www.impgroup.org/uploads/papers/6746.pdf (archived at https://perma.cc/KXX4-8M44)

GEFCO (2018) [accessed 27 June 2019] GEFCO launches its innovation factory to accelerate internal innovation, *GEFCO* [Online] https://www.gefco.net/en/newsroom/news/detail/news/gefco-launches-its-innovation-factory-to-accelerate-internal-innovation/ (archived at https://perma.cc/4F83-75ZX)

Gibson, R and Savage, C (2013) Know your risk, know your appetite for growth, *Operations Management*, **39** (1), pp 12–15

Gibson, R, Saghiri, S and Godsmark, J (2017) Supply Chain Innovations, *CILT Focus,* **12** (1), pp 29–31

Gourdin, K (2010) *Global Logistics Management: A competitive advantage for the 21st century* (2nd ed), Blackwell Publishing, Oxford

Green, W (2018) [accessed 11 May 2019] Five lessons from the KFC chicken crisis, *CIPS* [Online] https://www.cips.org/supply-management/analysis/2018/february/five-lessons-from-the-kfc-chicken-crisis/ (archived at https://perma.cc/QZ73-N2LF)

Grubišić Šeba, M (2018) [accessed 30 July 2019] Outsourcing Rules in the Public and the Private Sector, *Intech Open* [Online] https://www.intechopen.com/

books/positive-and-negative-aspects-of-outsourcing/outsourcing-rules-in-the-public-and-the-private-sector (archived at https://perma.cc/5M8U-QZU4)

Henderson, J (2017) [accessed 30 July 2019] KFC to "revolutionise" UK food service supply chain with DHL and QSL appointment, *Supply Chain Digital* [Online] https://www.supplychaindigital.com/scm/kfc-revolutionise-uk-food-service-supply-chain-dhl-and-qsl-appointment (archived at https://perma.cc/GHG3-6TVJ)

Honeywell (2016) [accessed 30 July 2019] E-Commerce Trends Driving Distribution Centers' Need For New Mobile Technology, Voice Applications To Provide Accurate, On-Time Delivery, Honeywell Survey Reveals, *Honeywell* [Online] https://www.honeywell.com/content/honeywell/us/en/newsroom/pressreleases/2015/10/e-commerce-trends-driving-distribution-centers-need-for-new-mobile-technology-voice-applications-to-provide-accurate-on-time-delivery-honeywell-survey-reveals (archived at https://perma.cc/K4WY-T7TG)

HSS (2019) [accessed 30 July 2019] Wincanton explores flexible automation to better meet strategic goals, *HSS* [Online] https://www.hsssearch.co.uk/3pl-automation-wincanton-strategy (archived at https://perma.cc/SY3P-V2GM)

IBISWorld (2018) [accessed 30 July 2019] Global Courier & Delivery Services Industry – Market Research Report, *IBISWorld* [Online] https://www.ibisworld.com/industry-trends/global-industry-reports/transport-post-storage/courier-delivery-services.html (archived at https://perma.cc/R73H-6M5A)

IBM (2006) [accessed 30 July 2019] Building value in logistics outsourcing: The future of the logistics provider industry, *IBM* [Online] http://www-07.ibm.com/innovation/in/adv/special/overview/download/building_value_in_logistic_outsourcing.pdf (archived at https://perma.cc/D2J5-JZ6S)

Inbound Logistics (2017) [accessed 5 July 2019] Freight Bill Audit & Payment: Getting More Bang for Your Bucks, *Inbound Logistics* [Online] https://www.inboundlogistics.com/cms/article/freight-bill-audit-payment-getting-more-bang-for-your-bucks/ (archived at https://perma.cc/FC4B-DJQE)

Insight Partners (2018) *Third Party Logistics Market - Global Analysis To 2025*, available at: https://www.theinsightpartners.com/reports/third-party-logistics-market?Anand-EMP (archived at https://perma.cc/E6N7-RP8E)

Integrated Marketing Communication Council (IMCC) Europe (n. d.) [accessed 30 July 2019] Glossary of Terms, *IMCC* [Online] http://www.imcceurope.com/pdfs/Integrated%20marketing%20communication%20glossary.pdf (archived at https://perma.cc/H9PE-3EU9)

International Air Transport Association (IATA) (2019) *World Air Transport Statistics, Plus Edition 2019 (WATS+)*, available at: https://www.iata.org/publications/store/Pages/world-air-transport-statistics.aspx (archived at https://perma.cc/ZF8V-HY9T)

International Air Transport Association (n. d.) [accessed 30 July 2019] The value of air cargo, *IATA* [Online] https://www.iata.org/whatwedo/cargo/sustainability/Documents/air-cargo-brochure.pdf (archived at https://perma.cc/2WV4-M2LV)

International Organization for Standardization (ISO) (2018) ISO 31000:2018 *Risk management - Guidelines*, available at: https://www.iso.org/standard/65694.html (archived at https://perma.cc/YEJ4-MXSE)

Jackson, M (2011) [accessed 7 June 2019] A sign of intelligence life, *Logistics Manager*, https://www.logisticsmanager.com/15452-mick-jackson-a-sign-of-intelligence-life/ (archived at https://perma.cc/L8XJ-KASF)

JD Logistics (n. d.) [accessed 7 August 2019] JD com Fully Automated Warehouse in Shanghai, *YouTube* [Online] https://www.youtube.com/watch?v=2--V-MkcYOg&t=54s (archived at https://perma.cc/9752-9SJG)

JDA Software (n. d.) [accessed 7 August 2019] Third Party Logistics: Redefining the model for innovation, *JDA Software* [Online] http://www.warehouse-logistics.com/Download/Flyer/jda_ms_bro_3pl.pdf (archived at https://perma.cc/XUS5-YZ7S)

John, G (n. d.) [accessed 7 August 2019] Companies confuse supplier performance with relationships, says State of Flux, *State of Flux* [Online] https://www.stateofflux.co.uk/ideas-insights/articles/companies-confuse-supplier-performance-with-relati (archived at https://perma.cc/8XVV-8WTJ)

Kapadia, S (2018) [accessed 7 August 2019] One-third of warehouses don't have a warehouse management system, *Supply Chain Dive* [Online] https://www.supplychaindive.com/news/WMS-voice-picking-adoption-2018-dc-measures-study/525012/ (archived at https://perma.cc/7ZYJ-734M)

Kaplan, R S and Norton, D P (1996) *The Balanced Scorecard*, Harvard Business School Press, Cambridge, MA

Knapp (n. d.) [accessed 7 August 2019] Pick it Easy Robot by Knapp, *YouTube* [Online] https://www.youtube.com/watch?v=iw2wnaCc1ls&t=16s (archived at https://perma.cc/AGM2-APAZ)

Kraljic, P (1983) Purchasing must become supply management, *Harvard Business Review*, **61** (5), pp109-17

Kremic, T, Tuken, O and Rom, W (2006) Outsourcing decision support: a survey of benefits, risks, and decision factors, *Supply Chain Management – An International Journal*, **11** (6), pp 467–82

Langley, J *et al* (2019) *2019 Third-Party Logistics Study: The State of Logistics Outsourcing*, available at: http://www.3plstudy.com/3pl2019download.php (archived at https://perma.cc/K4G7-3Z6Z)

LCP Consulting (2016) Outsourcing operations and processes, talk to Cranfield University

Leonard, M (2019) [accessed 27 July 2019] Walmart tightens on-time, in-full rate for suppliers to 87%, *Supply Chain Dive* [Online] https://www.supplychaindive.

com/news/walmart-on-time-in-full-87-suppliers/550083/ (archived at https://perma.cc/LU64-ZCBF)

Lieb, R and Lieb, K [accessed 30 July 2019] The Asia-Pacific Region Third Party Logistics Industry in 2013: The provider CEO perspective, *Penske Logistics* [Online] https://www.penskelogistics.com/pdfs/2013_asia-pacific_3pl_ceo_study.pdf (archived at https://perma.cc/FZ6J-XV3M)

Lofvers, M (2013) *How would outsourcing the logistics activities add value?*, available at: https://www.supplychainmovement.com/how-would-outsourcing-the-logistics-activities-add-value/ (archived at https://perma.cc/8BF4-4DR8)

LogisticsGlossary (n. d.) [accessed 7 August 2019] Fifth Party Logistics Model (5PL), *LogisticsGlossary*, https://www.logisticsglossary.com/term/5pl/ (archived at https://perma.cc/9V2R-GRB9)

Markets and Markets (2017) [accessed 30 July 2019] Artificial Intelligence in Transportation Market by Machine Learning, Application, Offering, Process, and Region - Global Forecast to 2030, *Markets and Markets* [Online] https://www.marketsandmarkets.com/Market-Reports/artificial-intelligence-in-transportation-market-261260227.html (archived at https://perma.cc/Q5VL-L8E7)

McIvor, R (2000) A practical framework for understanding the outsourcing process, *Supply Chain Management: An International Journal*, 5 (1), pp 22–36

McIvor, R *et al* (2009) Performance management and the outsourcing process: Lessons from a financial services organisation, *International Journal of Operations & Production Management*, 29 (1), pp 1025–48

Mello, J E, Stank, T P and Esper, T L (2008) A Model of Logistics Outsourcing Strategy, *Transportation Journal*, 47 (4), pp 5–25

Melton, J (2019) [accessed 7 August 2019] Kroger and Ocado plan robotic grocery fulfillment center outside Atlanta, *Digital Commerce 360* [Online] https://www.digitalcommerce360.com/2019/07/12/kroger-and-ocado-plan-robotic-grocery-fulfillment-center-outside-atlanta/ (archived at https://perma.cc/YY2G-3VU7)

MetricStream (n. d.) [accessed 30 July 2019] Measuring Supplier Performance, *MetricStream* [Online] https://www.metricstream.com/insights/Supplier_performance_mngt.htm (archived at https://perma.cc/G453-F9H8)

Miller, R (2018) [accessed 1 February 2019] How transportation and logistics can position itself in a new world, *Ernst & Young* [Online] https://www.ey.com/en_gl/automotive-transportation/how-transportation-and-logistics-can-position-itself-in-a-new-world (archived at https://perma.cc/8NBQ-9TCR)

Moseley, R (2004) When working with metrics – the fewer the better is the rule, *Inventory Management*, 4 (10)

Motor Transport (n. d.) [accessed 30 July 2019] Motor Transport Top 100, *Motor Transport* [Online] https://motortransport.co.uk/top-100/ (archived at https://perma.cc/66B2-EAAH)

Murphy, P and Poist, F (2000) Third-party logistics: Some user versus provider perspectives, *Journal of Business Logistics*, **21** (1) pp 121–33

NOVONOUS (2015) Logistics Market in India 2015-2020, *Digital Journal* [Online] http://www.digitaljournal.com/pr/2558651 (archived at https://perma.cc/8CGD-8W7P)

O'Byrne, R (2017) [accessed 1 August 2019] What is Outsourcing? *Logistics Bureau* [Online] https://www.logisticsbureau.com/what-is-outsourcing/ (archived at https://perma.cc/6YFV-QKR4)

O'Marah, K (2018) [accessed 30 July 2019] 3 Supply Chain Lessons From the KFC Fowl-Up, *Forbes* [Online] https://www.forbes.com/sites/kevinomarah/2018/03/01/three-supply-chain-lessons-from-the-kfc-fowl-up/#64569b651cb1 (archived at https://perma.cc/5BHH-YBFX)

Parasuraman, A, Zeithaml, V A and Berry, L L (1985) A conceptual model of service quality and its implications for future research, *Journal of Marketing*, **49** (4), pp 41–50

Peters, T and Waterman, H (1982) *In Search of Excellence*, New York, Harper & Row

Porter, M E (1985) *Competitive Advantage: Creating and sustaining superior performance*, The Free Press, New York

Post & Parcel (2018) [accessed 7 August 2019] FedEx places reservation for 20 Tesla Semi trucks, *Post & Parcel* [Online] https://postandparcel.info/94708/news/infrastructure/fedex-places-reservation-for-20-tesla-semi-trucks/ (archived at https://perma.cc/W2EG-W9ML)

Post & Parcel (2019) [accessed 7 August 2019] 24/7 deliveries are the future of e-commerce, says ParcelHero, *Post & Parcel* [Online] https://postandparcel.info/104554/news/24-7-deliveries-are-the-future-of-e-commerce-says-parcelhero/ (archived at https://perma.cc/6MXP-JLBZ)

Power, M, Desouza, K and Bonifazi, C (2006) *The Outsourcing Handbook: How to implement a successful outsourcing process*, Kogan Page, London

Prahalad, C K and Hamel G (1990) The Core Competence of the Corporation, *Harvard Business Review*, **68** (3) pp 79–91

Priday, R (2018) [accessed 30 July 2019] The inside story of the great KFC chicken shortage of 2018, *Wired* [Online] https://www.wired.co.uk/article/kfc-chicken-crisis-shortage-supply-chain-logistics-experts (archived at https://perma.cc/SN99-E6JE)

Procurement Leaders (n. d.) [accessed 12 August 2019] Strategy Guide: Supplier Relationship Management, *Procurement Leaders* [Online] https://www.procurementleaders.com/AcuCustom/Sitename/DAM/052/sample-strategy-guide-SRM-0613_1.pdf (archived at https://perma.cc/SZ67-TMYM)

Robinson (n. d.) [accessed 7 August 2019] The Uberization of Trucking – Will We EVER See It Happen?, *Cerasis* [Online] https://cerasis.com/uberization-of-trucking/ (archived at https://perma.cc/9M9R-NYVZ)

Rouse, M (n. d.) [accessed 29 July 2019] (2003) Definition: Core competency, *SearchCIO* [Online] https://searchcio.techtarget.com/definition/core-competency (archived at https://perma.cc/H6ZJ-CNDQ)

Rushton, A and Walker, S (2007) *International Logistics and Supply Chain Outsourcing: From local to global*, Kogan Page, London

Sanchís-Pedregosa, C, Machuca, J A D and González-Zamora, M (2011) Logistics Outsourcing: Performance Models and Financial and Operational Indicators, *International Journal of Mechanical and Industrial Engineering*, 5 (11), pp 1311–16

SAP (n. d.) [accessed 7 August 2019] VIDEO 6.6 SAP Vision and voice warehouse system, *YouTube* [Online] https://www.youtube.com/watch?v=fJ-SDVU1JO8 (archived at https://perma.cc/F95X-4VNA)

Schwarting, D and Weissbarth, R [accessed 5 June 2019] Make or Buy: Three pillars of sound decision-making, *Strategy&* [Online] https://www.strategyand. pwc.com/media/file/Strategyand_Make-or-buy-sound-decision-making.pdf (archived at https://perma.cc/92SD-KGCP)

Schwemmer, M (2017) *Fraunhofer SCS Top 100 in European Transport and Logistics Services 2017–2018*, available at: https://www.dvvmedia-shop.de/ buch/logistik/503/top-100-in-european-transport-and-logistics-services-2017/18 (archived at https://perma.cc/FTW3-YH3J)

Simchi-Levi, D (2013) *Operations Rules: Delivering Customer Value through Flexible Operations*, MIT Press, Mass

Sit, S-S (2018) [accessed 30 July 2019] KFC was 'warned DHL would fail', *Chartered Institute of Procurement and Supply* [Online] https://www.cips.org/ supply-management/news/2018/february/kfc-warned-that-dhl-would-fail-its-supply-chain-says-union/ (archived at https://perma.cc/QDH8-8PVY)

Slack, N, Chambers, S and Johnston, R (2001) *Operations Management*, 3rd ed, Pearson Education Limited, Harlow

Slater, A G (2005) *Vulnerability in the supply chain.* University of Huddersfield, adapted from lecture notes

Starship (n. d.) [accessed 7 August 2019] Starship Campus Delivery Service with Robots, *YouTube* [Online] https://www.youtube.com/watch?v=Ftc0AVQEF6s&f eature=youtu.be (archived at https://perma.cc/ZS9A-7UN3)

Sparkes, M (2014) [accessed 12 August 2019] 'In a sense, Acorn did take over Apple', *The Telegraph* [Online] https://www.telegraph.co.uk/technology/ news/11220574/In-a-sense-Acorn-did-take-over-Apple.html (archived at https:// perma.cc/9HJF-TD6Y)

StartUs Insights (n. d.b) [accessed 10 July 2019] Disrupting The Logistics Industry: A Breakdown On Startup Driven Innovation, *StartUs Insights* [Online] https:// www.startus- insights.com/innovators-guide/disrupting-logistics-industry-breakdown-startup-driven-innovation/ (archived at https://perma.cc/8ASJ-ALTB)

Statista (n. d.a) [accessed 30 July 2019] eCommerce – outlook, *Statista* [Online] https://www.statista.com/outlook/243/100/ecommerce/worldwide (archived at https://perma.cc/KH62-NM2Z)

Statista (n. d.b) [accessed 30 July 2019] Fourth-party logistics (4PL) market size from 2018 to 2027 (in billion U.S. dollars), *Statista* [Online] https://www.statista.com/statistics/992952/fourth-party-logistics-market-size-worldwide/ (archived at https://perma.cc/S4M5-2V44)

Steele, P and Court, B (1996) *Profitable Purchasing Strategies*, McGraw Hill, Australia

Supply Chain Digest and JDA Software (2017) [accessed 30 July 2019] 3PLs are Buzzing with Innovation, *JDA Software* [Online] https://jda.com/-/media/jda/knowledge-center/thought-leadership/scdigest_report_final.ashxJinks

Swisslog (n. d.) [accessed 30 July 2019] Yusen Logistics, Singapore Swisslog reference English, *YouTube* [Online] https://www.youtube.com/watch?v=uL6ZKaUNTsU&feature=youtu.be (archived at https://perma.cc/YMU5-BHRB)

Tech Insider (n. d.) [accessed 30 July 2019] Ocado's new robot can recognise and pack 50,000 grocery items, *YouTube* [Online] https://www.youtube.com/watch?v=FtOt-tE0YB4 (archived at https://perma.cc/6DM5-L636)

Tench, D *et al* (2013) [accessed 30 July 2019], Case Comment: Woodland v Essex County Council, *Supreme Court of the United Kingdom* [Online] http://ukscblog.com/case-comment-woodland/ (archived at https://perma.cc/FQ6T-2DS7)

Toyota (n. d.) [accessed 7 August 2019] Toyota BT Autopilot Jurassic Sae 160, *YouTube* [Online] https://www.youtube.com/watch?v=nvgJBAB4SlQ&feature=youtu.be (archived at https://perma.cc/MGF9-9E89)

Transparency Market Research (2017) [accessed 30 July 2019] Global Logistics Market: Soaring Popularity of E-commerce to Help Market Display Exponential Growth, says TMR, *Transparency Market Research* [Online] https://www.transparencymarketresearch.com/pressrelease/global-logistics-industry.htm (archived at https://perma.cc/Q3EU-JWSA)

Transport Intelligence (TI) (2018) [accessed 12 August 2019] Total Logistics 2018, available at: https://www.ti-insight.com/briefs/total-logistics-2018-reveals-fundamentals-trends-size-share-key-logistics-markets-globally-regionally/ (archived at https://perma.cc/8QQA-YQYV)

Transport Intelligence (2019) [accessed 12 August 2019] Global Contract Logistics 2019, available at: https://www.ti-insight.com/product/global-contract-logistics/ (archived at https://perma.cc/U32C-J6WC)

Transport Topics (2019) [accessed 7 August 2019] Is Amazon a Logistics Company? All Signs Point to That, *Transport Topics* [Online] https://www.ttnews.com/articles/amazon-logistics-company-all-signs-point (archived at https://perma.cc/KT8N-HCES)

UPS (2019) [accessed 7 August 2019] UPS launches first revenue drone delivery service in U S, *YouTube* [Online] https://www.youtube.com/watch?v=z-T9hLObvvA&feature=youtu.be (archived at https://perma.cc/AM8X-HPHP)

Venkatesh, A and Vulugundam, A [accessed 30 July 2019] Impact of GST on supply chain strategy and its effect on warehousing and transportation, *Mahindra Logiquest* [Online] http://www.mahindralogistics.com/logiquest/pdf/2015_pdf/LogiQuest_EastCoastExpress_NMIMS.PDF (archived at https://perma.cc/J8HJ-9TTM)

Vitasek, K (2013) *Vested Outsourcing: Five rules that will transform outsourcing* (2nd ed), Palgrave Macmillan, New York, NY

Vitasek K *et al* (2018) [accessed 30 July 2019] Vested for success case study: Intel and DHLSC's European Expansion of Vested, *Vested* [Online] http://www.vestedway.com/wp-content/uploads/2018/05/Intel-DHL-EMEA-TEACHING-case-study.pdf (archived at https://perma.cc/5SN7-ZRRA)

Wagner, S M and Franklin, J R (2008) [accessed 30 July 2019] Why LSPs don't leverage innovations, *Supply Chain Quarterly* [Online] https://www.supplychainquarterly.com/topics/Logistics/scq200804innovation/ (archived at https://perma.cc/A3CW-E6N3)

Walker M (2013) [accessed 11 August 2019] Outsourcing transport and warehousing: How to be Successful, *Logistics Bureau* [Online] https://www.logisticsbureau.com/outsourcing-transport-and-warehousing-how-to-be-successful/ (archived at https://perma.cc/L9DR-RU63)

Warehousing Education and Research Council (WERC) (2019) [accessed 1 June 2019] DC Measures Annual Survey & Report, *WERC* [Online] https://werc.org/page/DCMeasures (archived at https://perma.cc/EK9N-94QZ)

Wilson, D (2018) [accessed 7 August 2019] UPS Ware2Go matches merchants with local warehouse and fulfilment, *Tamebay* [Online] https://tamebay.com/2018/08/85335.html (archived at https://perma.cc/8L2K-V7VG)

World Bank (n. d.) [accessed 30 July 2019] International LPI Index, *World Bank* [Online] https://lpi.worldbank.org/international/global (archived at https://perma.cc/6LL5-NCUS)

Zimmerman, M, Sonthalia, B and Deshmukh, R (2017) [accessed 30 July 2019] Crowdsourcing comes to logistics, *A T Kearney* [Online] https://www.atkearney.com/operations-performance-transformation/article/?/a/crowdsourcing-comes-to-logistics (archived at https://perma.cc/R2B9-7FMC)

INDEX